OUR HUMAN HERDS

THE THEORY OF DUAL MORALITY

Abridged Version

STEPHEN MARTIN FRITZ

Edited by Denise Morel

First published by Dog Ear Publishing
8888 Keystone Crossing
Suite 1300
Indianapolis, IN 46240
www.dogearpublishing.net

ISBN: 978-145756-912-8

This book is printed on acid-free paper.
Printed in the United States of America

To

This book is dedicated to that miniscule fragment of humanity that reads books like this. You are the remnant that keeps general philosophical conversations alive across the centuries among people who will probably never meet.

Acknowledgements

I thank Elizabeth Fritz and Nicholas Fritz as well as Harold Froats and Kevin Hodak for their proofreading work and for their many ideas that found their way into this book. I am indebted to Julian Fritz for every piece of interior art, to James Egbert for his advice and support, to Andrea Bochi for her design of the book's covers, to Nicholas Froats for his permission to use his photo for the front cover, and to Michael Fortson for contributions to the website. I owe a great debt and a special thanks to Denise Morel for tirelessly editing this enormous work, reviewing each argument for soundness, adding new ideas of her own, and for making the entire thing presentable.

Preface

This is an attempt to understand and explain the complex and often contradictory nature of human action through a philosophical theory I call "Dual Morality." It lays out a clear, simple, and comprehensive framework describing our moral spectrum.

In this abridged version, Section I (The Theory of Dual Morality), which comprises the first five chapters, is presented in full. This is followed by excerpts from the remaining 23 chapters of the larger and more comprehensive unabridged version, to provide an overview of the areas that are further investigated there. In the larger unabridged version, the lessons of dual morality are applied to all walks of life and all eras of history.

Dual Morality builds upon the genius and insights of social activists, politicians, scientists and philosophers from around the world and throughout history. I make a determined effort to include observations, not only from these thinkers, but also from popular writers, novelists, and journalists from all walks of life. Figuring out right and wrong has always been everybody's business. By putting together the insightful but fragmented observations of these thinkers, we acquire a more comprehensive understanding of why we are who we are.

For more information visit the website:
www.ourhumanherds.com

INTRODUCTION

In our time, the conversation concerning culture, morality and human behavior, like everything else, has become a research area dominated by specialists. Some study remote tribes in jungles, others focus on narrow neighborhoods in India, or contrast urban with rural life. Others investigate apes or insects to cross-correlate their behaviors with our own, and many do locally crafted experiments in college classrooms. All publish their findings in journals, usually read only by similarly interested members of their field, and remain unknown to the laymen.

Historically, thinkers have tried to explain moral effort and moral conflict as beginning with a battle between passion and reason. The control of the emotional by the rational has dominated conversations about morality for centuries. We find this in the dialogues of Plato and in papers written by today's cultural anthropologists.

In the book, *Culture Theory*,[1] published in 1984, Richard Shweder contributed a chapter he titled '*Anthropology's Romantic Rebellion Against The Enlightenment*,' or '*There's More to Thinking Than Reason and Evidence*.' Here he attempts to better understand moral behavior by dividing it first into three aspects: Rational, Irrational, and Non-rational. Then he goes on to point out how theorists have tried to explain these in different ways depending upon whether they favored the *Enlightenment* approach, with its focus on man's intentional rationality, or the *Romantic* approach, which emphasizes our nonrationality (or a-rationality).

The ancients and the moderns both present morality as a process involving the objective and the subjective. Thinking and feeling are discussed by many without explaining exactly what these two cooperating and conflicting mental processes are. In this book we define 'thinking' and 'feeling' clearly, and show how they relate to each other, and how their relationship creates the activity we know as *moral expression*.

We live in a scientific age. Morality and other aspects of mind are investigated clinically in much the same way as malaria or CO_2 emissions might be. But discussions about human action are not at all restricted to specialists. What we do and why we do it is on the minds and on the tongues of plumbers, politicians, parents, poets, and priests. From every walk of life, everyone has something to say about what is right and what is wrong. Here we listen to them all.

Cicero and the ancient Stoics believed morality was linked to emotional control. Some modern researchers like Dutch Primatologist Frans de Waal[2] believe morality is intricately connected to emotional expression like sympathy and empathy. Both Cicero and de Waal are saying morality is fundamentally the proper expression (or proper lack of expression) of emotion. Neuroscientist Samuel Harris[3] proposes that morality can be found in atheism and does not need its historic religious foundation. Social psychologist Jonathan Haidt[4] explains morality through six fundamental moral principles; and evolutionary biologist Richard Dawkins[5] describes it as an aspect of genetic expression. All make valuable points we address and incorporate.

We are not only interested in how morality comes about, but what it is. What is moral and what is immoral? What should I do and why should I do it?

Pope Francis said recently, "*We all have the duty to do good.*" So we ask, "*What is good?*" Gandhi said, "*The truth is the truth.*" So we ask, "*What is truth.*" In the following pages, these questions will not only be asked, but will be answered directly. We will discern what is duty, what is good, and what is truth; why we understand such things in the way we do, and how they are used together to create human culture.

Harvard University Professor of Psychology, Joshua Greene,[6] suggests that it is through reason and passion we understand morality, and that it is an aspect of grouping or herding behavior. Another modern philosopher, Jesse Prinz,[7] uses sensibility theory to explore moral relativism. One hundred and fifty years ago, philosopher Fredrick Nietzsche[8] rejected the comparison of human beings with herding creatures (such speculation was also popular in his time) and felt the higher nature of superior people defined what was best and what was right. He wanted to reject moral relativism. This book will show how and why Greene, Prinz, and Nietzsche can all be correct.

In an attempt to bring the findings of specialized researchers to each other's attention, in 2011 Oxford University Press began publishing a series of books titled, *Advances in Culture and Psychology*. In a chapter titled "Horizontal and Vertical Individualism and Collectivism,"[9] Shavitt, Torelli, and Riemer divide human cultural action into four distinct patterns. – Horizontal or Vertical along with Collective or Individual. They suggest cultures can be understood as one or another of these four types: *Horizontal-Individual, Vertical-Individual, Horizontal-Collective,* and *Vertical-Collective*. This book, *Our Human Herds*, will address similar observations and show how and why aristocratic cultural verticality has been losing ground to democratic and egalitarian horizontalism since the Renaissance. We detail the development of circumstances that allowed the French Revolutionaries to side with slave holding American Revolutionaries in their claim that, "*All men are created equal.*" We go farther and explain why such an egalitarian outlook is so popular today and why it was so notably absent in the writings of the ancients.

Variations in what we have considered moral and immoral have been observed through all of time and in every culture. This book explains them through a new conceptual model called **Dual Morality**. Using it, the findings of our technical specialists mesh easily with the observations of the philosophers, politicians, rabbis, economists, journalists, jihadists, comedians, poets, and everyday people. We create a single, clear, and universal moral framework. We put forward an approach for understanding what morality is, why it has been explained in so many different ways, and where it is likely to go tomorrow.

Notes

1. Richard Shweder, *Culture Theory* (New York: Cambridge University Press, 1984).

2. Frans De Waal, *The Age of Empathy: Nature's Lesson's for a Kinder Society* (New York: Harmony Books, 2009).

3. Samuel Harris, *The Moral Landscape* (New York: Free Press, 2010).

4. Jonathan Haidt, *The Righteous Mind: Why Good People Are Divided By Politics and Religion* (New York: Pantheon Books, 2012).

5. Richard Dawkins, *The God Delusion* (Boston: Houghton Mifflin Co., 2006).

6. Joshua Greene, *Moral Tribes: Emotion, Reason, and the Gap Between Us and Them (*New York: The Penguin Press, 2013).

7. Jesse Prinz, *The Emotional Construction of Morals* (New York: Oxford University Press, 2007).

8. Frederick Nietzsche, *The Genealogy of Morals* (New York: Barnes and Noble Books, 1996, originally published in 1887).

9. Sharon Shavitt, Carlos J. Torelli, and Hela Riemer, "Horizontal and Vertical Individualism and Collectivism," in *Advances in Culture and Psychology,* Vol. 1, edited by Michele J. Gelfand, Chi-yue Chiu, and Ying-yi Hong (New York: Oxford University Press, 2011), 310-350.

TABLE OF CONTENTS

SECTION I
The Theory

The following five chapters lay out the details of the theory of dual morality and quad-realism. Repetition of terms and examples is unavoidable and should be anticipated.

- In Chapter 1, <u>Solving the Most Difficult Problems in Life</u> outlines the scope and parameters of the theory of dual morality.

- In Chapter 2, <u>The Group</u>, human socialization is discussed in general terms.

- In Chapter 3, <u>The Individual</u>, the origin and importance of human individuality is outlined.

- In Chapter 4, <u>The Two Sides of Truth</u>, what we mean by "truth" is determined.

- In Chapter 5, <u>Truths and Facts</u>, subjective, intuitive and instinctive goals are contrasted with tangible ends and the determination of facts. The clear distinction between these two terms is vital to understanding moral certitude.

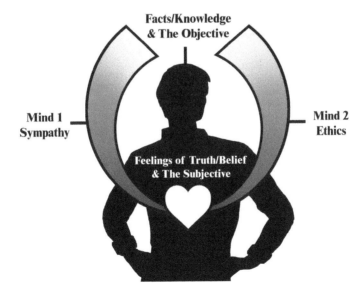

CHAPTER 1
Solving the Most Difficult Problems in Life

WHAT IS MORALITY?
THE ORIGINS AND MEANINGS BEHIND RIGHT AND WRONG

Morality is about life and death

Three hundred years ago, if a woman was raped and became pregnant we'd kill the rapist and spare the baby. Today, we spare the rapist and kill the baby.

Two hundred and fifty years ago Americans fought the British for their freedom. Ninety years later they fought each other for the right to own slaves.

Centuries ago, many cultures condoned polygamy; today we put people in jail for it.

One hundred years ago, we only approved of heterosexual marriage and people were put in prison at hard labor for homosexual behavior. Today leaders all over the western world are calling for the legalization and acceptance of homosexual relations and gay marriage.

How, in the course of a few generations, could the moral standards of a society flip so completely?

This book explains such changes. It is about how and why we see right and wrong as we do, and why right and wrong can alter over time. It is about how morality was viewed in the past and why it was so viewed, how it has changed in our present, and what it means for our future. In the process, we will discover the origins of moral outlook itself, and how it shapes all human institutions from our forms of government to our beliefs about family, atheism, and God.

We will discover how our innate moral outlook leads "necessarily" to both moral relativism and moral absolutism. We will find out how human moral understanding gives rise to liberals and conservatives, operates with emotional motivators like pleasure and happiness, creates terms like personality and character, and presents us with questions like, "What is the meaning of life?"

By the time you are done reading this book, you will have concrete answers to all such questions.

Philosophy as algebra

In this book philosophy will be approached as it was by the ancients, conversationally, and as a unifying discipline encompassing science, politics, art, religion, and everything else. There has been the tendency, beginning with Spinoza I think, which attempts to create mathematical or logical systems of relational understanding and limit philosophy to only such things. This has led to the modern preoccupation by philosophers with symbolism, language, true-false propositions, and epistemology. Consequently, the discipline has become esoteric and of little value to the man-in-the-street. Here I try to make philosophy relevant to everyone again. I do so by focusing my attention on the day-to-day matters that fill our lives, like family, government, love, greed, sex, television, hatred, happiness, history, and fun.

There is another modern tendency, namely, to conflate and treat as synonymous the terms *truth* and *fact*. In this book we return to the practice of distinguishing the two, of treating matters of fact as independently verifiable occurrences, and matters of truth as the personal significance of them. Through the disciplines of history and science we ascertain facts; through philosophy we try to figure out the significant truths revealed or illuminated by fact. This book returns philosophy to its larger and original purpose of figuring out which facts are worth worrying about and why.

Right and wrong

Right and wrong are how we evaluate our decision making. The right decision leads to good and proper results; the wrong decision leads to bad consequences. Right and wrong is inexorably linked to good and bad. Knowing the difference between what is right and good and what is wrong and bad is what we call moral understanding. Using that understanding to act appropriately is what we call moral action.

As the book unfolds, it will become apparent why so much of human morality revolves around three major issues: sex, violence, and wealth distribution. But the details of these issues take many forms. In the chapters that follow, we will discuss the many aspects of moral and immoral behavior. My goal is that by the time you are done with this book, the moral questions that have plagued us, and that seem unanswerable, will all be explained. The questions posed and answered will include conundrums like the following:

Morality is about treating other people justly

In 1776 slavery was legal in every one of the thirteen British colonies in America. It was these same slave-holding colonials who held their fellow human beings in bondage who made a great commotion for independence on the basis of freedom. What exactly is freedom and how is it that a free society also condoned slavery?

Great thinkers like Aristotle and compassionate feelers like Jesus never advocated the elimination of slavery. Are we today somehow *smarter* or *more generous* than these famous leaders from the past? More importantly, if our culture and our greatest thinkers and feelers found slavery to be right in one century but wrong in the next, is there any chance it might be condoned again at some future date?

Morality is about equality

Were all the early political battles over liberty and democracy hypocritical because most did not include women being given equal social status with men? We will find out why behaviors that seem incomprehensible today were once viewed as the most decent and moral outlooks. For example, in the nineteenth century, Britain's Queen Victoria came out against women's suffrage saying, "The Queen is most anxious to enlist everyone … in checking this mad, wicked folly of 'Women's Rights'… It is a subject which makes the Queen so furious that she cannot contain herself."[1] The most powerful woman in the world certainly was not anti-female. Why was she against sexual equality at the polling booth?

Morality is about controlling our desires

Controlling sex and the ramifications that spring from it has always occupied a center stage in moral discussion. Profanities in many languages center on sexual or scatological acts. So much of modern social and political debate has involved sexually related matters.

Jonathan Eig has recently published a book about morality and equality. The book examines the purpose, control, and proper direction of human desire. It is called *The Birth of the Pill*. Eig of course is talking about *the birth control pill*. In his book he details the struggles many went through to prevent or ensure its development. Individuals within Western culture battled for or against it with both sides claiming to act in the name of morality.

Writing of American culture in the 1950s, Eig tells us how laws once passed to create a moral society were being challenged everywhere. Morality itself seemed to be changing:

> Thirty states and the federal government still had anti-birth-control laws on the books...

> It was the midpoint of the century. Scientists were taking up matters of life and death that once had been the domain principally of artists and philosophers…

> Young men returning from battle were looking for new
> adventures … During the war, new rules of morality had
> applied. Sex had become a more casual endeavor as foreign
> women traded their bodies to American soldiers for
> cigarettes and cash … many of the women back home had
> been exploring their own new moral standards. The war
> had thrust women into the workplace, putting money in
> their pockets and liberating them from their parental
> homes. They'd begun dating and making love to men they
> did not intend to marry …
>
> In the years immediately following the Civil War,
> [Anthony] Comstock had made it his mission to fight smut
> in America, almost single-handedly creating a strict set of
> anti-obscenity laws… With the backing of influential
> businessmen … Comstock became famous for guarding
> America from pornography and disease. In 1873 he
> persuaded Congress to pass a bill banning the use of mail
> for transporting "any obscene, lewd, lascivious, or filthy
> book, pamphlet, picture, paper, letter …" After that, every
> state in the union enacted its own anti-obscenity laws …[2]

For the guardians of the old morality, fighting obscenity was simply one battlefront in the war to control sexual expression and negative social consequences. Birth control might have its merits, but making it readily available would give everyone, especially youngsters, encouragement to have sex outside of marriage and for nothing more than the satisfaction of carnal desires. A split was becoming apparent in our moral outlook. Some thought *the better* and *most moral* people were those who controlled their desires. Others thought the best life was lived by finding ways to *satisfy our wishes, including gratifying our desires*. We will discover that changes in the way we define the goals of our life occur with increasing or decreasing wealth and safety, and that these changes alter our view of right and wrong.

Morality is about leading happy, healthy lives

In the same book, Eig records the trepidations of a young woman who desired sex and gave in to her desires, only to fear the results. She supported established moral norms. She believed, as others of her time did, that the sexual liberality that birth control made possible was somehow immoral. She was torn between the urges to satisfy her desires, versus satisfying the moral demands of her society. Eig quotes the girl:

> I knew birth control existed, but I didn't know anything
> about it … To go out and actually get it [birth control]
> would mean that I planned to do these things, to have sex.
> Since I knew it was wrong, I kept thinking I wasn't doing

> it, or I wasn't going to do it again. Each time was the last
> time. Birth control would have been cold blooded.[3]

Eig tells us about Margaret Sanger, a socialist who did not pretend to champion the cause of birth control in the name of health, but promoted it as an aspect of moral equality. She admitted to wanting women to be free to have sex whenever they wished:

> It was Sanger who popularized the term "birth control" and almost single-handedly launched the movement for contraceptive rights in the United States. Women would never gain equality, she had argued, until they were freed from sexual servitude.[4]

Sexual servitude... Socialism... Democracy... Freedom... how are all these social debates connected? What have all these things to do with morality?

People different from me can't be trusted

We will look at why we have had a recurring mistrust of people unlike ourselves throughout history, and at how tolerance for differences expands in times of ease and contracts in times of trouble.

In 167 BC, Antiochus Epiphanes ruled over a kingdom in disarray. He wanted to tightly unify his realm by eliminating the old and traditionally divisive practices of the Jews and to bring them in line with others in his Hellenized nation. He did not want one portion of his people following one set of customs while others did something else.

To wipe out their archaic customs, he prohibited circumcision and encouraged all Jews to eat pork. Refusal was treason. In every nation, disobedience or disregard of the laws rightfully ordered by the leadership is immoral. But as with all law, many complied while others did not. To get his people to follow his edict, he was forced to resort to ever-harsher punishments. When two mothers had their newborns circumcised, Antiochus made an example out of them. He ordered the babies killed and hung around their mothers' necks. The mothers themselves were then led to the city walls and thrown off to their deaths.[5]

The king imagined he was doing right because he believed he was doing good. His culture needed to be united. Just as with any other type of struggle, some individuals were unavoidably sacrificed so that the majority could survive and prosper. Sometimes we sacrifice soldiers in war, and at other times we sacrifice civilians in peace. The end, it is assumed, justifies the means. But does it?

Again and again throughout history we find morality coming back to the same few points: loyalty to the group and its leadership, following rules, the control of sex, the proper application of violence, and the correct distribution of wealth and material resources. But why is it largely about these things, and why do we debate them as we do? Are the changes in morality no more consequential than changing our taste in clothing? Women once wore hooped skirts and now wear pantsuits. Are these moral issues or just matters of shifting habit? Do moral attitudes change as quickly as styles of music, and for no better reason?

Morality has been addressed indirectly by an army of bright and influential writers from Plato to Burke, Adam Smith to Karl Marx. Each has contributed something, but somehow none explained everything. In this book we will show how they were all partially correct. The theory presented here, called "Dual morality," will allow us to combine the insights of all these philosophers to produce a single comprehensive moral system to explain all these things. It will help us make sense of the course of human history more clearly than any other philosophical approach of the past.

Dual Morality
Morality is a relationship between ourselves and others

A single consistent moral code does not answer all our questions, but a Dual Moral outlook can. There is an unbroken line of life beginning with the first single-celled life and you. For billions of years, each successful generation of intermediate forms was born, reproduced and died in uninterrupted succession to those of us alive today. To do this, each life had to make the correct decisions that guaranteed their survival. The most intellectually complex of those decision makers are human beings.

Making the correct decision leads to life and making the wrong one might end in death. Morality is making the right decision. Because we are a herding animal, our decisions do not just affect us individually. To survive, it is not just we, but also our group that has to do well. Without our group, we would certainly die. Doing right involves doing right by ourselves and doing right by others. Survival depends on it. Morality is what we call the process of doing right by ourselves and others.

The two moral patterns of our Dual Morality exist to guide us in the two great life-and-death situations we face:

- We are safe and there is enough for all.

Or

- We are in danger or there is not enough for everyone.

Human morality has its roots in this dichotomy. Acting properly in each of these circumstances improves our chance, and our group's chances, for survival. The cornerstone observation comes as we recognize that proper action is not the same in the first circumstance as it is in the second.

One of our two moral codes takes precedence within us when we find ourselves in conditions of safety and security; the other tends to dominate our outlook when we face threats and danger. When seeing the world in the first way, when we are safe and secure, we tend to be easy going; and since there is plenty, sharing becomes a priority. From this position of security our actions can be more eclectic. What is right and what is wrong are less pressing issues and can be debated. We are not in a life-or-death situation. When times are good, we relax. I call this our *Moral Mind 1* position.

Alongside this is our second way of seeing right and wrong. It is our morality of scarcity, want and danger. This outlook dominates us when there is not enough to go around, when we are under attack, or when we find ourselves in dangerous circumstances. This is what I call *Moral Mind 2*. In Moral Mind 2, right and wrong are more urgent and pressing things. We resort to this outlook when facing troubles, where we are forced to decide (individually or by tradition) who should be given more and who should be given less, and even who can live and who must die. We prioritize people as friends or foe; we ration our supplies; and we view dishonor or disloyalty as our greatest enemy, since the actions and reliability of others may lead to our own survival or cause our collective death.

On the following page, for the sake of illustration, Figure 1-1 plots out a spectrum of moral outlook. On the left is how we feel when we are safe and there is enough for all, and on the right is how we feel when times are tough and danger is near. A person in a comfortable situation feels and acts in a predominantly Mind 1 fashion.

At any moment in time, we evaluate our condition and conclude that we are somewhere on this line, and our morality adjusts accordingly. We see things in either a Mind 1 or a Mind 2 way.

By understanding our two moral outlooks and how they affect our actions, we will explain the progress, regress, and tremendous variety we find in human cultural history. We will not only explain war and peace, slavery and freedom, crime and punishment, but we will also discover how educational establishments are created as we find them; why dictators or democrats come to power; and we will be led inexorably to discover the nature of how we see (or do not see) our gods, our science, our families and our politics.

We begin with the recognition that humans throughout history have faced one or the other of the two primary determinant conditions: whether there is enough for all and times are easy, or there is not enough for all, and times are tough. *Acting rightly is acting properly in the conditions that face us now*. Our Dual Morality has ensured we are prepared to act rightly in either circumstance. Relative plenty and safety or relative scarcity and danger is the linchpin around which all of cultural history unfolds.

Figure 1-1

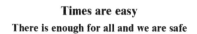

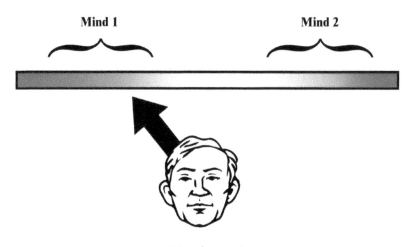

Moral propriety

Moral sentiment establishes what we recognize as right and best in every aspect of life. Morality, as the term is used in this book, abstractly generates our ideas of right and wrong. Morality is the outlook that guides feeling and leads to actions. Through the emotions, morality manipulates our will. We will discover why honesty, thievery and kindness are labeled circumstantially as moral or immoral.

We will find out that morality is more than right and wrong between individuals. Morality is more than discussions about stealing a woman's purse or beating the dog. Morality is acting rightly in all sorts of relationships.

It is through our dual moral nature that we have structured our families, created social institutions, and built nations. What is correct and what is best encompass much more than "Did Johnny tell a lie?" Morality determines everything we do. Why was dueling right and honorable in one era but wrong and despicable in another? Why was being a virgin on one's wedding night once expected, but now such notions seem archaic and even cretin? Why did we love kings in one century and despise the thought of them in another. By the time you finish this book, you will understand why both moral positions are not only possible, but also necessary. Being able to see right in both ways has been vital to survival.

Once we understand the dual nature of our morality, all the inexplicable problems of the past disappear. Not only do we see how it can be right and proper to believe in God, we also see how it is equally understandable that some of us should be atheists. We will discover that, with our moral framework, some "necessarily" must be liberals and others conservative, with many (utilitarian) pleasure seekers opposing (virtue/deontological) ethicists. Our dual moralism guarantees this is how things must be. There must be both believers and atheists, liberals and conservatives, pleasure seekers and those promoting ethical self-control.

With an understanding of our dual moral nature, we will find that the bickering between these seemingly opposite moral outlooks is not only necessary, but unavoidable, beneficial, and just what is needed to protect our group.

The genesis of the book

I began with intentions of writing a different book altogether. I started with a "How-to" guide for parents trying to teach their children to think. I felt the best way to teach someone how to do something was by having them do it – sort of like learning to ride a bicycle: at some point you just need to get on and ride.

I created a long list of perplexing questions, and suggested that parents set aside time every night, possibly at dinner, to ask these difficult and probing questions:

- Why are there different countries?
- Should there be different religions?
- How do we know right from wrong?
- Why do girls dress differently from boys?
- What is art and what is not art?

I deliberately chose controversial subjects and problems that allowed no easy answer – seemingly no right answers at all. I preferred the questions that most people would claim unanswerable. I finished the how-to book, but found no publishers.

Throughout the process, all these sorts of questions kept rattling around in my head. I wondered why they were so hard to answer. Why do we talk of liking people, and also of loving them? What is the difference between "like" and "love" anyway? Why do we feel obligated to continue to "love" our brothers and sisters, no matter how despicable they might grow up to be? Such questions were always on my mind.

Why do people write poetry? Why do couples who marry for life cheat on their spouses and get divorced? Should we follow laws we do not agree with? When opposing soldiers die for their country, which of them did right and which was wrong?

I began with a premise that these questions were impossible to answer, but this was unsatisfactory. After all, there were answers; we all just did not agree with each other about them. Take the question of good and bad music, for example; some people said Mozart and Beethoven created good music while the Rolling Stones and the Beatles just made noise. Some people said all music was equally acceptable, none better than any other, and that it was just a matter of personal preference, while others said there could be things like music critics and there was better music and worse music. Both sides claimed to be right. They did not say there was no answer to these questions; they simply believed a different answer. Some said:

-    All music and any art is just a matter of taste.

Others believed:

-    There is better art and worse art.

I examined the answers that have been historically proposed for these questions and, like Dmitri Mendeleev with his periodic table of chemical elements, the answers to these questions began to line up categorically.

	Some felt	Others felt
War:	Always wrong	Sometimes necessary
Slavery:	Always wrong	Sometimes necessary
Sexism:	Always wrong	Sometimes necessary
Sexual Preferences:	Equal but different	One way is better than another
Good and bad art:	Equal but different	One way is better than another
Religion:	Equal but different	One way is better than another

A pattern began to appear. I began calling the pattern of feeling in the column in the middle *Moral Mind 1* and the pattern on the right as *Moral Mind 2.*

It was apparent that folks who thought in one way about a subject tended to think in that same way about the other subjects. Mind 1 types felt and then thought in Mind 1 ways; Mind 2 people favored Mind 2 ways. These patterns were not new. They are as old as philosophy and as common as history. They have been called:

our sympathetic view	versus	our ethical view
our personal view	versus	our social view
our liberal view	versus	our conservative view

But by whatever name they've been called, it has been widely recognized that our morality, our right and wrong, always seemed to split apart in two broad patterns:

Questions about	Moral Mind 1	Moral Mind 2
Religion	We should be flexible; one person's beliefs can be as valid as another's.	The traditional religion of our people is best.
The Family	One family is as valid as another; what is important is love and acceptance.	The traditional family structure is best.
The Country	Borders should be open if possible; society is enhanced with cultural diversity.	Cultural traditions are weakened and diluted with people and customs from other locations.
Rights and Freedoms	The government's role should be expanded to guarantee rights, promote freedom, and ensure equality.	Restricting the power of government is how rights and freedoms are secured.
Criminality	The focus should be on prevention and rehabilitation.	Punishment is the best deterrent to crime. Spare the rod and spoil the child.
Ultimate social aim	To provide	To protect

I stopped trying to publish my book, *Teaching Your Kids How to Think*. But the exercise of lining up answers to the most difficult questions became a pastime. The concept of dual morality took shape as I realized all these impossibly difficult-to-answer questions really could be answered. In fact, not only could they be answered, they were being answered every day. The most contentious moral conflicts between people became easy to explain. *Moral conflict began to take shape, not as a battle between right and wrong, but as a needed and necessary struggle between right and right.*

What is morality?

Whenever we ask, *"What is the right thing to do?"* the question is posed as if there were only one right answer, and that it is our job to go out and find it. But what if there is not one right answer, what if there are always at least two possible right answers?

Starting at the beginning we have to ask, *"What is morality?"* What is the thing itself? *We recognize that morality requires a relationship.* Morality would have no need to exist if we were the only thing in the universe. If I was all that there was, I could do neither right nor wrong; no one else would be there for me to hurt; and there would be no God to judge me and none to condemn me. I could be neither disappointed nor rewarded; no one would be there to expect anything. For morality to exist requires something other than me.

"What is moral" is another way of saying, "What is the right and best way for one thing to act toward another?" How should soldiers treat civilians, mothers treat children, society treat rapists, masters treat slaves, people treat the environment? These are all problems of morality – What is the right relationship between two or more things?

What I found was that, for us, there was no single right way. But that did not mean that there was an infinite number of right ways either. Right and wrong always seemed to divide into these two familiar camps; not three or four, not 100 or 1000 and not just one. There were always two general ways to see right and two ways to see wrong. And so the name of this theory presented itself: Dual Morality.

Dual morality provides a survival advantage

Like the taste buds on our tongue, some of which are there to react to sour and others to sweet or salty, the ability to taste in multiple ways gives us an ability to distinguish healthful from unhealthful foods and is an advantage for survival. Seeing in multiple wavelengths of light allows us to discern the subtle details in the world around us. Similarly, being able to feel – that is, to judge – proper action in more than one way has been vital to survival too.

We have often faced challenges for existence. By being able to answer the question, "Is my well being assured or is it not?" in two ways, either "yes" or "no," and having a genetic plan for how to best react in either circumstance, has allowed us to react in the most advantageous way possible. When there is enough of everything, survival for us and the group is best ensured by feeling it right to share and for others to share with us; when there is not enough, it is best we feel it right to ration and prioritize, and the survival of ourselves and of the group depends on being recognized as one of the deserving. Survival has hinged on feeling right and wrong in one of these two ways.

Which of these two moral codes we choose at any moment depends on a combination of genetic preferences and environmental factors. But once the psychological choice is made, we decide right or wrong in accordance with whatever view, Mind 1 plenty or Mind 2 scarcity, we call into action. Everyday experience finds us employing both moral codes. We move in and out of them with ease. For example, in a home environment with our children, the atmosphere is one of safety, where provision becomes the top priority. Here Mind 1 dominates our behavior:

- We treat our children as equally worthy people.
- We feel all of them must survive.
- We encourage sharing and cooperation.
- If someone does something wrong, we react with an eye toward rehabilitation and correction.
- Wrong acts lead to reeducation and redemption.
- The smallest and weakest get the most careful attention.

The same is not true if we are in a workplace or social situation, where our job may be in jeopardy and lay-offs are imminent. Under this condition, we might act in a Mind 2 way, where:

- We need to be seen as better and others to be seen as worse.
- We feel not everyone can or should be kept on if the job cannot support everyone.
- Competition is encouraged.
- Everyone cannot and should not be equally rewarded.
- Wrong acts lead to punishment: termination.
- Better actions lead to superior rewards and greater distinction.
- We look up to the strongest and most well placed for guidance.

Each of these moral codes is consistent within itself and appropriate for the conditions where it is applied. Both moral methods have been necessary to ensure the survival of the individual and the group. The moral code in play informs us how to act to be seen as doing right and not to be doing wrong. Sometimes we are taken care of, and at other times we need to prove we can take care of ourselves. To survive, both moral orders have been necessary.

The two codes we carry within us are not complementary, and are often at odds with one another. Through the judicious application of the best code for the circumstances at hand, humanity has prospered. Choose the right code and thrive; choose the wrong code and suffer. But deciding which code is best for the circumstances is not always easy. In fact, as a social creature, the code that seems best from one person's point of view might not seem the best to another. Such is the origin of political debate.

This work describes our two codes, suggests how they developed, and uses them to explain how what has been right before can be wrong now and how what is wrong now could have been right before. It all begins with the answer to the single most important question that decides our morality: *Can everyone in our group survive?*

Can We All Survive?

If Yes   If No
/   \

Moral Code 1   Moral Code 2

Unable to exist outside the group, the question "Can *we* all survive?" is the psychological key to moral decision making. If the answer is "yes" and we are safe, we will receive a share of provision and protection and we will prosper. If the answer is "no," then everyone's survival is not ensured. If everyone's survival is not guaranteed, each of us needs to act in ways which impress others that we should be considered for a share of whatever insufficient provision and protection is available. How we individually (and the group collectively) see the current dilemma and how we/it answer this question determines how we all must feel and then act.

Does the current situation demand we be cooperative or competitive? We feel and then act in conformity to the demands of one or the other moral patterns. Feeling in a Mind 1 way or a Mind 2 way is far from a conscious decision. Like other mental impulses, those that are vital and most important to survival occur below the level of consciousness. Our conscious mind controls our hands and fingers. We decide to reach out and pick up a candy bar and eat it. But our conscious mind does not have to decide to keep our hearts beating or when to inhale or exhale. These things take place outside the level of conscious thought.

Our moral decision making often occurs outside of conscious thought too. We simply feel one way or we feel another – in Mind 1 ways or in Mind 2 ways, then we act accordingly. We are not always aware of why we feel as we do. How we feel is dictated as a response to circumstances and how we select which of our moral paths to follow comes to us subliminally.

Thought experiment

Imagine your world was made up of *only* the people in your community – not so small as to be a tiny tribe, but not a town either. Imagine it as a group of say, 200 people. Further imagine you and your group routinely faced two possible conditions:

Condition 1: Everyone in our group can survive.
Or
Condition 2: Not everyone can survive.

In either of these conditions, we face a moral dilemma: *How do we distribute our resources?* Do we distribute them evenly, so that everyone in our group receives an equal share? Or do we distribute them unevenly, with some getting more than others? In each case, which is the most moral choice?

Option A: Distribute resources evenly.

Or

Option B: Distribute resources unevenly.

Condition 1: Plenty (Everyone in the group can survive)

Obviously, Condition 1 is preferable to Condition 2, both for the individual and the group as a whole. And when everyone can survive, everyone certainly should. Feeling this and then acting to ensure it when under these circumstances is best for humanity. This has been most moral. Morality is acting rightly in the situation we face.

This has always been the starting point of our dual morality. When everyone can survive, it is imperative that we do the things that ensure they will. This is right. When our environment is safe and our supplies plentiful, we should feel it proper that we take whatever steps are necessary to ensure everyone will make it. *We share*, we look to give to those who have less, and we distribute goods and protection in such a way that everyone will be taken care of. In other words:

Option A is the most appropriate moral response in conditions of plenty and security.

The moral dilemma: How do we distribute our resources?

In one form or another, the scenario described above has been the great moral dilemma in all human existence. Either there was enough food, shelter, and protection for everyone to survive (and so we should believe everyone should) or there was not enough for everyone in the group to make it. If there is not enough, what should we do? Decisions have to be made on how to best distribute insufficient resources to ensure most of us survive – that is, the individuals and the group surviving in a strong enough position to successfully carry on and compete with other groups and the challenges of nature.

Condition 2: Scarcity (Not everyone can survive)

For most of human history, Condition 2 has been far more common than Condition 1. Starvation and death have always been close at hand. So how should we act in Condition 2? When we all probably cannot survive, which of the following outcomes is preferable?

Outcome 1: Ten percent *of our group will die.*

Or

Outcome 2: Five percent *of our group will die.*

We have no trouble picking out the second as the best outcome. We should pick the scenario where most survive. Choosing Outcome 2 is moral; choosing Outcome 1 is less moral. Human existence depends on feeling properly, so that we choose and act appropriately, that is, it depends on being most moral.

But our choice of outcomes has not really determined our means. To make sure only five percent perish instead of ten percent, we have to make some very hard choices about how best to distribute our resources in order to achieve that goal. In other words, we have to choose between Option A (Distribute resources evenly) and Option B (Distribute resources unevenly).

Option A: Distribute resources evenly

Our group has limited resources, limited territory, limited game, limited medicines, limited firewood, limited manpower for fighting or farming. These facts will not change any time soon. More babies will be born this year than our group can feed, house, and protect. If we share our food, water, shelter and everything else equally, everyone must get less than what they need to be healthy. If we share everything equally, everyone must suffer.

If we begin by sharing things equally, everyone soon begins to starve. Eventually the younger, older, and weaker fail. As soon as five percent die, their portion can be distributed to the others, leaving enough for all remaining to live. But by doing things this way, all have been weakened. By doing things this animalistic and unthinking way, an additional five percent will go on to die from having to suffer for so long, or having been unable to fight their enemies. Beginning from the position of an equal distribution of resources, as many as *ten percent of your group will die, still leaving the other 90 percent who survived depleted and weakened.* Five percent die soonest, another five percent die later from their weakened condition. Ten percent die eventually. So, in times of stress:

> *If we distribute resources equally,*
> *it is possible that ten percent or more may die.*

Option B: Distribute resources unevenly

With an uneven distribution of protection, and of food, water and shelter *right from the start*, only five percent of your group will die. With some getting more than an equal share from the beginning, the five percent will die sooner than they would in Option A. But only this five percent need die at all, and the remainder will not be weakened. With the remaining 95 percent getting enough from the start, they never pass through this challenging and recurring situation. In other words:

> *In tough conditions, an unequal distribution of resources*
> *right from the start can be the most morally correct position.*

Figure 1-2 below illustrates the position we take when times are tough.

Something like this difficult moral scenario is probably close to the condition most large groups have lived in throughout history. More people are born than can easily survive with the resources available. If we always felt and believed the equal distribution of goods was best, we would cause the greater harm much of the time. Believing only in this way would likely have resulted in the early extinction of human beings or any herding creature that felt so. Many herding animals distribute safety, security and food unevenly, usually by the fittest and strongest, holding the most productive and safest territory or position in the herd. Creatures that do this survive better than those that do not.

Throughout the animal kingdom, individuals and families have fought for the better territory, the more secure nesting sites and the best place at the watering hole. Might makes right. The strong survived, the morality of the warrior prevailed. But superiority is often demonstrated in ways other than fighting. Sometimes we prove our superiority with our looks, our words or other cooperative skills. Attaining a superior place in the herd also gets us the greatest protection and the most food. The battle for superiority takes place not just between herds, but also between members within the group.

Figure 1-2

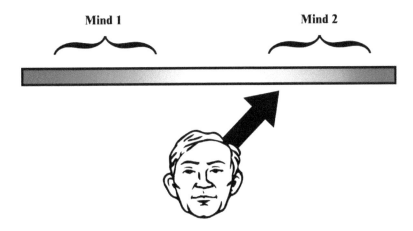

Times are tough
There is not enough for all and we are threatened

In times of trouble, morality rested on finding the best way to be unequal. When there is simply not enough to go around, culture has to be set up to distribute goods and protection to some more than others. In doing this, not only do most survive, but it is possible that things can be arranged so that the more vital members of the group can be better guaranteed to make it. *Inequality must sometimes be right and best.*

-   When we all can survive, it is morally imperative that we all do so.
-   When we all cannot survive it is morally imperative that the most vital do so.

In good times, we need to be more equal. In times of plenty, we need to feel that goods and protection should be distributed to all, even to stand ready to take from those who have more and give it to those who have less. It is morally right that we feel and act to influence the others in our group to make it so. In harsher times, we need to be less equal. We need to structure our limited resources in such a way as to preserve the most important.

These are descriptions of our two moral modes in action. In the good times of security and plenty, we needed to feel and act in terms of equality and sharing. In lean times of danger and insufficiency, we have to be ready to feel and act sacrificially, and in ways that distribute scarce goods to some more than others. *Both systems are moral.* Both systems do as much for us as they can in the circumstances they address.

This theory proposes that there is likely a connection between our two instinctive moral patterns and the original division of labor between the sexes. That is, our morality is rooted in what it meant long ago to be a good mother and a good man. In the chapters that follow, it will be shown that it is probably from this original division of labor that our two distinct moral patterns were first separated and perfected, and that later, sophisticated production and trade brought our two moral patterns together in beneficial conflict to resolve increasingly complex social problems. By retaining the two ways of seeing right and wrong, honed by the sexes and brought together by production and trade, humanity continues to be guided to success.

Horizontal and vertical

Neither of our two internal moral systems agrees completely with the other, nor should they. In one moral system, our code of plenty, our Mind 1, society is seen in a horizontal fashion. In this moral mode, we feel it right to stress equality and sharing. Everyone is as good as anyone else. The needs of one are equal to the needs of any. If anyone makes it, everyone makes it. This is an elemental human outlook.

Feeling in our other moral method, our Mind 2, we must be vertical. This is the moral outlook of danger, want, and suffering. These feelings promote an outlook where the people and things around us that are most necessary to the group should be so recognized, so as to be best protected and most certainly provided for. Their vital skills or position in the group mean they must survive even if others may need to be sacrificed. When not everyone can survive, the moral imperative must be that the best, brightest, bravest, most knowledgeable, or most experienced do so. This second way is an elemental outlook too.

In a survival situation where many may die, those who do cannot simply be chosen at random. I propose here that any group that developed ways to ensure that their best and brightest were never sacrificed, competed more successfully with groups who could make no such provision to their superior performers. When some have to die, we cannot allow it to be the most vital leaders, our doctors, our most fertile females, or the wise who know how to hunt or who can find their way to the watering holes. The groups that prioritized their people and resources did better than the groups who could not.

In a situation where the moral imperative is that some must get less than others, those less important to the group should be the ones to be put off. If we have no choice, and if it is inevitable that some of us will have to die, it is a group survival advantage to see to it that those who are least valuable to the rest are sacrificed before others.

In one moral mind, our mindset of plenty, we are all equal. Making decisions about more vital and less vital do not make sense. Such decisions need not, and therefore should not, be made. Since there is enough to go around, we can relax and accept everybody. If someone acts a little differently, we can shrug it off; times are easy. Everyone is as valuable as anyone else.

In our second system, the mindset of scarcity and danger, choices need to be made. We must be able to ascertain who is more expendable than others. People and things are prioritized. Under these conditions, where we all sit at the edge of a precipice, there is little toleration for new and untried ways; risk needs to be minimized. In tough times, we cannot afford to show weakness to others and chance being seen by the group as one of the expendables. We must show others that we are in some way better than or more valuable than some around us. In later chapters, we will map out how these moral conditions of tolerance for change on the one hand, or a loyalty to custom and tradition on the other, have shaped history and modern social institutions.

Nature advances no guarantees. We don't know if next year we'll be facing hardship or plenty. We must be morally prepared to act rightly in either case. The survival of the human species continues to depend upon it.

The two sides of truth

Morality is first a feeling and then an action. We feel what is right so that we may do what is right. And we feel right in two ways.

Mind 1	Mind 2
The mindset of plenty	The mindset of scarcity
The mindset of safety	The mindset of danger
The morality of equality	The morality of prioritization
The morality where deviation can be tolerated and even encouraged	The morality where deviation from tried practices may be dangerous and therefore should be discouraged
The morality that promotes emotional expression in times of safety	The morality that encourages emotional control in times of danger

We need look no farther than our mirror and into our own lives to reveal how we see things like this. But the picture is not complete until we recognize that within each of these two systems of moral truth comes an ability to feel them with different levels of intensity. After all, we can be in only a little danger, where we might want to be cautious and on guard; or we can be under immediate attack in a desperate situation where many are not likely to survive. Sometimes we are uneasy when walking in the woods where the leopard lurks; but our unease becomes intense when we spot the leopard rushing toward us. The levels of danger we face are not always the same.

Additionally, our good times can be long and deep or short and precarious. We may have enough now, but we might be able to look ahead to probable scarcity soon. Or, our riches might have been enjoyed for so long, that they appear everlasting. Then again, we might recognize that there is not much wheat left in the loft, and hunger may be just around the corner.

What we find is that the area between our two moral minds is where both conditions are weakest. Here is where we might be when we are not really in danger, but also not so secure as to completely let our guard down. This is the region between our moral outlooks. There is enough for now, but the plenty is not guaranteed; and we are not in danger at the moment, but our situation of safety is not ensured forever either. We are not threatened nor are we completely comforted. Neither of our moral outlooks is imposed.

Figure 1-3

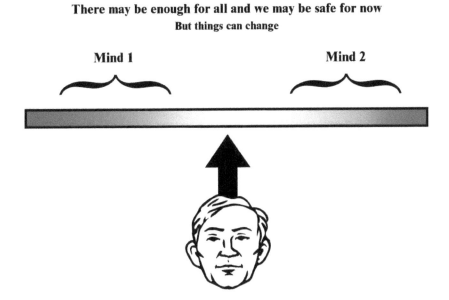

There may be enough for all and we may be safe for now
But things can change

In response to the environmental reality of the intensity and immediacy of danger or of plenty, we have the capacity to feel our moral responses with a matching intensity. We can feel in two moral minds, and we can also feel weakly or strongly within either of them. In times of abject poverty and desperation, we might choose to fight and to kill for a scrap of bread; conversely, when surrounded by mountains of food, we feel strongly that denying even a morsel to anyone makes no sense. If we color-code our moral intensity, we create a useful visual representation of the human moral spectrum: the stronger the color, the more completely the environment of plenty or scarcity faces us:

MIND 1	MIND 2
A hint of Mind 1	A hint of Mind 2
Slightly Mind 1	Slightly Mind 2
Strongly Mind 1	Strongly Mind 2
Intensely Mind 1	Intensely Mind 2
Absolutely Mind 1	Absolutely Mind 2

To better describe with a picture what I am trying to say in words, I'll frequently rely on two types of illustrations: the one above, where our two moral codes examine the same issue side-by-side, and a second way, where our feelings are gauged by a circle. By bending our human moral spectrum line-diagram (Figure 1-4) around so that the two ends of moral intensity meet (Figure 1-5), we create a circle – a moral circle that represents each of us, and that can represent all of us.

When we are feeling as depicted on the left side of the chart, we look for dangers from within the group. Times are easy and what danger exists comes from those unwilling to share the abundant resources that are plentiful enough for everybody. When we are feeling as depicted on the right side of the chart, we are wary of dangers from outside the group. We are under threat. There is not enough for all and others may be coming to get what little there is.

And whether on the left or the right, we can experience these feelings either mildly or intensely.

Figure 1-4

The Moral Spectrum

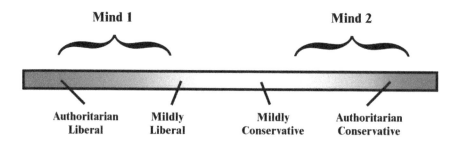

If we wrap the ends around to meet each other, the graph above can also be depicted in this way:

Figure 1-5

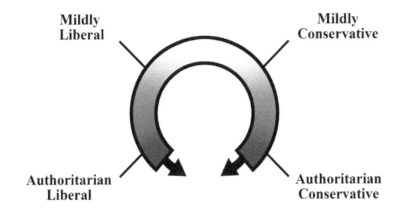

Mildly Liberal

Mildly Conservative

Authoritarian Liberal

Authoritarian Conservative

Fully wrapping the two extremes around, we create a circular pattern I call the "Moral Compass." Using this we can plot the moral position of individuals, collections of individuals, or entire societies:

Figure 1-6

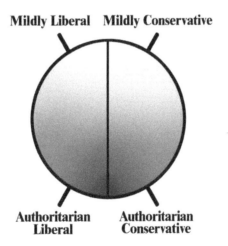

Mildly Liberal   Mildly Conservative

Authoritarian Liberal

Authoritarian Conservative

The circle pictured in Figure 1-6 above displays our dual moral choices and the degrees of intensity with which they can be felt. We can pinpoint how we feel by placing our emotions at some point around this circle. Near the bottom we feel our moral preferences for Mind 1 sharing and equality intensely; but near the top, we feel these same things only mildly. On the other side of our circle, near the bottom, we feel our Mind 2 conservative ethical impulses strongly, but near the top, say at the one o'clock position, we feel mildly protective. Both moral minds, along with our feelings of moral intensity, can be graphed on this circular chart, which we call our "moral compass."

Dual Morality contends that we need to feel differently at different times. This is just another way of saying that our morality can be expressed in assorted ways depending upon the situation we face. We recognize from our own experiences that our own feelings bounce around this chart. Sometimes we are more easy-going and liberal, and at other times we are more demanding of others and less forgiving of their deviations from standards. Sometimes we are on the left side of the circle and sometimes we are on the right side. Additionally, sometimes we are near the top, where our moral feelings are slight and at other times near the bottom where we feel strongly that only the moral position we hold can be tolerated.

The Moral Compass

The moral compass diagram will make it easy to plot how we move morally leftward or rightward in reaction to the circumstances we face. The diagram will be used to plot the moral climate of cultures and societies too. A very conservative society may be described at the three o'clock or eastward facing position on the compass. A very liberal political commune where everything is held in common would be described near the nine o'clock or westward facing position. At the very top of the circle, or facing due north, we are least emotional and most rational. Here, both moral outlooks are suppressed. And at the very bottom, the six o'clock position or pointing south, we are just the opposite. Here we feel our strongest moral compulsions to provide and protect. Using these four quadrants of moral feeling-then-action:

- North - amorality
- South - ultimate morality
- East - ethical verticality
- West - horizontal equality

We will diagram and explain the entire spectrum of human moral activity. These diagrams will show how and why we act as we do when we do. We will discover why slaveholders can demand only their own freedom, why movie stars are often liberals, why the miraculous is so prevalent in religions, and why we know it is right to love our children more than we love the kids next door. *We will uncover why society MUST BE composed of both relative liberals and relative conservatives, and also how and why both believers and atheists develop in every culture.*

Quad-Realism

From this point on, we will use a phrase that expresses the four points of this compass as the four general methods we have to understand right and wrong. We can see things in four fundamental ways: I call this "Quad-Realism." It combines the idea of a left/right Mind 1/Mind 2 dual moralism with the recognition that our morality is felt either weakly or strongly. Sometimes we see things unemotionally, and amorally, as if we were facing north on our compass. At other times we feel things with fervor and passion, as if we were facing south. But our morality is experienced most often and most distinctly as we face in an eastward or westward direction, where we see things in a generally liberal and sympathetic or generally conservative and ethical way.

Figure 1-7

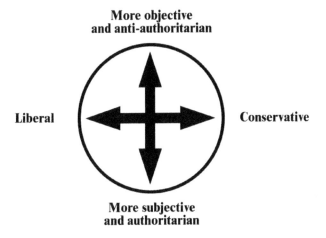

More objective
and anti-authoritarian

Liberal   Conservative

More subjective
and authoritarian

Applying our pictograph to real-life situations, we can see how institutions and occupations emerge to satisfy and provide emotional direction for each of these moral needs, outlooks, and intensities. At the extreme of moral intensity, toward the bottom of the chart, ultra-subjective human-oriented righteousness is felt. Individuals and institutions come into existence to cater to this end of the emotional spectrum, the people we call priests or gurus. At the other end of the spectrum and at the top, an amoral nonhuman universe is recognized and understood by putting our human morality on hold. Here human beings seem no more special than a blade of grass or a bit of dust. With no morality, there is no subjective value to constrain us. This ability to look outside human society and beyond human moral agency gives rise to our sciences. People who act in these ways we call "unemotional." In these hardly-moral (or amoral) conditions we find technocrats.

Reality for most of us is lived between these extremes of intensity. Life happens between our peaks of northern amorality and southern ultimate moral urgency.

Figure 1-8

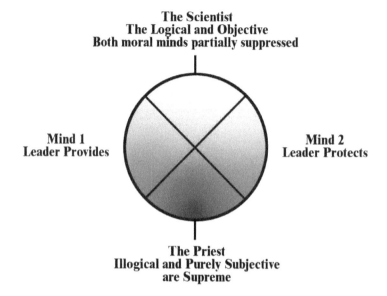

The Scientist
The Logical and Objective
Both moral minds partially suppressed

Mind 1
Leader Provides

Mind 2
Leader Protects

The Priest
Illogical and Purely Subjective
are Supreme

The Philosophers

Leaders and thinkers from the past have usually tried to explain the world from one or the other moral viewpoint. Some, like Jean J. Rousseau[6] and Pierre Proudhon,[7] operated primarily on the left side of our diagram, feeling that ultimate correctness and human progress lie just out of reach, available to all of us if we would just impose a bit more equality on everyone. On the other side, the Mind 2 ethicists like Edmund Burke[8] or the religious Ayatollahs atop Iranian society imagine a better life waiting just beyond our grasp, accessible if we all just follow the best examples of others who have come before us, or the superior leaders who are around us now.

The liberals who see right in horizontal equality and conservatives who see right in vertical superiority are both looking to better the world, but each feels a little differently about it; so each sees its improvement, as well as right and wrong, in slightly different ways.

Along with these, the scientifically oriented explain the world in terms of physical experience and logic and are plotted in the northernmost quadrant of our compass, and those whose emotions find themselves in the southern quadrant search for the meaning of life in faiths and truths deeper than mere facts. The thinkers and philosophers are prone to mistakenly take their own emotional preferences as what is correct absolutely. And their theories are shaped around justifying their own moral preferences. In doing so, most philosophers ended up explaining only part of what we observe in real human society. *They argued for how they thought society should be, rather than explaining how and why it really exists as it does.*

We will look back through history and examine the philosophers who have tried to explain right and wrong in the world, as largely either Mind 1 or Mind 2 affairs, the great social liberals or conservatives. We will also look at those thinkers who argued for ultimate reality as pure logic, cold fact, and hard experience – the scientists; as well as those who felt right and wrong to be found in the discovery of pure subjective and internal truth – the religious. We will decipher liberal from conservative, the subjective from the objective.

Figure 1-9

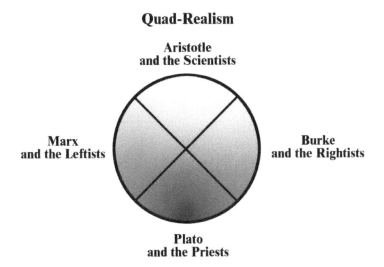

Dual Moralism/quad-realism shapes our feelings and then spurs our actions. It is responsible for the structure of human society as we live it. Along with our left and right wing politicians, our families and our friends, our priests and our scientists, our armies and our welfare agencies, we will eventually come to the ultimate question on the meaning of life. This question will pass from seeming impossible to answer, to obvious and even easy.

We will discover how dual moralism shapes our understanding of ultimate ends; how, when in Mind 1, we feel things in terms of the present and of plenty. These feelings orient our actions and direct our goals toward what is present.

The other side of our dual moralistic outlook aims for pleasure over time, and looks forward and back, trying to satisfy social needs.

Does history repeat itself?

Conceptualizing morality as a dual system within us helps us understand how and why political parties develop, and why they divide into left-wing and right-wing elements. These two sides of us, politically labeled "liberal" and "conservative," emerge in all democracies. Even their minor parties and factions are labeled as either leaning "left" or leaning "right."

Liberal and sympathetic party of current need	Conservative party of ethical tradition
Great Britain	**Great Britain**
Labour	Conservatives
Japan	**Japan**
Democratic Party	Liberal Democratic Party
India	**India**
Indian National Congress	Bharatiya Janata Party
Mexico	**Mexico**
Coalition for All Good	National Action Party
Philippines	**Philippines**
Liberal Party	Nationalist People Coalition

We will show how, at their extremes, Mind 1 societies come to look like Mind 2 societies and why collectivist societies are ruled by individuals and indivdualist societies (democracies) are ruled by the collective.

Figure 1-10

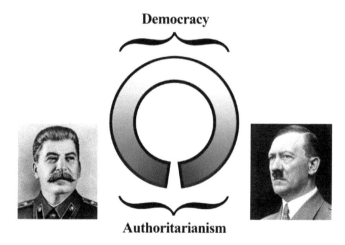

Democracy

Authoritarianism

We will investigate the connection between the political conception of "rights" and our moral understanding of them. When Schopenhauer claims, "It is accordingly easy to define *human* rights: everyone has the right to do anything that does not injure another,"[9] we show why problems crop up as we disagree over exactly what constitutes an "injury." Is someone "injured" in an abortion? Am I "injured" if my neighbor paints his home a garish color? Am I injured by higher taxes or do I benefit from how they will be used?

We will discover that moral conflict is beneficial. As Bernard Williams said in his book, *Ethics and the Limits of Philosophy*, "Disagreement does not necessarily have to be overcome. It may remain an important and constitutive feature of our relations to others."[10]

Morality, *right action toward others,* necessarily involves conflict and disagreement. Dual morality is biologically based internal conflict. It is a subjective, genetically-based debate, which assists us in finding what is most right – right now. With multiple moral codes, not everyone agrees with the moral position others are feeling. Contrary to popular belief, our perpetual moral conflict is far from a catastrophe; it has proven a boon. The group prospers most when some are encouraging sharing while others are emphasizing protection. By keeping the group potentially alarmed to all moral dangers, we remain on our toes against any of them.

Reason or passion

Our dual moral minds operate in a world of both truths and facts. We will investigate what these terms mean and how common it is for our truths to run afoul of our facts. And we will find that it is there, in the effort to turn our truths into facts, that we uncover the *Meaning of Life*.

Though science has progressed at a fantastic pace, it cannot supersede human morality. We grasp that the sun rises and sets outside of human need, but any and all appreciation for the sunrise comes from an underlying urge to do good for ourselves and others. We only pretend we can be creatures of pure reason and logic.

Yet nor can we act only in the sphere of pure truth and absolute subjectivity. *Reality is experienced at the point where the subjective meets the objective.* Human moral impulse is what gets us out of bed in the morning and guides our every action in the real world. If we had no moral compulsion to do for ourselves or others, we would never do anything. If we had only moral compulsion without any physical action we would sit in a trance until we expired. At either the extreme of pure truth or that of pure logic we would be stones.

We can never survive by being completely logical or thoroughly emotional. If we only looked inward at our needs, we could never satisfy them. Satisfying needs requires we interact with the world outside. If we only looked outward, we would have no motivation upon which to act; motivation is an internal thing. Reality is experienced by sensing both outwardly and inwardly. Feeling needs inwardly and then satisfying them outwardly. Right action is understood as both the suppression and expression of our two moral patterns of feeling through right action.

Caring is a moral thing. Logic and reason take no side when a shark bites a surfer or a surfer bites a shark. Logically, actions are observed and recorded, but not judged. Judgment is a function of emotion, and of our dual moral minds.

THERE CAN BE NO ME WITHOUT WE
There can be no we without me

In his pamphlet, *The Emotions: Outline of a Theory*,[11] Jean-Paul Sartre writes of emotions being like a sort of magic that animates us. His philosophy suggests that without a creator, we have no purpose, but this is not so. Purpose does not need to be imposed upon us from without; it can be biologically generated from within. We find purpose in many of the things we do. Our purpose, though internally generated, is just as real to us as if it were inflicted upon us from outside or above. Morality is - moralities are - the emotions we must share to maintain our group existence. All human action, from war to peace, capitalist production to socialist redistribution, marriage to sodomy laws, citizenship to science, and belief to atheism will be explained as complex outgrowths of dual morality and quad-realism.

We are capable of feeling it right that one person is superior or inferior to others. With the capacity to feel in this way, we create institutions and titles with names like "princes" and "paupers." We have innate abilities to treat the lesser people in lesser ways. How much worse can we treat people in lesser conditions and still remain in the realm of decency?

We are capable of feeling it right that all people are equal to others regardless of condition. When the unrepentant criminal miscreant must be seen as in some way equal to the saint, how equally can we treat our unequals and still remain within the realm of moral decency?

The answers to both questions depend on how deeply our culture need express Mind 1 or Mind 2 moral outlooks, which give rise to moral equality or moral inequality.

Inexorably we will link Marx with von Mises, masculinity with femininity, the prince with the pauper, the democrat with the republican, and the theist with the atheist. We will uncover that it is through their combined efforts that we remain on a moral, by that I mean *successful*, path to survival.

This is more than a speculative work in sociobiology. It is a system of fundamental philosophy designed to continue the conversation begun by Pythagoras and Socrates, continued through Hobbes and Hegel, and applied to everyday lives by Martin Luther and Martin Luther King.

Armed with an ability to see correctness from two vantages, where right can be defined as the group sacrificing for the individual, or where it can be understood as the individual sacrificing for the group, I propose to describe, using the insights of so many thinkers before me, how right and wrong come into being and how they are applied; and to explain clearly why right is right, why wrong is wrong, and most importantly, **why right can also be wrong at the very same time**.

Notes

1. Lytton Strachey, *Queen Victoria* (New York, Harcourt, Brace And Company, 1921).

2. Jonathan Eig, *The Birth of the Pill* (New York, W. W. Norton and Company, 2014), 4

3. Ibid., 19.

4. Ibid., 3.

5. J. H. Haynes, *The History of Torture* (Sparkford, Great Britain: Haynes and Company Ltd.), 5.

6. Jean Jacques Rousseau, *Discourse on Inequality*, written in 1754, translated by G. D. H. Cole, [Online] *The Constitution Society* < http://www.constitution.org/jjr/ineq.htm [Retrieved December 2016].

7. Pierre Proudhon, *The Philosophy of Poverty*, written in 1847, translated by Benjamin R. Tucker, [Online] *The Anarchist Library* < https://theanarchistlibrary.org/library/pierre-joseph-proudhon-system-of-economical-contradictions-or-the-philosophy-of-poverty > [Retrieved December 2016].

8. Edmund Burke, *Reflection on the Revolution in France* (New York: The Bobs-Merrill Co. Inc., 1955, originally published in 1790).

9. Arthur Schopenhauer, *Essays and Aphorisms*, translated by R. J. Hollingdale (New York: Penguin Group, 2004), 161.

10. Bernard Williams, *Ethics and the Limits of Philosophy* (Cambridge: Harvard University Press, 1985), 133.

11. Jean-Paul Sartre, *The Emotions: Outline of a Theory* (Secaucus NJ: Carol Publishing Group, 1948, republished 1993), 60-62.

Chapter 2
The Group

HERDING: HOW THE MANY BECOME ONE

Attending a seminar with about thirty other people, our group was released for lunch, and directed to an eatery across the street and about two blocks from where we were staying. We walked over and ate, with instructions to come back after an hour. The group strolled over and returned from the restaurant all at about the same time.

We staggered there and back alone, or in groups of twos or threes. The pairs or trios chatted among themselves, seemingly oblivious to the scenery around them. If asked, I am sure they would all have said they were not paying the least attention to anybody other than their pals walking beside them. We were dozens of little independent flocks. I myself walked alone.

Glancing ahead, I noticed a curious coincidence. Everyone had to cross the small street that separated the cafeteria from the hotel, and though everyone seemed completely unconcerned with what anyone else was doing, each cluster of people crossed the street at the same spot, between exactly the same two parked cars. Interesting.

I initially thought the first few groups crossing at the exact same point might be together. But then I noticed that none deviated. Not one individual or small group crossed anywhere else. Everyone walked up to exactly that same point on the street and crossed at the same precise spot, passing between exactly the same two cars. I continued to watch.

I turned around and looked behind me, then looked back ahead. Our seminar group formed a long meandering line of people, which for some reason were all crossing at the same place. The road on both sides was lined with cars about evenly spaced and it appeared that there was no obvious reason to cross at one location rather than another. But there it was, there WE were. Every clutch crossed at the exact spot the first intrepid pioneer had chosen for reasons unknown to the rest of us.

The randomly chosen crossing point dared first by some unknown leader had somehow gained value for the rest of us. Without thinking, and seemingly at some unconscious level, we all followed his example. Not a single soul crossed at any other point. Like so many wildebeest braving a river of crocodiles, our nameless leader first waded across at that point, and we followed. These thoughts were lazily floating through my mind when, as if I were a disembodied soul looking down and observing my own actions, I found myself in the middle of the road before I realized that I too had crossed the street between exactly those same two parked cars.

It was no coincidence. We do it all the time. We look for examples about everything and we trust what others do. We do it often, we do it everywhere, and we are so accustomed to doing it we take no notice of it. It was on that day that the path to this book was born. I wanted to know how and why we follow whom we do, why we think the instructions and examples of others are worth following. More than that, I wanted to find out how it is we come to decide anything at all. How is it that we determine what is best. I wanted to figure out what was at the radical root of right and wrong.

Herding and social organization

Forming herds and being part of groups is what we do. We are gregarious creatures. From baseball teams to families, cliques at school to hunting clubs, political parties and nations, we are joiners. We know who we are because we are like others around us. It became apparent to me early on that our groups, clans, and cliques are organized in two basic ways: either we are all equal and alike, like a school of sardines, the spectators of a football game, or a seventh grade class being shuffled about on a museum tour; or, the group can be a hierarchical entity with specific leaders, middle-managers, and followers, like a troop of baboons, a Cub Scout pack, or the employees of a factory. Usually we are a little of both. Doing right by others, doing what was expected of us, and ascertaining what we should expect depends on which of these two organizational patterns we are part of.

We follow and we lead. When crossing the street, was I a sardine, doing what those close to me were doing, or was I like a baboon following a more knowledgeable leader? We were a mob all headed in one general direction, yet we followed a distinct and previously laid out path. We were organized both like the sardines and baboons at the same time. In this case, morality, that is, doing rightly, was both doing what others beside me were doing and also following a superior. Years later, I would conclude that what I witnessed was just one in an innumerable array of instances where right is apprehended by us psychologically as a choice between these two acceptable possibilities.

Sardine-style organization	Baboon-style organization
The crowd exiting a stadium, following the flow of others next to them	The military, following the lead of those above and directing others below

TO DECIDE IS TO BE MORAL
Morality is not simply right vs. wrong
It is also right vs. right

How do we decide anything? That became the question I was determined to answer. We decide so many things, what to eat, who to marry, who to vote for, and when to put mom into a nursing home. What do any of these things have in common? How do we determine what to do? How do we know what is right and where to begin?

I did not have to think too long on this subject before I realized that we learn where to cross a street in about the same way we have learned everything. The language I speak, the clothes I wear, the food I eat, and everything else I do is done because someone else did it before me and instructed me on how to do it. I began to wonder, did I really ever decide anything for myself?

I had been taught so much by my parents, my peers, and my superiors. I had been shown by television and influenced by magazines. But then I turned it around. I also did some teaching. I had preferences. I liked some things and disliked others. I tried to sort it all out.

I started by looking at what members of groups had in common, like styles in clothing, language and mannerisms. How was it that some cultures preferred togas and others pants? It was easy to see how circumstance affected choices. All humans might need protection from the sun or the cold and all might be capable of figuring out how to clothe themselves. And this clothing was likely to be made from whatever resources were available – grass skirts, animal hides or woven cloth. But why did those long accustomed to wearing grass skirts come to hold this choice in esteem, while looking askance at the cloth-wearing strangers who met them? Why do we become attached to our circumstantial cultural choices, and assign moral value to them? It became clear that for some reason, long-held preferences come to be taken as "the best" choices. Today in the West, we are fine with the mini-skirt or the sombrero, but some might think it a poor choice to wear the hijab or the turban. To stand out in this way might bring the wearer negative attention or even ridicule. Why?

Could these things really be viewed as moral choices? Then I remembered the mini-skirt and the bikini. The girls first to brave these clothing choices were morally suspect. The first man to discard the toga and wear pants must have suffered the same fate. What did it mean to be good and do right, and how do we know?

About a decade ago, young black men started wearing their pants low, sagging around their butts; it seemed a typical act of individuals trying to establish some colorful distinction within their group or sub-culture. It was looked down upon by older folks and people not identifying with them or their sub-culture. Then, shortly after that, young white guys began to imitate the practice.

Did the originators in the black community smile or frown when they were being imitated by persons outside their immediate association? Was it a matter of developing cultural distinction only to have it stolen and misappropriated, or was it assimilation? And what of the folks who never approved of the habit? Many people thought it was deliberately sending out a message of non-conformity. When was a person "cool" for wearing one's pants hanging down, and when was he a reprobate thug? When was the practice a black thing, and when did it become a youth thing? Was the image of being cool or being a thug in the hands of the wearers or the viewers? The act of leading, following and impressing is what we are describing here.

Just exactly how we will choose to demonstrate that we fit in, or that we do not, varies. The details of how such things are accomplished are irrelevant. Like the bowerbirds that collect whatever is at hand to line up their bowers to impress the females, humans exaggerate or amplify whatever is at hand to bring distinction or express conformity. Others follow the example set by leaders in order to identify which sub-groups are winning their support.

More than with mere clothing options, what was best (or right) and what was worst (or wrong) varied wildly and involved everything. It occurred to me that morality and goodness were not always choices between right and wrong, but were often between right and right. Those wearing the turbans felt they were more correctly dressed than the guys beneath the fedoras. Those with the saggy pants were, considering their circumstances, more appropriately dressed than if they had been wearing a suit. What made one choice more appropriate than another?

Standards. The first girls who dared to wear the mini-skirts were accused of giving into their own pleasures and vanities. No one had to wear a mini-skirt. No one had to wear his pants sagging down. The problem involved who got to set the standards (to pick our crossing points) and who was expected to follow them. Why does the new assault? Somehow the older, accepted styles retained more moral value. But how was this possible? Just because our mothers and grandmothers wore certain dresses did not make their older styles more correct! Or did it?

Following the crowd

Moms everywhere were known for scolding their kids against following the wrongdoing of their peers. Every mother has heard her child justify doing some questionable thing by saying, "Everyone else is doing it."

And every child has heard her mother respond with something like, "If your friends were jumping off a bridge, would you jump off too?"

The moral lesson mom was teaching was that there was some standard of right and wrong outside whatever our crowd was doing. Was she right?

The observant child might have noticed that mom varied the style of shoes she was wearing or the hairdo she sported based on what other mommies of her generation were doing this year. Why was it okay for mom to follow her crowd, but not okay for children to follow theirs? Mom was telling us that we had to learn to distinguish between two possibilities. Sometimes we can do what we want, and at other times we must do as we should. Sometimes we do as we please, but at other times we should do as we have been taught.

I read the old philosophers and political theorists. They seemed to say about the same things our mom said, though in a more complex and highbrow manner. They concluded, as mom had, that the question always came down to choosing between doing what was fun and doing what was right. Everybody always pointed out the difference between having fun as we found it in the moment and doing right by some standard set by others. I was on the track of right and wrong. The answers seemed to lie in this direction: to follow the crowd, or follow the proper leader; to have fun or do what was right. Why did most things seem to come down to choices between these options?

Having fun or doing right

On the opening page of William Godwin's book, *Enquiry Concerning Political Justice*, published in 1793, a list of principles is given from whence to proceed whenever morality was being examined. The first principle he listed was just a rewording of the choice we always seemed to be facing: "The true object of moral and political disquisition is pleasure or happiness."[1]

Wasn't this just what our moms have been telling us all along? My friends and I were seeking pleasure, but they wanted us to do more — to do right, to seek happiness. It might be fun to jump off that bridge, but when we hit bottom, we would not be laughing. Wearing saggy pants may be fun for a while, but if we expected to get anywhere in this world, we better pull them up and do right.

Defining ultimate ends in terms of either pleasure or happiness has been recognized by moms and other philosophical moralists as the great moral tug-of-war that has been going on since time immemorial. Having fun is not always the same as doing right. Having fun was good in the moment but it was the other thing, doing right, that was to be preferred as most beneficial over time. What is it about these things that make them special? Why are these two different goals the corner-posts of all that we seek?

I found that the goals of pleasure and happiness were alluded to again and again. I was about to discover how and why these are the great destinations and end points that provide us a target to aim for as we seek meaning in our lives. These are the two ends of our dual psychological outlook, pleasure being happiness in the moment, and happiness being pleasure over time.

THE NATURE OF CRUELTY
Our fiercest battles are never waged between right and wrong but between right and right

Sometimes moral choices seem simple, like deciding how long or short to wear a skirt. At other times they seem more complex, like which candidate to vote for or how to advise our son after we find illegal drugs in his closet. The march of history has been little more than a chronology of moral choices and how people made them.

History passes over the mundane and records the morally significant. During the Middle Ages when slavery was accepted everywhere, the moral question in Europe was whether Christians should be enslaved or whether the institution should be limited to the heathens. As material wealth progressed and slavery was on its way out, the moral issue turned on who continued to support the institution and who opposed it absolutely. In every era, the issue of war or peace finds its way into cultural conversations. And today we have others, like whether to provide taxpayer funding for abortions or increases in teachers' pay.

Today we are in a culture dominated by Mind 1 morality; this has not always been so. In Mind 2 times, the moral end points we aim at are different, so the moral choices we face are not like those we face now in our Mind 1 times. If we recall the difference, Mind 1 is our morality for conditions of plenty and safety. This certainly describes how most of us live now. But things have not always been so easy. For most of the past, our other outlook needed to prevail: our morality of want and danger. Depending on how we see the world, we will ascertain right and wrong in different ways. This has a bearing on how we judge the appropriateness of actions.

Recently, a professional athlete spent months in prison for staging dogfights. He was found guilty of being cruel to animals. Animal cruelty has only recently become a major social issue in the West. That is, it has only been a topic of debatable political moral significance in the past 200 years. In many cultures, particular animals have been held as sacred for centuries, and some cultures have adopted vegetarianism. But a widespread belief that animals and people share the same moral protections is recent. Our society has not yet developed a consistent attitude on the matter, though we are moving toward a consensus where animals have rights and expectations once reserved only for people.

We cannot fight dogs or chickens, but we can hunt birds and we can kill certain animals just for fun. Why is shooting animals for sport acceptable cruelty? If we raise them to eat them, then we can kill animals too. Is that not cruel? What defines animal cruelty, and why is it an issue now when it was never an issue before?

It is apparent at a glance that tolerance of man's cruelty to animals parallels our tolerance for cruelty to each other. In times when people were owned, chained or whipped, it made no sense to object to animals being treated this way. Back when painkillers and antibiotics were non-existent and children suffered and died with regularity in the arms of their parents, could tears be spared for the better treatment of criminals?

Patterns in moral behavior take shape slowly. Today in the developed nations, when pain and suffering are not everyday occurrences, we have little stomach for them. But when pain was all around, inflicting it on others could be seen as not only tolerable, but beneficial. When we suffer ourselves, it seems we more easily accept the suffering of others. When life was cruel to us, we did not worry much about the neighbors being cruel to their pets, their kids, or their livestock.

A moral pattern began to take shape in my thinking: In easier times, being easy becomes right; in harder times, being hard seemed necessary.

Is it right for others to suffer if their suffering is good for us?

A couple of hundred years ago, a belief developed that eating the flesh of animals who suffered fear and pain at the moment of death imparted invigorating nutrients into the meat and then into us. Bulls were tortured before being butchered, pigs and calves were whipped to death before eaten. It was thought not only to improve their flavor, but also to impart energetic properties to the food. There was nothing wrong with it – and if it worked, something very right about it.

Beating animals to death or skinning them alive was believed by some chefs to improve flavor. In a book titled *The Cooks Oracle*, published in 1821, William Kitchner recoils at the old practice he describes as diabolical:

> Take a Goose or a Duck, or some such lively creature, pull
> off all her feathers, only the head and neck must be spared:
> then make a fire round about her, not too close to her, that

the smoke do not choke her, and that the fire may not burn her too soon … within the circle of the fire let there be set small cups and pots of water wherein salt and honey are mingled… The Goose must be all larded, and basted over with butter: put then fire about her, but do not make too much haste, when as you see her begin to roast; for by walking about and flying here and there, being cooped in by the fire that stops her way out, the unwearied Goose is kept in; she will fall to drink the water to quench her thirst, and cool her heart, and all her body … and when she roasteth, and consumes inwardly … always wet her head and heart … when you see her giddy with running, and begin to stumble, her heart wants moisture, and she is roasted enough. Take her up and set her before your guests and she will cry as you cut off any part from her and will be almost eaten up before she be dead: it is mighty pleasant to behold![2]

Ghastly! Mr. Kitchner was no sadist, but apparently some cooks who came before him seemed that way. How is it that such behavior could be found normal and acceptable in one generation while feeling intolerably egregious in another? Today we are fined for whipping animals; yesterday we were appreciated for skinning them alive.

THE MORAL FORK IN THE ROAD
Can we all make it?

/   \

If "yes," we are guided by Moral Mind 1   If "no," we are led by Moral Mind 2

Culture is structured in such a way that:	Culture is structured in such a way that:
Everyone matters equally.	The more vital members matter most.
Everyone should be heard.	The opinions of the better people count most.
We look down to the smallest, weakest or poorest for guidance on how to act and how to distribute goods.	We look up to the biggest, strongest and most powerful for guidance on how to act and distribute goods.
People can decide things for themselves.	Standards have been set for us to follow and succeed.

Culture is structured in such a way that:	Culture is structured in such a way that:
We are most concerned with what others near us are doing.	We are most concerned with what the better people are doing.
Competition is unnecessary; sharing is what is called for.	Competition reveals who is better and who worse; we need to prevail when in competition.
All people should be looked out for and treated equally where possible.	Our group and those closest to us can be treated better than others. A hierarchy of treatment from best to worst can go along with those most vital to least vital to our group.
At the extreme of plenty and security, even animals and things can be felt as having equal needs and equal worth to people.	At the extreme of danger and want, even valuable individuals might have to be sacrificed and die for the good of the others.

We do what is right vs. Right is what we do

Moral practices vary between cultures because cultural practices themselves change with circumstances over time. But one pattern became clear to me: Whenever a group did anything for a long period of time, the practice took on an air of moral certitude. To learn from the past, it was imperative that we first must feel that the lessons to be found there are likely to be valuable.

Women may have woven the first grass skirts because dried grass was the only material available. But after generations of wearing grass skirts, the material and the style took on a moral precept of its own. Repetition creates credibility. Those who acted in this way survived and were important people in our lives. When other materials came available, the long accepted grass skirt continued to be preferred for some time as best and right.

In some cultures, the grass skirt became the conservative choice of all girls. Good girls, that is, girls who knew and understood the lessons of their mothers, wore grass skirts. Those of the current generation often rose up to challenge the practice, but everyone understands that to challenge it now is to be daring and possibly dangerous. What we have always done, with grass skirts as with all other things, comes to be understood – biologically – as what is right. The reason for this seemed obvious.

When we do what the successful people before us have done, we have a better chance at being successful too. Clearly humans who thought this way have advantages over others who could not or would not learn from the past. Learning from those around us and before us, especially those who were doing better than we are, profits us. The psychological habit of mimicking the better people in order to become better ourselves was a mental advantage.

This seems self-evident. It is the basis of the instinct to culture. Yesterday matters, people older than us know something valuable, and we can learn from it and them today. Actually, this must have been a complex social adaptation that took place among herding animals long before the emergence of man. We must be able to recognize who is doing best, and then be internally compelled to do as they do. Mimicry, exhibited in the proper ways and at proper times, is an asset.

With an advanced brain, humans took this a step further. Not only can we learn from the best that are around us now, but through stories and histories we can also learn from the more capable people of long ago. All herding animals learn by mimicking the older and stronger among them. Humans prove themselves superior by recalling and imitating the successful people from other times and distant places.

It is easy to see how a reverence for the past or an inclination to emulate the capable is vital. By being a part of a herd, we do not have to acquire every experience ourselves or genetically inherit every trait through instinct. We can learn from those around us as well as those who came before. Acquiring culture is the process of personal improvement – that is, doing what others do. Being *the most cultured* has always meant doing what the best and brightest have done.

We should not always do exactly what the people of the past have done. Survival sometimes requires we decide differently for the here and now. New circumstances can arise for which there is no historic precedent. Sometimes we have to try new and different things when facing problems our ancestors never faced.

Dual morality has incorporated these choices: of doing something new now or doing what others have always done. Moral Mind 1 is usually called into play when doing something new and now, Moral Mind 2 is more often relied upon when following patterns established in the past. We will later discover how this time perspective fundamentally alters moral behavior.

Mind 1	Mind 2
We do what is right - right now.	We do what has been proven right before.

Having it both ways

When discussing morality, we often imagine we should confine it to the monumental and serious questions of the age, like abortion, the death penalty, or war. But morality is simply the assertion of what is right in relation to the goals we seek. Right and wrong come into play in everything we do: the tiny decisions along with the great ones.

We need to know what is happening around us now, and react as is most appropriate today. This is certainly a pressure we will always face. Then again, following the patterns of before has the advantage of experience and predictability. These outlooks shape our two moral orders. The first, giving priority to the opportunities that present themselves in the present, gives a nod to success in the present. Following today's fashions, safety in numbers, and joining the crowd, all give rise to pleasure in us. When feeling this way, sympathetically driven, we consider our moral goals present and circumstantial.

In the other moral outlook, we try to apply the lessons of yesterday to the circumstances we face now. We follow traditional fashions, examples from the past, and uphold tradition. When feeling this way, when ethically driven, we consider our moral goals established, proven, and customary.

Moral Mind 1	Moral Mind 2
The morality of now	The morality of yesterday and custom

Learning to act in both moral outlooks gives us an advantage over those who might only know one or the other. We need to know what people today might be doing now, in current circumstances, as well as how things have been done before. Doing what seems right, right now, is often something different from doing what was shown to be right yesterday.

Most importantly, the morality of today – Mind 1 – is determined by people today: by me and my contemporaries. The morality of yesterday has already been determined by someone else, by mom or by lawgivers. In Mind 1, I can decide; in Mind 2, others before or above me have made the choice already.

Mind 1 The morality of now	Mind 2 The morality of then
The morality of what our contemporaries, our friends and our equals are doing	The morality of what has been right all along; the morality of our betters
The moral choice that makes sense right now in the situation I am in	The moral choice that has been long ago determined as right in this circumstance
My peers and I decide.	Others have decided.

We sometimes imagine morality can be a set of moral absolutes: *Thou shalt not kill* or *Thou shalt not commit adultery*. In practice such absolutism is always mitigated by circumstances. *Thou shalt not kill* becomes:

- *Thou shalt not kill - except in self-defense.*

or

- *Thou shalt not kill except when drafted into the army and told to do so.*

Everywhere we look we find that, in practice, morality is a twofold thing. It is doing what is right for me and my close associates right now, or doing right as others see it for the good of the group. Morality is both doing right for me and doing right for you. Sometimes these are the same thing; sometimes they are not.

Mind 1 I decide	Mind 2 Others have decided
I can decide what is right for my group.	Through custom, tradition and established institutions, my group decided (before I was born) what is right for me.

Morality is expressed both by following long accustomed social practices and by doing whatever it takes when facing current circumstantial demands. These two standards often clash. Each of us decides right based on one or the other of our dual internal moral patterns; but we all do not decide it in the same way. Some of us favor the practices of now and others the patterns of before; some accept the latest trends, others the methods of times past.

Custom as Mind 2 morality

Morality comes to us as a feeling; morality is emotional direction. Morality is instruction on what to do in order to prosper personally and in order to help others proper too. If our group lives in a grove of oak trees and we travel north at daybreak to drink because it is then that the lions sleep, and we travel west at noon to eat from the fruit trees, then travel south at dusk to gather fire wood, and later return home at dark for safety, these habits are more than just whims. Established patterns of behavior that have profited others in the past need to be retained by us, and valued today.

These ways are proven. Acting in these established patterns allowed those like us who came before to survive. These same practices will likely help us now. If we practice these patterns, others around us will know what to expect from us. They can rely upon us to act in these ways. If we do these things, the others can count on us, and through predictability we help each other survive. The group has moral expectations of us. They depend on us doing the right thing, for their sake as well as our own.

When a renegade group member wants to deviate from the pattern, he is suspect. He endangers himself. If he encourages followers, he puts them at risk as well as the rest of us. Jumping off a bridge has always been seen as bad. Following leaders who are now doing this is to become bad yourself. Mom says, "Don't do it!" It's common sense. Common sense is the sense that is common.

To do "good" is to follow the proper leader
or the proper practices

We are a herding species; we travel in groups and follow leaders. Evil itself is often best understood as following the wrong leader. We have only to look at our electioneering slogans or Christmas carols to grasp how ingrained this idea is in the psyche. Good leaders preserve us from danger; bad leaders take us astray. Vote for me and prosper; vote for the other guy and suffer. Or we sing:

God rest ye merry Gentleman
Let nothing you dismay,
For Jesus Christ our Savior
Was born upon this day,
To save us all from Satan's power
When we were gone astray ...

Going astray is following the wrong leader. Follow one supernatural being and you are good; follow the other and you are bad. Evil is doing bad things, which occurs when we follow bad leaders.

The people crossing the street ahead of me at the seminar manifested the same old moral understanding we humans have always displayed for thousands of years. We played it safe. The first leader crossed at this point and made it across, and the rest of us followed the example and succeeded too. We benefit from the apparently sound decision. We followed rightly. We followed subconsciously.

Large groups have a number of leaders. We can decide whom we follow. When we have choices, what is morally right can be more than one thing at any one time. The larger and more diverse the group, the more likely not everyone will agree as we will face making a number of moral decisions.

There was a time, we can suppose, when human groups were small and everyone knew everyone else. It was a time before our group was so big that corners of it spoke different languages and practiced assorted religions. Long ago, we were one. We were one big family, we were the army when attacked, we all prayed to the same gods for a shared blessing. If we came across food, we shared it. We all killed together and we shared together.

In those times, leaders who were just like us led us to success in all these areas. They directed our prayers, guided our hunts, told us how much to share, and commanded us in battle. The great leader found food and fought off enemies. The best leaders, human or otherwise, both provided and protected. These became the two faces of human moral judgment: provision and protection.

Provision/protection becomes central aspects of moral understanding. Look around: our political parties as well as our patterns of home life center on these things. We must acquire food and seek safety in shelter. We must have enough to eat as well be protected from the elements, enemies and criminals. Dual morality is the process by which we fulfill these basic needs: provision and protection.

To Provide: To have enough food, warmth, and material goods for survival.

To Protect: To be safe in our homes and territories so that these material goods can be acquired.

Leadership itself becomes a binary thing:

Can We All Make It?
Yes or No
/ \

Mind 1 If we can all make it, we all should make it.	Mind 2 If we cannot all make it, we must decide who does and who does not.
The moral imperative is: **to provide.**	The moral imperative is: **to protect.**
The proper and equal distribution of ample resources distinguishes the superior leader.	The proper prioritization of limited resources distinguishes the superior leader.
Sharing what we have is right, because we have enough for all.	With not enough protection or food for all, we must prioritize people and things; if we all cannot make it, it is vital to the rest of us that the most important come through.

Our two moral methods are built around the two distinct conditions that face all creatures – safety and plenty, or starvation and danger. It is for the purpose of handling these two fundamental social circumstances that what we call our moral sentiments developed in the first place. And it is here – to provide and to protect – that our two moral modes are rooted. When the group is in danger and starvation threatens, we instinctively become traditional. Frivolity goes out the window and we get serious. We marshal all our resources to save ourselves. First among these are the lessons from our past. How others made it before us gives us clues to how we might survive today. Morality tells us that thinking this way is right and best.

On the other hand, tradition can handcuff us. The group needs to try new paths and visit new waterholes and different groves of fruit trees. Tradition sometimes needs to be challenged. We have developed an affinity and a place for change as well. When times are easy and dangers few, we are more daring. We tolerate the new and the untried. We experiment.

We seek the novel when we can, and value the traditional when we must. Being able to appreciate both as best serves our needs and gives us moral flexibility.

Can We All Survive?
Is there enough for all?
Yes or No
/   \

Mind 1: Times are Easy	Mind 2: Times are Hard
New ways can be tried.	Old ways have proven themselves.
Subgroups doing different things develop and are tolerated.	Subgroups are eliminated as deviant, maybe dangerous; we must unite toward a common purpose.

   Proper moral training equips us to act rightly in either situation. But morality is a deeper thing than cultural training. We have evolved two mental moral outlooks: If we all can make it, sharing becomes the preeminent moral imperative; if we all cannot make it, some of us can live while others may have to die, and methods have to be developed to determine who those will be. We feel these things. These basic outlooks are more than cultural anomalies; they are instinctive, biologically-based behavioral patterns. The details of what came before or what is happening now might change, but preferring the before or preferring the now is largely an instinctive response.

Mind 1 There is enough for all – and we are safe	Mind 2 There is not enough for all or there are physical dangers
Leadership focuses internally. The equitable distribution of plentiful resources within the group is what is required most by the leader's management.	Leadership focuses externally. External threats or deprivations must be faced. The prioritization of people and things is what is demanded of the leader.

DUAL MORALITY - TWO WAYS TO ORGANIZE SOCIETY
THE HORIZONTAL AND THE VERTICAL

   It is clear that if we imagine there is enough for everybody, we further deduce that everyone should get enough. If there is not enough for everybody, mechanisms need to be in place to establish who gets more and who gets less. When facing one environmental condition, a general atmosphere of equality would and ought to reign; and under the other, a condition of advantage and disadvantage needs to be set up.

If not everyone can make it, the most important need to be sorted out for preservation. How can we do this? If some of us matter more than others, those who matter most should be closest to the leader's attention. If we look around us, we discover this is exactly how herding creatures socially structure themselves.

By whatever name we give them – herds, flocks, schools, or prides – each organizes in one of two ways: horizontally or vertically.

Can We All Survive?
Yes or No

/   \

Mind 1 We organize horizontally	Mind 2 We organize vertically
Everyone is about equally important to the leader.	Some are closer and more important to leadership than others.
We share resources.	We prioritize resources.
We share leadership responsibilities.	We prioritize leadership responsibilities.
We get about the same amount as others.	Some get more than others; some less.
All should survive.	Some are unavoidably expendable.

Depending on the survival strategy and environment, all grouping species socially interact in either a top down hierarchical fashion or in a broad and equal way – many do both. Some species have evolved to perpetually exhibit one method more than the other. These organizational patterns correspond directly to the challenges faced by the species: general plenty or perpetual danger.

Looking around, we discover that all herding animals tend to organize themselves horizontally or vertically. Humans and other creatures with complex social structures do both.

Horizontal or vertical morality

Horizontally organized species such as flocking starlings or schooling sardines have no apparent leadership, and every individual is assumed to have equal obligations and equal opportunities. Food may be eaten as a group, but is not acquired in a coordinated group effort; everything is equally available to all. Safety, when needed, is understood as the jostling to attain a central physical position within the group. To be in the middle is safest. This does not mean starlings or sardines never face times of shortages. I use these examples here merely to demonstrate that, in nature, these organizational patterns recur for a reason. Sardines, like flocks of starlings and pods of dolphins, find resources scattered plentifully around them; selecting out the single leader in a group of thousands is neither feasible nor necessary. The species survives by relying almost exclusively on one organizing pattern – the horizontal. One starling or one sardine is interchangeable with another.

For the social creatures organized horizontally, like vultures, lemmings or reindeer, no clear line of superiority and inferiority is evident, at least outside of breeding seasons. No clear leadership develops. These creatures follow abundant food supplies and internally they are motivated to do whatever the creature beside them is doing. If all before them rush to the right, they move right. If all before them turn around and retreat, they do the same. They trust the decisions of the herd members around them.

They are the ones jumping off the bridge if their pal beside them is doing it.

Vertically organized species have established leaders, hierarchies, followers, and subordinates. They are structured in a top-down fashion. Though one member is equal to another at the social level he occupies, he lives among others whom he knows are either above or below him. These groups include the social insects like bees that have a queen who must be preserved, and whom all others would die to protect. She is more vital than the rest – and every other bee feels it.

Primate society is often structured in this fashion, as are lions and hyenas. Some members of the group lead and others follow. Some get a first share or larger share, while others wait their turn. Some are more important than others.

Groups that use this strategy more exclusively gain from having their members prioritized with the smartest, meanest, strongest, or in some other way the fittest, working their way to the top and making most of the group's decisions. A hierarchy from the most to the least able is established. Resources for these species are not abundant everywhere and often have to be fought over. It does not mean that there are not times when these groups are safe and resources abundant; it only means that the species evolved where a more vertical social structure was right most of the time.

Vertical structure does best for creatures facing constant danger and limited supplies. Those nearest the top, those proven most fit, are assured the safest place and easiest access to limited goods. Those at the bottom are most likely to suffer, but as the least fit, they are objectively the most expendable. Tough times make for hard choices. In vertical societies, gaining and maintaining social status is vital to success; place is everything. Wolves and baboons fall into these categories. It pays to be near the top of the totem pole.

Zebras and other grazers under constant threat from predators often use a mixed strategy. They have leader-stallions and followers, superiors and subordinates, and some are assumed to take on more risk to protect and provide for than others. The leader also takes them to the greenest pastures; after that they are on their own. We reach into the animal kingdom for examples of socialization patterns. Human beings are neither sardines nor baboons – but examples of socialization patterns similar to our own are found everywhere in nature.

Mind 1 Resources Are Plentiful and Dangers Few	Mind 2 Resources Are Scarce and Threats Abundant
Organize horizontally – sardine-style.	Organize vertically – baboon-style.
The loss of any one is no more damaging to the group than the loss of any other.	The loss of some group members is more threatening than the loss of others; these more vital elements need better provision and protection.

Higher animals socially cooperate in both ways, though there seems to be species-specific preferences for one type of social organization over the other. Humans, the most complex of the herding animals, developed the ability to operate in both manners too, and we have taken these social structures to levels unmatched in the animal kingdom.

Our human ability to institutionalize behavioral patterns gives us supreme flexibility and allows us to benefit from the most varied social structure of any creature. Hierarchical animals have troop leaders; humans have kings, presidents, and beauty contest judges. Other herding animals post lookouts; we develop police forces and border guards. Other herding animals compete among groups; humans have wars. Though we are more socially complex than other creatures, our patterns of social structure are fundamentally similar. The moral basis of right and good, and the directions under which our human institutions operate, are rooted in basic herd morality, which is found everywhere.

The dual roots of our moral nature are expressed through our institutions. When we socialize vertically, we develop kings and serfs; when we horizontalize, we discover equality and democratically recognize every citizen. One or the other moral outlook will likely be on display, depending on the nature of the threat to us.

Morality is acting rightly in the situation we face at the moment. But with two moral capabilities, what is moral can be two different things at the very same time.

Do we fight or flee, share or hoard; do I leave that extra two dollars as a tip for the waitress or do I keep it for my own future needs? What is right, right now?

Intuitively we believe when we go wrong, when we act in ways other than what is morally best, we suffer. Acting rightly is acting morally. But we find that with two moral spheres, there are two ways to act rightly – two opinions on what we are to do – both bouncing around in our heads at the very same time.

THE ORIGINS OF DUAL MORALITY

> Why a dog, whenever he sees a stranger, is angry; when an
> acquaintance, he welcomes him, although the one has
> never done him any harm, nor the other any good. Did this
> ever strike you as curious? – Plato, *The Republic*[3]

Philosophers of every stripe have commented on the dual nature of morality. Herbert Spencer spoke of it being of two types, which he called the "industrial" and the "martial."[4] Some have referred to it as the morality of the family and of the group; some have called it the intuitive versus the rational. Thinkers pondered different names for the dual social experience we witness. It is no coincidence that our two moral forms line up smartly with our two major social patterns of interactive experience – our family and our group. It is from here that the deeper roots of our morality became focused and sharpened.

We are always either among family members or we are out in the public in the realm of strangers and acquaintances. The moral codes we employ change depending largely on which of these situations we are in. Broadly speaking, when we are surrounded by family, we share, we pay attention first to the smallest and weakest, and we view it right that everyone survive.

Our public selves discern right in our other way. Publically, we follow the person in charge. Groups follow the experienced, the strongest, or the bravest. At home everyone eats – we are equal; on the street, services and expectations are given and received unequally. At home we look first to the small, the sick, and the weak; on the job we look up to the superior for instruction. In the outside world of sports and construction, those who make the most get the most; the weaker, the shirkers, and the incapable get less. At home, those who contribute least may be fed first; outside the home, those who do not contribute may get nothing. Both can be right.

The good times

When do we share? What are the politics of equality? Horizontal herding patterns emerge when our times are safe and our resources plenty, such as those we find in democracies. Leadership in these situations is temporary, tenuous, and sometimes hardly existent. The security of the home spills over into the streets and promotes this mindset; everyone must be provided for and the weakest shall get the most attention. This social outlook creates the circumstances conducive to republics, democracies, and communes. These forms of government emerge in times of wealth and commercial exchange where socially we are surrounded by security and plenty. In such social situations, decisiveness is not likely vital. Threats are few; expanding wealth and sharing it receives our attention. We are tolerant. Risk and change are okay. The richer and safer society becomes, the more we bring "family style" morality into the public square.

In easy times we let our hair down. Our art can spin off in a hundred directions, our relationships are flexible and our tolerance great. If I do all right without having to worry about what you are up to, then I really do not have to be concerned with your habits. As long as each of us knows the other is provided for, we have little reason to be concerned with anybody else.

The hard times

Our second Moral Mind is called upon when there is not enough for everyone or when the group is in danger. Where these conditions persist (as they did throughout most of human history), leadership assumes a top-down hierarchical structure, is long lasting, often attained through struggle and vacated only at death. These cultural patterns develop to bring their limited resources to bear quickly on any problem.

Vertical social structures are institutionalized to limit the chaos that would occur if we had to fight among ourselves every day for place and position. Social classes coalesce. Kings, dictators and emperors proclaim where we will go, and the rest of us follow.

It matters not if we are speaking of Julius Caesar, Napoleon, Mao Ze Dong, Shaka Zulu, or Crazy Horse; those favored by the leader enjoy more of the limited fruits available to their culture than others. Where everyone cannot survive and threat is ever present, hard choices have to be made. But they are not always made by us individually; sometimes they have already been made for us. Not even the tyrannical leader gets to choose all his lieutenants or every one of his aristocratic pals. Cultural battles within the group lead to the establishment of hierarchies in every sphere, which the king or tyrant recognizes. Even dictators need social allies.

It is not surprising, and is in fact instinctive and morally proper, that in times of want or stress, the strong central leader assumes dictatorial dimensions and sometimes makes sweeping decisions. In our own times, when our group was threatened, presidents ignored the metaphysical constraints of constitutionality or democratic precedent and set up internment camps for the Japanese, like Franklin Roosevelt, or snooped into everyone's emails and telephone conversations, like

George W. Bush. Under threat, the dynamic leader is trusted to decide for all of us. Respect for the individual is temporarily set aside, and most of us cheer. We need to be protected. Things may need to be sacrificed.

Method 2 is ever on guard within us, and sees the greatest threat coming from outside the group, or from within the group only when members do not follow the rules. With danger and want all around us, infractions cause a loss of status, and status is vital in Method 2 surroundings. Doing what one is supposed to do is the best method of guaranteeing personal safety. Breaking the rules sets one outside the group's protection. Criminals become like outsiders, hardly worthy of serious consideration.

Together Moral Minds 1 and 2 tug us back and forth, keeping us and our herd both safe and well cared for. Dual morality focuses our attention sometimes on the external and sometimes on the internal threats. Together our dual morality has made us the most successful species on the planet.

SOCIETY ORGANIZES HORIZONTALLY AND VERTICALLY

Moral Mind 1 Society organizes HORIZONTALLY THERE IS ENOUGH FOR EVERYONE TO MAKE IT AND NO THREATS ARE APPARENT TO THE GROUP.	Moral Mind 2 Society organizes VERTICALLY NOT EVERYONE CAN SURVIVE. THERE IS NOT ENOUGH TO GO AROUND.
We are all equally valuable.	Some are better than others.
Democratic equality – leadership is temporary and rotated as it bubbles up from the group.	There is an ultimate leader, a king, a dictator, an aristocracy, a peasantry, castes, even slaves.
The present counts most.	Lessons from the past teach us much.
The biggest threat comes from misappropriation of resources within the culture. The individual is protected by the group.	The biggest threat comes from outside the culture or rule breakers. The group is protected by prioritizing individuals and controlling actions.
The many sacrifice to save the one.	The one is sacrificed to save the many.
The leader follows the group.	The group follows the leader.
Production is viewed in terms of cooperative coworkers.	Social structures include superiors and subordinates.
Worker cooperatives	Management and unions

Moral Mind 1 **Society organizes HORIZONTALLY** THERE IS ENOUGH FOR EVERYONE TO MAKE IT AND NO THREATS ARE APPARENT TO THE GROUP.	Moral Mind 2 **Society organizes VERTICALLY** NOT EVERYONE CAN SURVIVE. THERE IS NOT ENOUGH TO GO AROUND.
Culture is described through concepts like *the people/the pubic/the masses*. Religion is understood as a vague amorphous spirituality of ultimate equality and universal satisfaction of all needs and desires, and a sharing goodness.	The State, and The military and society at large are all viewed as hierarchical class systems culminating in ultimate leaders. Religion is where we take our subservient place to perform infinite duties.
A classless society; security and provision are available and better ensured by the elimination of class.	Social classes struggle to protect their position for themselves and their offspring.
Universal humanity/spirituality – equality of faiths and creeds	Our country, our faith, and everything of ours are better than other people's nations and faiths.
Majorities rule.	Experts and aristocrats know best and are to be acknowledged and followed.
Fun is praised. Emotions are expressed and enhanced; emotionalism is the excitement behind life. Sexy is the ultimate goal and compliment.	Stoicism is praised. Emotions show vulnerability and are to be hidden or controlled, particularly sexuality.
Life is pleasure.	Life is duty.
Organized like: starlings/sardines/wildebeests	Organized like: zebras/lions/chimpanzees

Liberals and conservatives

We look to elders, superiors and experts for guidance, but we also look around and do what others are doing. We follow the leader and follow the crowd; we inform and we conform. Being the most complex of creatures, our social structures are more varied and intricate. Our cultures become systematized and categorized. We call our vertically oriented systems monarchies, aristocracies, dictatorships – with leaders called popes, cardinals, and priests; or generals, colonels, and sergeants; or corporations, CEOs, managers, and supervisors; or castes and social classes. We have given our horizontal cultures names like democracies, communes, cooperatives, and families. The simple social structures observed throughout the animal world have been turned into the intricate cultural patterns repeated across human experience.

But we are not all these things equally all the time. Cultural and environmental forces determine which moral method gains the upper hand at any moment of our personal life and at each period of history. Individually we bring both moral minds to bear on every act we do and every question we face, but one or the other method tends to gain the upper hand. Each of us tends to favor our Mind 1 or Mind 2 outlook. As a group, we tend to be a mostly Mind 1 or Mind 2 crowd. If we display a Mind 1 pattern, we are sometimes called the sympathetic or liberal type; if we favor a Mind 2 view, we are usually referred to as the ethical or conservative type. If one or the other of these types of people is in the majority, then our culture is referred to as liberal or conservative.

We often sit in different social situations and come to think more easily in one mind or the other. The safe, secure and rich often become the liberals gliding naturally into a Method 1 outlook. The middle classes, who imagine their social positions tenuous and loss of place threatening, trend Method 2 conservative. The lowest social classes, when they look up to those in a higher social station or a superior economic position, can be motivated to promote the ideals of Mind 1 equality. But when those same people moving in the lower levels of society interact with those near their own social strata, they can be harshly Mind 2, struggling to preserve the small advantages they have acquired only with great effort. All are right.

How we approach the world anticipates how we will likely find it. Each of us concludes independently how much we are threatened or secure. When we assume the universe operates (or should operate) in a certain way, lo and behold our minds generally conclude that it does. If we lean toward Method 1, the criminal or foreigner is apt to be pitied. In Method 1 Mind, we are not afraid of the external; all people and all groups are equally worthy of consideration. In this mind, it is the internal-rich and not the external-foreign who alarms us. It is the unequal distribution of internal goods that poses the biggest threat. Those of us in Mind 2 feel differently. These folks find the group's resources are thinly stretched; there is possibly not enough to go round; the foreigner or criminal need to be put out of the group – for everyone's good.

A Mind 1 outlook is promoted in times of plenty. In such a condition we not only move to spread resources around to everyone in the group, but our fear of others outside the group diminishes. In easier times, the feelings of "them-or-us" dissipate. Everyone is "us." We become one big family of man.

It is easy to decipher that welfare programs find their original impulses in our Mind 1 moral feelings, and our militaries exist as institutions rooted in our Mind 2 concerns. But more than this: our scientific disciplines are sometimes manned by people reflecting the moral temper of the outlook that motivates them. Our scientists as well as our priests can be Mind 1 or Mind 2 leaning people. Their moral outlook influences the things they value and the events they find important.

C. Wright Mills
(1916 - 1962)

C. Wright Mills was a popular and influential social scientist of the mid-twentieth century. Through books and articles, he influenced public and professional perception on how to better understand groups and social classes, how they organize themselves and how they interact with each other. In 1951, The Society for the Study of Social Problems established the C. Wright Mills Award for works that address humanistic problems in original and scientific ways.

In his book, *The Sociological Imagination,* Mills explained the ultimate aims of the social sciences. As a social scientist, Mills valued and moralized in a certain way. He presumed that applying his truths to social studies, such as cultural anthropology, was right. Truth for Mills was largely a Mind 1 affair. We best understand Mills as a Mind 1 feeler through statements like the following:

> What social science is properly about is the human variety, which consists of all the social worlds in which humans have lived. These worlds contain primitive communities…great power states…classical China and ancient Rome, the city of Los Angeles and the empire of ancient Peru …The human variety also includes … an Indian Brahmin … a pioneer farmer of Illinois … a Hollywood starlet, a Roman patrician. To write of 'man' is to write of all these men and women—also of Goethe, and the girl next door.[5]

Sociologists like Mills have been both admired and criticized, not just for their desire to study other cultures, but also for the egalitarian way they view these cultures and for the direction toward equal rights and protections in they wish to move our own. For Mills and others who think like him, the people of the world are different, but are fundamentally equally worthy of investigation. Collectively, cultures are different, but also fundamentally equal.

Sociology is ultimately directed by the concerns of sociologists; and most of them, like Mills, have often been accused of operating primarily in Method 1, sympathetic and liberal morality. Finding all cultures equally worthy of study and ultimately equally valuable, Mills reveals himself to be operating in this mindset. The propensity to judge one group as worthy as another is the distinguishing trait and hallmark of the sympathetic Method 1 mind.

Those who address social problems through Method 2 dismiss the emotional conclusion of Mills and other like him. Those holding a Method 2 viewpoint generally do not go into fields like sociology or anthropology and dismiss people like Mills and his ilk as just a bunch of leftists. Why do sociologists and anthropologists lean toward Method 1? Similarly, why is it that our urban centers are reliably more politically liberal than the countryside?

In modern American politics, the urbanized areas of California, Oregon and Washington State earn the trio the title of "the Left Coast." Fifty years ago, conservative republican presidential candidate, Barry Goldwater, complained of the leftward bias of the other end of the country – the East Coast. He got in a bit of a pickle when he suggested that the nation might be improved if it cut off the liberal eastern seaboard and kicked it into the ocean. So how and why are liberals and conservatives shaped?

Each of us develops a preference for either the Mind 1 horizontal or Mind 2 vertical outlook. We can be labeled as leaning liberal or conservative. These moral dispositions govern far more than just our political persuasion. Being by nature a liberal or conservative defines how we approach all manner of moral problems. The fact that each of us operates around one of these two poles of moral possibility is easily seen. We may be genetically predisposed to lean toward one moral mind or another, but as with all other behavior, our environment plays a big part in who we are and what we understand as right.

These dual emotional dispositions are forever searching for amoral, factual, and scientific proofs to justify themselves. It is never enough to feel something is right; we want it demonstrated with scientific accuracy. We strive to correct wrong. We want to make what is wrong right. And so both our moral minds commandeer the human capacity for logical deduction to demonstrate why their version of morality makes logical sense. Scientists like biologist E. O. Wilson in his recent work, *The Social Conquest of Earth*, makes his own reference to a duality of our behavioral bi-moralism when he states:

> One part prescribes traits that favor success of individuals within the group. The other part prescribes the traits that favor group success in competition with other groups.[6]

But recognizing that we have a dual moral nature does not help us in deciding which moral path is best to apply to the problem facing us right now. That is a subjective judgment. Modern welfare economics may look objective and scientific because it is typically cloaked in mathematical symbols, statistics and graphs. At its core, economic welfare analysis, like military budgets, or school lunch programs, or the sociology of Mills, are but examples of distributive ethics brought about by subjective moral doctrine. "Who should get what?" is more a feeling than a mathematical deduction.

Vertical morality

Method 2 vertical morality (the morality of danger and want) assumes there can be better and worse people, better and worse cultures, better and worse anything. Understanding this moral position, we grasp why sociologists like Mills are dismissed by many conservatives. In Moral Mind 2, the goings-on of the better and more advanced people are by definition more worthy of our time and our study than the piddling around of the lower (i.e. less capable) orders of humanity. This is easy to demonstrate when comparing cultures of vastly different technological abilities.

"After all," say the Mind 2 ethicists, "if, after 100,000 years of human existence, one culture still finds itself living a hand-to-mouth existence and is hardly more able to master their surroundings or fight diseases than can the lice, cockroaches and other vermin with which they share their dwellings, while another culture has landed men on the moon, ended starvation and controlled disease, is it really difficult to determine which culture is best and where our research time is most valuably spent?"

Comparing human culture and the environments they create for themselves is not like looking at other animal populations. If we wish to discern which environment is best for starlings or for deer ticks, the answer is found by comparing the number of individuals within any given area. If one million starlings live west of the Mississippi river and ten million starlings live east of the Mississippi, we conclude that life east of the Mississippi is better if one were a starling. If there are one million deer ticks per square mile in the state of Maine but only one thousand deer ticks per square mile in New Jersey, Maine must be a better place to live if you were a deer tick. One starling or one tick's life is presumed to be lived about as well as another's. Not so the human being. Just because more than one billion people live in India or China and only 200 million live in Japan, we do not conclude that human life in India or China is better lived than in Japan. For people, the quality as well as the quantity of life counts for something. How we figure that out involves morality.

For a person with a Method 2 moral outlook, all cultures may be scientific curiosities, but they are hardly equal. For the Mind 1 feeler, equality is presumed. All that is necessary is the equal distribution of provision and protection. For the Mind 2 feeler, the distribution of provision and protection is a function of how we distinguish the better from the worse cultures. When feeling in Mind 2, we say things like, "Just look around. Does the Borneo bushman send his researchers paddling in dugout canoes to London to study Europeans? Of course not."

In a purely amoral examination, a culture is a culture; and so the amoral or logical-rational view is often conflated with the Mind 1 outlook. Is the cultural anthropologist who studies the tiny tribe and compares its practices to those of developed nations acting more like an amoral scientist or more like an equalizing social liberal? The Mind 2 among us are often not too sure. They can accept the findings of the former, while challenging the presumptions of the latter.

Such vertical feeling is not limited to the Mind 2 feelers of the advanced democracies. In the Asian or Middle Eastern nations, their Mind 2 feelers find just as many justifications to prefer their own cultures to others. They dismiss the West as decadent, or self-indulgent, irreligious and vulgar. The nineteenth century Native American of the Sioux tribe was threatened and starved and therefore likely to be of a Mind 2 moral outlook. He believed the old ways of his people were right, and the ways of the white man wrong. He was in no rush to change his loincloth for a suit. To do so would be immoral.

When we look back and scratch our heads, wondering why more Native Americans did not rush to adopt the farming and trading practices of the Europeans, we now understand how most were limited by their biologically-based moral outlook. They could not see it as right.

MORAL PURPOSE
The vicarious life

I am not from New York, nor have I ever lived there, yet a couple of decades back I said to my father, "The Yankees are the best team in baseball."

My father was a lifelong Red Sox fan and took umbrage. What developed between us was a minor competition involving the two teams. Whenever the Yankees were ahead in the standings, my dad would complain that they were "buying the pennant" with their over-the-top payroll; whenever the Red Sox were on top, he rejoiced with jubilation and on par with the defeat of Goliath by puny David. I was never a sports fan, but the banter was fun.

Slowly I became interested in the games, taking pleasure when the Yankees won and laughingly making excuses for their losses. I displayed a fundamental characteristic of the herding human; I identified with a group, gained pleasure with their successes, felt depressed with their setbacks, and imagined I somehow gained or lost when they did. Getting vicarious pleasure and feeling vicarious pain from the success or failure of others are the foundational emotive abilities that pave the way for us to find meaning in our lives.

We feel we are getting ahead when others whom we identify with do. Though I have never played on the team and never contributed to their effort in any way, it felt like I gained something when the Yankees won. In daily life, each of us has innumerable opportunities to express this emotion of vicarious identity. I gain when my kids gain; I suffer when my country suffers. I live through others.

What I view as my causes and my success can go on completely independently of me. The capacity for vicarious moral understanding explains many things. If my cause can go on without me, I gain or lose as my cause does, regardless of how little I actually contribute towards it. It is but a small step to imagine that, even without any participation at all by me, my cause endures. Even if I die, my success or my failure retains meaning. My cause somehow can go on even without me! My cause is more than just me. I am more than just me. I am part of a larger whole.

There is no modern soccer-riot that would have surprised a Roman or a Greek, or any other large nation where the people were rich enough to support public games. We think in group terms, and group competition is in our nature.

Here the Roman official Pliny the Younger, in the first century AD, complains in a letter to a friend. He sounds like a typical condescending middle-aged guy. The letter could have been written from any city at any time. It could have been written by me before I began following the Yankees:

> I have spent the last few days quietly, but very pleasantly, involved with my notes and books. 'In Rome' you say. 'How could you?' There were, of course, chariot races, but I am not the least bit interested in that kind of entertainment. There's never anything new or different about them, nothing which you need to see more than once. And so I am amazed that so many thousands of men time after time have such a childish desire to see horses racing and men driving chariots. Now, if they were attracted by the speed of the horses or the skill of the drivers, this would not be unreasonable. But as it is, they are only interested in the team uniforms. It is the team colors they love. In fact, if, during the race itself, right in the middle of the race, the team colors were suddenly switched, the spectators would immediately transfer their interest and support, and abandon those drivers and those horses which they recognized from afar and whose names they had been shouting just a moment before.[7]

The ability to live vicariously and to identify with institutions, teams or titles as if they had real existence is the fundamental aspect upon which all herding psychology depends. Sympathetic vicarious feeling allows us to personalize the experiences of others. We can objectify institutions and treat them as people, and so we hear phrases like, "The Yankees learned their lesson" or "Corporations can have a voice in politics," or "The Mongols are your enemy." We treat these constructions of imagination as if they had memories, motivations, and feelings too. Individuals come and go; the herd survives. And so it does us good to know what the herd will do, regardless of what any of its constituent members might be up to.

We fear when other people fear; we cry when they are pained. Without this sharing of the emotional experience, we could not function as a reliable member of the group. Our feelings must mimic the feelings of others either around us or above us. But we are more complex than other herding creatures that share some semblance of a vicarious existence. When one or two individuals from the buffalo herd run in panic, it might send vicarious ripples of fear through their herd and cause a stampede. When some members of a flock of geese lower their heads and begin to feed in a cornfield, the others may relax and feed too. But as with other emotions, the ability of humans to interact vicariously with other members of their group has developed to an extraordinary level.

If we are Christians of the Baptist persuasion, we smile with satisfaction when our preacher announces that the Baptist sect is the fastest growing denomination in our area, though we ourselves had nothing to do with its growth. We pat ourselves on the back because we are "Americans" and we glow with pride as we recall anything ever accomplished by "America." Everything from the digging of the Panama Canal, the defeat of the Germans at Normandy, or the landing on the moon is viewed as a glory we somehow share in, though we had nothing to do with any of it. Anatomic psychology suggests that if any Americans did it, every American past, present, and future shares in the act. Our herd extends through time and space.

We are a grouping animal and never alone. Books and authors exist and communicate with others they never met and presume to have some sort of existence through time as well. We are part of greater things, larger numbers, and people who came before and will come after. It is from them we get our identity, discover our purpose, and find happiness. Happiness itself is a transcendental emotion, that is, it exists as a concept not only of the present but as an evaluation of life in relation to a broader past and deeper culture.

Television and movie watching, like old-fashioned storytelling, teaches us of other people in real or imagined situations. We get pleasure from it. Like a pseudo-relationship, observing others through a box in my living room seems to psychologically convince me that I am not alone. I need to feel a part of the group. I am with others, and I am involved. I listen to music. I identify with current songs and particular sound patterns shared and enjoyed by others of my group. I discover what my kind of music is by accepting that my music is the music of my peers.

I send email messages and read blogs to remain in contact with friends and faceless comrades. I talk on the ever-present cell phone and maintain, as best I can, the ideal that I am perpetually surrounded by, and in constant contact with, my acquaintances. There is safety in numbers, and satisfaction too.

We have no desire, no daydream, no goal or lasting reward that is not imagined in relation to others beyond ourselves. We strive toward a Mount Olympus or Heaven where others like us exist in morally perfect perpetuity.

THE CREATION OF YOU AND ME
How the one becomes like the many

By the time we are grown, we are remarkably opinionated on a range of issues we have spent little time studying or experiencing. We know our country is best, though we are only vaguely familiar with its history, territory, or laws; and we know even less about other nations. We consider ourselves a conservative or a liberal, though exactly what these terms mean we cannot precisely articulate. We have never read an actual piece of legislation, yet we take positions on a few bits of the current legislative agenda as articulated by the social leaders we follow. Politicians, like commercial advertisers, manipulate our emotions for support, but we do not look at it as manipulation (by our side anyway), but see it as sharing information to organize an effort toward cooperative social goals.

We take a stand on the origins and ultimate fate of the entire universe, though we have never studied cosmology; and express opinions on the fate of souls after death, though we have never looked into theology. We articulate a position on global warming, nuclear proliferation, the immorality of today's youth, and why the country is going to hell in a hand basket. We know all these things probably without reading a book on any of them. In adult life, few read many non-fiction books on any topic. In late adolescence or early adulthood, we established a favorite sports team, religion, career field started a family, and established a food preference, and we have not deviated much in years.

In every area we are remarkably similar to other members of the group we were raised among. If we are brighter than average, we are likely to have slightly more articulate arguments for the exact same positions held by the least astute of our clan. We are fine representatives of our herd. In most attributes, we are interchangeable with the next guy. If you want to know what I think about most things, ask any of my neighbors; other than a leaning toward one moral mind or the other, our views and habits probably do not differ much; our houses, manner of dress, language, and food items are likely very similar.

We emerge from the womb not merely loving our parents before we ever meet them, and they loving us before ever knowing us, but also equipped with instincts and emotions to emulate those we are about to call family. We are born receptive to every practice of our herd, articulated and transmitted to us first through our mothers. We are born with preformed questions our herd will answer in their own (soon-to-be our own) cultural way.

Through mom and dad, we adopt not merely our herd's language but its faith, prejudices, superstitions, loyalties, gesticulations, foods, clothing and bathing habits. We pass through youth and are released from her bosom a fully functioning herd member, ready to stand shoulder to shoulder with our peers. Our parents are judged successful by how closely their kids think and act just as they were told to do. We are proclaimed successful young adults based on how closely we think as our leadership thinks, act as our leaders act, and believe pretty much what they and most others believe. If we do things a bit differently, it should be to improve upon how to accomplish the same things others have been trying to accomplish. The only social aspect where we are likely to differ from others is our preference to judge in either Method 1 or Method 2 Minds. We are either generally liberal, believing pretty much like all liberals do, or conservative, feeling like most other conservatives.

We are individuals, just like everybody else.

We are born ignorant of who we are but not of what we are

We are born into a family, which itself is embedded in a group. We are born with an urge to seek out the moral patterns that will help us survive in either circumstance. For most of history, Mind 1 was "family mind," the morality of sharing and of looking to the weakest for our clues on how to act. "Social mind" was Mind 2. Mind 2 life is lived beyond the home. We looked up toward leadership and to the strong and successful for habits to emulate. We wanted others to look up to us.

Long before C. Wright Mills wrote of a *Sociological Imagination* and before E. O. Wilson developed his concept of sociobiology, Aristotle observed that man is a *political*, and by it he meant *social*, animal. The philosopher explained, in his book, *The Politics*,[8] that the state preceded the family – a strange proposition for us today, trained to see the family as the founding structure and beginning of all society. But the philosopher's meaning becomes clear when we realize that by "the state" he meant the group, the nation, the culture, the race, or by whatever name you want to call the human herd with which we identify. We are all born into a tribe.

Show me the circumstances in which children will be raised and we can reasonably predict much of what they will think and believe 20 years later. As every homesick immigrant couple learns to their chagrin, a baby taken from any continent, any culture, and any genetic background, and raised among Americans, becomes an American. Raise children among Germans and they become German. We are reflections of those around and above us.

Biology demands we emerge from the womb created of a mother and father. What mom and dad know and think will be passed to us, and what they know and think is likely to be pretty much what their neighbors know and think. Families exist as embedded structures within the culture and serve as training grounds that prepare us for full-fledged membership. The formative years of our lives, the years where we learn who we are (which herd we belong to), occur between birth and puberty. If raised in Japan until about the age of 13 or 14 and then taken to another country, a child will likely feel "Japanese" forever, probably speak with a Japanese accent, and yearn to return "home" someday if only for a sentimental visit. Puberty marks a fundamental change in us. It establishes an imprinting with our herd. Speaking anecdotally, it seems we are susceptible to varying alterations in our behavior at different times in our lives.

In common experience we find that if a youngster is transplanted to a new location prior to puberty, he will likely imprint on his new land and hold less sentimental attachment to the country of his birth than the one he is being raised in. We are receptive to different cultural lessons at various times in our life. Language and nuances of speech and manner can be changed prior to puberty; after puberty changing these is more difficult. Patriotic identity to one group or another can be adjusted for about a decade after puberty. If we spend the first twenty years of our life in America, or Spain, or Greece, we will probably always feel American, Spanish, or Greek, no matter where we might move to later on.

Cultural aggressiveness, that is, an urge to teach and tell stories about the superiority of our own culture to others, begins in early adulthood. Nationalistic, patriotic and even xenophobic young adults are all around us. Our social institutions reflect our applications of these things. The founding leaders of the United States recognized this tendency to be dedicated to the land of one's birth and upbringing; the only requirement in the Constitution to attain the presidency is that the candidate be born in America and be 35 years old. Cultural consanguinity and a little experience, more than any requirement of training or disposition, makes him a trustworthy leader of his country's people. The president only has to be born in America and be at least 35 years old – beyond the age of rash militant demagoguery, but not yet so old as to have lost all daring.

Immigrants who enter new lands past puberty feel, in some tiny way, as strangers in a strange land. They often feel that way for the remainder of their lives. They retain quiet attachments to their former homes and hope to pass on the love of the old- country to their children born in the new land. This is a fool's errand. The adult immigrant may have been forced for financial or political reasons to emigrate and in his heart remains an expatriate; but he cannot intellectually pass on those "feelings" to his kids. You cannot be intellectually talked into loving a country any more than you can be intellectually talked into loving someone else's kid or someone else's god.

Our compulsion to self-identify with our herd, like our need for family identity or religious identity, is age dependent. The foster child, like the foster citizen, loves and is most loved the earlier the attachment is made. The newcomer is examined by preexisting members of the group with curiosity and suspicion. The adult who comes to America from elsewhere will probably never be 100 percent American in his heart, and both the immigrant and his new neighbors know it. But this is only a problem of one generation. The children born and raised in the new land generally become fully fledged members of the new group and have only slight interest in the far away motherland of his patrimony. No matter how the immigrant tries to instill love of the old country into his children, the herd they are born into is imprinted as "their group" and the land they are born in is now "their land."

The state, as Aristotle called it, or the "herd," as I have chosen to call it, does precede the family; but it is through the structure of family that we first train and interact with our group. The herd is created and renewed one unit at a time. We are born not knowing if we are boys or girls, French or Spanish. We are born ignorant of our century, our gods, and our leaders. We do not know if we have a king or a president, a pope or a witch doctor. But being human, we emerge endowed, like the seed of the mighty oak, to grow in phases where answers to these questions will be provided for us, even before we know enough to ask them. The process terminates in our emergence as functioning members of a greater community. We are all born ignorant of who we are, but not what we are. We are a herding species and will be taught to think, do and act in all the right ways to ensure our acceptance and success. We will be taught to feel, then think, then act, rightly.

The making of a herd member:
childhood/adolescence/adulthood

Children begin as reflections of their parents for their own good. The things our parents love become what we love, their fears our fears. In our youth, we imitate them and do as they do; they lead and we follow. The parent-child relationship is far from democratic. Parents love their kids, and the years when their children were small are often remembered as the best times in a parent's life. But mom and dad are in charge.

Children do not come to parents so that they may be molded into wonderful children; childhood is but a staging area for adulthood. Parents are not judged successful only by how well their toddlers behave, but also by how successfully these children mature. It is not through the pleasing of parents that a child's destiny is fulfilled, but through success with his peer group as an adult.

We take over the world from our folks. To do this we must pass through a phase where we leave their side and sidle up to our friends, establishing alliances, gaining mates and learning trades. By our teenage years, we have acquired the basic socializing skills and cultural practices we need to assimilate. We identify with our peer group and express a passion for the enthusiasms of the current age and our own emerging leaders.

Generational peer identity is strong and expressed at every step. If we go to a large family reunion or block party, we initially segregate ourselves by relations. Each of us sticks close to others we know. But as we grow comfortable with the group, we subdivide mostly by age. Those under eight years old stick close to their mothers who will often corral them all together; those between eight and puberty hang together; teens and young adults find another corner to congregate; middle-aged people find a place by the food; and the elderly snooze together in the shade. Peer group identification is vital to herd health and is displayed whenever large groups are casually gathered for prolonged lengths of time. The sexes will often separate as sub-segments within their age group. We look for people like ourselves.

In my youth, rock-and roll music and the Beatles were all the rage, and wearing long hair and strange footwear were external signs of identifying with the subculture. I grew out my hair and wore those shoes, believing I was acting as a discerning individual. I felt emotionally that these were the things I preferred. I did prefer them. I did not *feel* I was copying others or following a crowd. I believed I was leading. I was an individual, just like the thousands of others all around me.

Who I distinguished myself from was not my peers but my parents. In my era there were others of my age group who shaved their hair close and listened to country music. They were following different leaders in a separate cultural milieu, and though one of these types seemed odd to me, and a bit like a clone of any other one, each of these country kids undoubtedly imagined himself a unique actor on his own dramatic stage. Those kids might have imagined he was distinguishing himself from me. We dressed, sang, and spoke in accordance to the group we followed.

In early adulthood I was settled into domestic bliss doing pretty much the same things every day, seeing the same people, and retelling the same jokes. In my twenties, as is the case with most of us, my friends were paramount. I wanted them over to the house all the time. Spending time with them fishing or beer guzzling was an important part of my wellbeing. I was slowly changing.

In my thirties my routine was a rut, but a secure and predictable rut, and ruts are just the right atmosphere for raising kids – predictable and unthreatening. In my teens and twenties, what was new in my life involved me, new people, new ideas, new songs and new jobs. In my thirties, what was new was the latest skill acquired by my kids: they learned to cross the street, say a new word, or ride a bicycle. Their development was what was new in my life, but relative to them, their parents were stable, boring and predictable. The ability to live vicariously comforted me again. The tiny accomplishments of my kids — to do well in a school play or shoot their first squirrel – was somehow an achievement for me. Domestic bliss.

From about 25 to 60, we are in the prime of life. Looking around us, it is at this stage people are most involved in all aspects of adulthood. We are no longer merely political protestors; we are political participants. We are the culture; what we do and how we direct resources establishes what gets done.

After 60, with hormonal levels dropping and intellectual as well as physical abilities falling away, we recede to take our place in the corners of society as the old story tellers, scolds, amiable grandparents, and the last reservoir of memories, hanging around on the off-chance some youngster might put us to use as a babysitter or by asking us to tell a tale from long ago.

Dogs are not smarter than cats but they are more moral

Dogs were bred from a herding species; domestic cats were not. Our mutts possess the emotions and instincts of a herding creature, more varied than cats and more in tune with our own. Dogs look to the other members of their pack for clues on what to do, when to feel good and why to feel bad. Cats do not. Our moods, failures, and enthusiasms matter to the dog, but are of no concern to our cats.

A dog that has tipped over the trash and made a mess will likely be hiding under the bed when its owner comes home. The cowering pooch looks for and learns the things that bring praise or scorn from those who share his life. Doing right by the group is important to the domestic canine. If it makes a mess, it hides. The pooch feels badly. It eventually emerges contrite, with its tail between its legs, knowing it has done something wrong. Anticipating a scolding, thinking it is deserved, man's best friend seems sorry it has done something wrong in the eyes of the group.

The dog has an aspect of a-rationality we call a conscience, and its conscience is bothered when it lets down the members of the herd it loves. The dog understands right and wrong in relation to others of the herd. The cat knows right and wrong only in relation to itself and its own individual wellbeing. The canine is a social creature. The dog is a *moral animal*. The cat is not.

The cat that has eaten the owner's parakeet may in some way anticipate a scolding, but it will do little more than stay out of sight. It will show no signs of regret or contrition. It saw an opportunity and it took it. A cat has no group, so it needs no conscience. Remorse, guilt, and feelings of inferiority are strange to it; the cat need have no ability to recognize authority or responsibility. Without a herd, its survival has never depended on these things.

A herd member, be it puppy, starling, or human, is born with a capacity to feel and express and read social emotions. We are empathetic beings. Social creatures discern right by watching others around them for cues to action. The telling difference in styles rests on whom the creatures look to for these clues. Mind 1 creatures look around themselves and down; Mind 2 social animals look upward to superiors and betters.

The dog and its human owner live as much for each other as they do for themselves. The dog, fundamentally a Mind 2 being, looks toward his superior master for direction. The cat lives first and always for the cat alone. If she is in heat, she will seek a mate; if pregnant she and her offspring will become a temporary herd as she raises her brood – carrying out temporary responsibilities as they relates to her kittens. Unaccustomed, semi-social emotions will temporarily well up within her. Outside of these special circumstances, she is alone. The loner needs no morality. Consequently, the cat sits amorally, without any need to see things either in a co-equal and sharing way, or in a hierarchical manner.

Conscience, guilt, pride and envy are all aspects of how we find meaning through our relationships. The guilty conscience, the prideful one, or the happy one is a mental condition that informs us through reflection of how our actions might affect our standing among others. An act is construed as good or bad and makes us confident or anxious based on how it promotes our general progress in Mind 1 or Mind 2 morality. Morality enhances relationships; immorality destroys them. We are born with an innate presumption embedded in our psyche, that if we find a perfect morality we can find happiness; extreme immorality leads us to anguish. Beginning with this presumption, and endowed with an ability to understand good and bad in either Method 1 or Method 2 mind, we act to improve our condition.

The Golden Mean
Aristotle[9]
(383 – 322 BCE)

Aristotle has been called "The Father of Science." Impressive! His logic-based philosophy put Western culture on track to exploit the scientific and technological discoveries of the late Middle Ages, which propelled us into the modern world. A seminal thinker, Aristotle's contribution to answering the problems posed through moral sentiment has never been equaled.

Much has been made of right and goodness being found in moderation; avoid the tendency to act in extreme ways and you avoid most social conflicts. Aristotle understood that every emotionally based decision could be spoken of in terms of an extreme: the extremely frugal verses the profligate; the timid coward versus the rash fool; the sports fanatic verses the indifferent. He advises us that to succeed we must seek the middle point between wherever our society defines these extremes. This has been called "The Golden Mean" and something like it occurs repeatedly in the philosophy of many moralists.

Courage is acting rightly; it is the mid-point between rashness and cowardice. Liberality is the mean between the profligate spender and the miser. But exactly where this mid-point might be is not exactly the same for everybody and at all times. Every culture faces unique challenges, so its need for courage in war or its interest in sports varies. In light of this, some cultures put great stress on bravery; others on social participation in a particular sport. Regardless of the situation, every culture will set limits to where it defines its extremes. Understanding where your own culture delineates its extremes – as too much or too little – in either of these areas, and acting between these guideposts, will be what is considered virtue in your culture.

Other wise men have spoken of the value of moderation. Gautama Buddha also spoke of following the Middle Way, and Confucius warns us to avoid excesses. Thomas Aquinas[10] and so many more weigh in on this same idea: to do rightly is to act temperately, not too much one way or another.

Figure 2-1

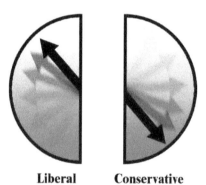

Liberal   Conservative

**Acting out, questioning the current pattern
Pushing the group to an extreme**

Emotions cannot be precisely weighed or measured. Mathematical formulas cannot be established for them. At best, what the advice of the philosophers has amounted to is for the educated and experienced person to gauge situations, evaluate the emotional expectations of those around us and act accordingly: everything in moderation. As herding creatures, we are instinctively capable of doing this. We read the situation, apply the appropriate emotional reaction to it at a moderate and middling level, and benefit accordingly.

The experienced and educated human, dog, starling, or chimpanzee does this every day. But when a member of the herd breaks the rules, acts out and defies convention, others take notice. The starling that does not turn left when all others do, or the subservient dog that disobeys its owner sets itself up for either a rebuke or a concession. Either the group will try to correct the renegade, or the renegade will correct and redirect the group.

Primatologist Jane Goodall observed just such an interesting drama involving two chimpanzees named Goliath and Mike.[11] Mike was a lower level male, and a relative weakling in his group of chimps at Gombe Stream Tanzania. Goliath, the highest-ranking male, sat stone-faced near the center of their herd, being undisturbed by the commotion of youngsters and lower-ranking males like Mike. Stoic steadiness among chimp leaders seems to reassure followers just as it does for us humans. Being unflappable means something; it steadies us. We will discover that emotional control is a prime Mind 2 attribute, and chimpanzees are fundamentally Mind 2 hierarchical creatures.

One day Mike the weakling learned to roll first one, then two, and later three empty kerosene cans in front of him in a charging display. The empty cans made a wild racket, which unnerved everybody. Controlling this seemingly confused riot of noise was Mike. At first the other males tried to remain sitting and unconcerned. Such a breach of chimp social etiquette could not be ignored. Either Mike would need to be corrected, or Mike would establish a new leadership position for himself.

Eventually the riot unnerved Goliath along with the others. Mike controlled a powerful new force. Eventually, even the mighty Goliath paid homage to Mike, panting nervously and grooming him. Formerly, Mike had ranked near the bottom of his group; mastering the fear created by the noise of the cans, he moved to the very top.

Mike became the leader. He proved himself the fittest male of his group. His invention demonstrates that the most able is not always the most physically strong. Cleverness and ingenuity are part of the equation. Mike's mastery of strange and seemingly dangerous objects made him seem emotionally in control when others reacted to them at the extremes of fear or cowardice. The top position of the troop came with perquisites like greatest admiration of males and most access to females – much as it does with us. Respecting Mike and deferring to him became the right and correct thing to do.

Self-control was still a primary chimp virtue. But these extremes of control came under the authority of Mike. We can imagine that Mike might thereafter sit back stoically, looking around at the others, with his cans by his side. Modern theories of government claim that a key factor of legitimacy for any government is the retention of violence it reserves for itself. In a way, Mike's behavior reinforces this notion. He is the chimp in charge, controlling the mechanism that frightens all others.

We are a herding species. We lead and follow others. But just what it means to be "in charge" varies. In Moral Mind 1, we lead and follow casually, horizontally oriented as to react to whoever is around us. In Mind 2, we are vertically oriented, looking for direction from superiors or experts. In Mind 1 we follow the crowd; in Mind 2 we follow leaders. Ideal moral reinforcement comes when we can do both: follow the boss-leader who is being followed by the large crowd. Doubly reinforced, all our social signals tell us we are doing right.

Public opinion or professional opinion

It is common to assume that the opinion of a majority of herd members is the same as wisdom. If two heads are better than one, then two thousand heads must be that much better still. Yet, part of us also believes the opinions of social leaders and experts mean more than the opinions of the common man or the masses of them – no matter how many they may be. We want to know what everyone around us is thinking, and we look to what our leaders and experts believe. Armed with information from both groups, we make up our minds on what to do or what to believe. When these two fountains of social direction agree, we are reassured; when they do not we are conflicted.

We are pushed and pulled by each of these. We instinctively seek direction; we look around at the herd for cues to right action. Part of us holds the views of many as the surest and safest bet, while another part looks up at the leader and the expert. Some of us are more inclined to trust one form of authority over the other. Some of us believe there is safety in numbers; others seek assurance through the superior. This dichotomy is another manifestation of our dual moral nature.

Henry Mencken was a bright Mind 2 feeler who had no deep respect for the common man. To him, the common man was no more impressive in bunches than individually. Mencken was a natural critic of the extreme democratic principle. If the common man knew little about so many things, how could he be expected to run a government? How could someone who could not find Gibraltar on a map or tell you the purpose of his own gall bladder, or name the century in which Shakespeare wrote, or much of anything else, select the president? According to Mencken,

> "The existence of most human beings is of absolutely no significance to history or to human progress. They live and die anonymously and as nearly useless as so many bullfrogs or houseflies. They are, at best, undifferentiated slaves upon an endless assembly line ... The familiar contention that they at least have some hand in *maintaining* civilization ... is plainly not valid. If all human beings were like them,

civilization would not be maintained at all: it would go back
steadily and perhaps quickly.[12]

But we do let them select the president. And we seem to do all right by it.

Too much Mind 1

When a well known religious leader is discovered in *flagrante delicto* with the wife of a member of his congregation, or when an elected official is caught on camera taking bribes, it is not unusual for some television or radio commentator to ask his audience to call in or go online and "vote" on what should be done about it. With no more knowledge about a subject than can be presented in a four minute telecast, we are encouraged en masse to pass judgment and give a position on what is to be thought and what is to be done about it. It is conducted in an atmosphere of self-righteousness, with a presumption that whatever the uninformed mob thinks about it, this is somehow important and even ultimately right.

It matters not the complexity of the topic; someone will suggest we need to find out what the majority thinks about it. It can be about the removal of a movie star's thyroid, the displacement of an indigenous tribe in the Amazon jungle, what the king of England should name his next child, or the projected fate of the sun. For us, collective group thought is valuable and oftentimes even to be preferred to the position of the educated specialist. When feeling in our Mind 1, it is majoritarianism that is to be preferred over any Mind 2 meritocracy. The majority opinion may mean little, but we instinctively want to know what it is.

We are not educated and experienced in all areas; sometimes we just need to be told what the group at large thinks, and that is good enough for us. When we put gas in our tank, we do not need to know what the Octane Rating means. We just select the type others do, or sometimes the kind some authority told us to use. Few need to know what octane is. I suppose if I needed to know it, someone would have told it to me by now.

Two million heads are better than one. Legally, the votes on these telecasts are for superficial entertainment purposes only. The fact that they are popular and participated in by thousands in spite of their being legally meaningless tells us how much we value just knowing where our opinion stands among the group around us, and how much we want to have our voice heard on every topic, regardless of how statistically puny and outnumbered we may be.

The view of the many must always be ill informed and shallow when it turns its attention to any particular. Without the guidance of some specialist who has investigated the matter, what do I know about anything? There are few things we all know a lot about but not many. We are reasonably well educated on the personal experiences of our day-to-day life. We know something about our jobs and a hobby or two. Beyond that, we are ill informed.

A majority of the general public, by logical deduction, must forever be incapable of reaching deeply informed positions about almost everything. What do I know about thyroids or their removal? What do I know about the storage of nuclear waste? What do I know about the proper materials that should go into car tires? What do I know about the leader of Kazakhstan? I know what my leaders have told me, and whichever one I prefer to trust, I feel confident in repeating his position. That his position may be as ill informed as my own is unlikely to come up. Leaders lead.

Too much Mind 2

In a recent presidential election, one of our local comedians compiled a list of all the recommendations being made by both the democratic and republican candidates for the presidency. He then switched them, and asked committed democratic and republican supporters about them. Democratic voters were told their candidate thought the American military needed to be strengthened, the national borders more tightly controlled, and voter identification efforts needed to be strengthened. To those committed to the republican candidate, he questioned their support of their candidate's (supposed) statements like the need to expand national health care, the creation of a more equitable tax system, and increasing the minimum wage. In every case, the supporters did not question the veracity of the list. Instead, they began justifying their candidate's positions. It was as if it did not matter what the facts were; once they had made up their minds who they were voting for, their job was to support him, not question him.

Everyday experience teaches us that we fill our doctor's prescriptions and swallow their pills as directed. We trust they know what they are doing. When our car begins to make strange noises, we take it into a mechanic we have selected and trust him to do whatever is necessary to fix it. When looking at the world in a Mind 2 manner, the high authority is to be preferred to the opinions of peers. Brand names matter.

We are motivated in two ways. Experience teaches us that this is so, though we have never before explained why this is so. But smart people understand that we are motivated to act according to both methods of influence. I buy my tires from the company I trust … as determined by the commercial I saw last, which told me not only that these tires were recommended most by experts but also that everyone else was buying them. What more could I ask for? To sway us, speakers try to appeal to both our moral minds. We are convinced about what to do through a combination of arguments.

Mind 1	Mind 2
Everyone is buying/voting for *X*.	The smarter and superior people are buying/voting for *X*.
Product/candidate *X* is good for everyone.	Product/candidate *X* is especially right for our kind of people.

THE MIND INVENTS TERMS FOR OUR MORAL CONCEPTUALIZATIONS

Mind 1
Equality/Fairness

Feeling that it is okay to follow the person to the right of me or the one to the left, it is clear that in one Mind I see people as equally worthy of consideration. Imitating those near me, whoever they may be, presumes initially that I find them worth imitating. In Mind 1, terms like "liberal" evolve to mean neither servile nor aristocratic.

In a moral outlook that finds everyone worthy, liberty can become license. As long as no one gets hurt, anything goes. There is enough to go round, we are safe, well provisioned and protected, and so we relax. In such times, experimentation is less discouraged. In Mind 1 times, we hear phrases like "open-minded" or "I am a citizen of the world."

Words like equality and fairness come to define our horizontal moral outlook. The circumstances that give rise to Mind 1 feelings — plenty, ease and safety — also promote personal independence. We hardly need to know the neighbors we no longer depend upon. This economic reality contributes to the general outlook of equality: the person we hardly know to the left of us is considered about the same as the person we hardly know to our right.

In casual associations of pleasure, we decide where to eat by a show of hands. Parents often ask the children where they want to go for a meal. When planning a day trip with our pals, everyone is encouraged to suggest a destination. In easier times, we resort to more horizontal and democratic methods of decision making. We use terms like "fairness" and "cooperation." But in times of trouble, we usually switch to our other outlook and see things in a more vertical fashion, using different terms to describe the relationships between participants.

Mind 2
Loyalty/Honor

Our loyalties define us, and our loyalties distinguish us. I am an American. This means I am loyal to causes articulated by the social and political leaders of America and not necessarily to the leaders or causes of others. I can be relied upon to act on behalf of those causes and on behalf of those leaders. If I am a Yankees' fan, I sing their praises, watch their games, feel good when they prosper and bad when they do not. If I am loyal to my family, I promote their causes, devote my income to their benefit, and do not share my affections with other women, which would threaten the stability of our home. Loyalty is a measure of who can be counted upon to act in our interest. Disloyalty is an act against us. Loyalty is vital to a herding creature.

Duty and honor are Mind 2 terms. They define what our responsibilities are and the respect we can expect for ourselves if we carry them out. Duty and honor are distinguishing terms; they separate those who are more capable and trustworthy from those who are less. Loyalty, honor, and duty differentiate and establish verticality between people. They signify who are carrying out their responsibilities and who are not. Responsibilities are not shared. When we apply concepts of better and worse to social situations, we are looking at them in a Mind 2 fashion. It does not matter if we are evaluating an aspect of private life, public life, economic life, or spiritual life; if we are seeing things in a Mind 2 fashion, we use Mind 2 phraseology like duty, honor, loyalty and betrayal. Such terms are applied to describe relationships between husbands and wives, parents and children, citizens and their nation, or parishioners and their gods. When we hear phrases like those in wedding vows – "To love, honor, cherish, and obey" – or in family life – "Honor thy mother and thy father" – or in spiritual life – "... giving honor and glory to God" – we are simply observing examples of where we reapply the same formal herding relationship to our various walks of life.

When we speak of being loyal and doing our duty, we are describing a vertical relationship. Vertically structured groups operating in a Mind 2 aspect, such as the military, or street gangs like the Crips and the Bloods, or corporations and organizations, all recreate our intuitive vertical structures of authority, with leaders, assistant leaders, and followers; or presidents, vice-presidents, and middle-managers;   etc.

Moral Mind 1	Moral Mind 2
Everyone is equal.	People are better or worse; there are ladies and gentleman and those who are neither.
We do not care what others think of us; terms like honor have no real place.	Our honor needs to be defended and loyalty is demanded.
As long as we are all equal, there is no special place to fight for.	We fight to retain respect and place.
Fairness and cooperation are encouraged.	Status matters and competition is necessary.

WE STRUGGLE TO INFLUENCE WHILE BEING INFLUENCED

Social power means influence. We try to exert it always. How many others can I get to do what I do, like what I like, and think what I think? Listen to your own conversations. We perpetually try to convince others to enjoy what we enjoy, eat what we eat, support the teams or causes we support. We sell them on the notion that *what I am doing is best*.

We are salesmen for ourselves whenever we are spokesmen for our causes. After all, *if I can convince others that all my pastimes are great, then it follows that the people who participate in them are superior to others … people like me*. Praise the things I do and praise the things I like, and you indirectly praise me. We are familiar with this pattern of behavior in politics, but each of us employs it whenever we express preferences.

If I like a certain restaurant, I promote it. I encourage people to take up the hobbies I prefer. I promote golf, fishing, or stamp collecting. If I read detective stories, I work them into my conversations. If I take a vacation, I return to tell all my acquaintances about it. Promoting what I do and what I like is a backhanded way of promoting myself.

Political leaders gather our support, not by convincing us to agree with them, so much as by assuring us that *they agree with us*. When we vote for democrats over republicans, we are saying that these candidates, whom we have never met and know little about, have convinced us, in the tiny fraction of time we have paid attention to them, through slogans and shallow rhetoric, to side with them over their rivals for the most powerful positions in the group, by assuring us that *they are on our side*.

To lead

Adolf Hitler, Napoleon, and Abraham Lincoln were all demonstrably effective leaders. Their influence was far-reaching and effective. Each had millions of supporters and millions of sworn enemies willing to kill and die to promote or defeat their aims. Regardless of the soundness of their causes, they showed a knack for convincing thousands of people to run into cannon fire – figuratively, following right behind them.

The speeches of these men must have been inspiring. We have some of them. Abraham Lincoln's words are among the best political and philosophical writing by any American politician. Exactly why their words worked on the crowd better than those of their opponents is an interesting psychological study.

Today, Adolf Hitler is remembered only to be deplored. But, deplorable as he may have been, there is much we can learn from him and from the millions who followed and adored him. Unlike either Napoleon or Lincoln, Hitler wrote on this very topic of leadership. He detailed at some length how the leader moves people and creates followers. In his day, nationwide radio was rare and television non-existent. A leader had to acquire and direct followers largely through newspapers. Hitler evaluated his potential supporters not as individuals, but as groups. He wrote about how to understand the readers of newspapers so as to better comprehend how to sway them:

> Readers can be divided into three groups: Those who believe everything they read; those who no longer believe anything they read; and those minds which critically examine what they read and then form their own judgments about the accuracy of the information.

> The first group who believes everything they read is the largest and strongest because they are composed of the broad masses of the population…This group includes those who have not been born with the gift of, or trained for, independent thinking and who believe anything which is printed in black and white…Since they are unable or unwilling to weigh what is offered to them and evaluate it for themselves, their approach to every daily problem is totally determined by how they are influenced by others. This may be an advantage if their understanding is fed by serious and truth-loving persons, but it will be disastrous if led by scoundrels and liars.

> In number, the second group who does not believe anything they read is considerably smaller. It is partially made up of those who once belonged to the first group of total-believers. Then, after continued disappointments, they

> have switched to the opposite extreme ... These people are very hard to deal with because they will always be suspicious, even of the truth. They are useless when it comes to any positive work.

> The third group who reads and evaluates for themselves is by far the smallest...Today, there are too few of them to have any significant impact...Today, when the voting ballots of the masses are final, the deciding factor is the highest number – that is the largest group and this is the first group I discussed.[13]

The Hitler administration may have been as diabolical and murderous as Timur the Lame and as unsympathetic to the Jews as Edward I of England, but unlike the other wannabe totalitarians, he left us his thoughts in written detail. We can learn from them. With a nod to Winston Churchill and Marcus Aurelius, who each wrote a bit on such subjects, no other leader left behind as detailed a written blueprint for leadership in the making.

Hitler and his German followers of the 1930s are fine examples of how a people seek leaders when they believe their backs are against the wall, in extreme Mind 2 circumstances. They circle the wagons around the group and nation; they stack, verticalize, and prioritize materials and people. Hitler exploited this to outrageous extremes. The Fuehrer may have killed others when he served as a common soldier in World War I, but we accept this as understandable and even heroic. He may have killed others with his own hands, but for this he is not held accountable, as he was following the lead of others.

Hitler did not hurt or kill anyone directly in World War II. But for his leadership in this effort he is despised. The man personally gassed neither gypsy nor Jew. He never fought from a tank or a plane; the world warrior battled from the podium. *The potential to support everything he wanted to accomplish had to have been present in his people themselves first, before he or any leader could rise up and direct it to such diabolical ends as he did.*

Hitler was an extreme Mind 2 moralist. He did everything possible to merge his image with the immortal leader at the top of an ideal "state" or "group" or "the folk" as it was called. In a Germany recently defeated in World War I, with a large segment of the population facing starvation and feeling surrounded by enemies, a Hitler-like character naturally appeals to such emotions.

That he took advantage of his nation's trust and ordered commands far outside Aristotle's/Confucius'/Buddha's golden mean makes him immoral in the particular. He was vicious and an extremist in a Moral Mind 2 fashion. But that his irrational desires ran in a Mind 2 direction is categorically understandable. His error was not in choosing an immoral aspect of mind; this he did not do. His error lied in the lengths he resorted to in order to achieve his Mind 2 ends of promoting the wellbeing of his group before competing herds.

In this Mind 2 outlook, patriots dream their kind, their group, their race, their nation, and their god are more than good; they are virtually infallible. Stephen Decatur's famous words come to mind, "Our country ... may she always be in the right; but our country, right or wrong."

Mind 2 is group oriented. It might be called our nationalistic moral outlook. It is the morality we lean to in times of threat and want. At its extreme, others outside the group need be considered only if they do not compete or detract from our herd's ambitions and safety. In times of want or danger, we need to prioritize people and things so that our group survives. It is the end that matters, and those at the top must be given a free hand to achieve it. The many do well when they support the superior leader. Here is Hitler again; he could be giving a pep talk to any would-be political campaigner:

> The purpose of [the political message] is not to be a constant source of interesting diversion for the unconcerned, smart gentleman, but to convince the masses. The masses are slow moving, and it may take a long time before they are ready to even notice something. Only constant repetitions of the simplest ideas will finally stick in their minds.[14]

He reminds his readers that the follower need only be convinced that the leader understands the problem; the follower need only be convinced to agree with the general moral direction things need to be taken. Either we need to be more ethical and return to former priorities, or more equal in the here and now.

The citizen has no mind and no stomach for details and policy. Like the hired auto mechanic, the leader need only reassure his drivers/voters that he is against the same problems as they are, and that he is capable of fixing them. Exactly how the filthy deed is done, or even how much it might cost in the long run, is something to be worried about later. The good leader, like the mechanic who seems reliable, will be trusted:

> It is a mistake to try to create [the political message] in the same way you would create a document for scientific instruction. The great masses' capacity to absorb information is very limited ... For these reasons, any effective [political message] must be confined to a few points, and these must be expressed in simple stereotyped formulas. They must be used repeatedly until the very last man cannot help but know the meaning instantly...The

> greater the scope of the message, the more necessary it is
> for the [political message] to follow a simple plan of
> action…[15]

We are reminded of the political slogans of recent times, which invariably include one variation or another of:

- Hope for tomorrow
- Time for a change
- Cut taxes
- Believe in America
- Yes we can
- Peace through strength

These are simple emotionalist words in the air. When Germany was on the brink of losing World War II, Hitler remained true to his extreme Mind 2 moral beliefs. If Germany faltered, it was not the fault of "Germany" (the cultural concept or "the folk" as it existed in the mind); it was the fault of stupid or disloyal individuals. In his final days, he proclaimed that if the Third Reich was defeated, then it must mean that in some way Germany was the weaker nation and did not deserve to survive.

Modern Germany is more prosperous, safe and comfortable. Mind 2 morality takes a back seat. Today's German politician is more likely to be successful by appealing to the people's Mind 1 sentiments of sharing resources and providing for the unemployed. It is the worker who needs to be cared for, not the nation's industrial base or its military – It is the poor and weak, not the industrial leaders and fighters, who get the political favors now.

Mind 1 - Provide and equalize	Mind 2 - Protect and prioritize
Socialistic mind	Nationalistic mind
Worker's rights	Strengthening business production
Wealth redistribution – to provide	Build up the military – to protect

Subcultures vs. nationalism

At the 1968 Olympic Games held in Mexico City, Tommie Smith won the 200-meter race and the gold medal. He was an African American, and his culture was in transition. Standing on the platform to receive medals, he and John Carlos, another African American who had won the bronze, held clenched fists in black gloves. For this act, both were expelled from the games.

The political statement made by the athletes was judged improper. The men displayed loyalty to a cause that was not recognized nationally at that time. The raised and clenched fists were statements of solidarity with domestic American subgroups agitating against the oppression of blacks in parts of the United States.

The clenched fist gesture was deemed a message of loyalty to a fragment of the nation and could be construed as a disloyalty to the other parts of it. It was not representative of the American herd as a whole. The two athletes returned home to a mixed reaction of adoration and envy from similarly minded supporters – and death threats from those who disagreed with them.

In 1968, Smith and Carlos were controversial figures. The internationalist and universal aim of equality they advocated were not yet the prevailing views in America – at least not expressed in the ways that appealed to these men. Today, if the incident is recalled at all, both are likely to be praised as iconic leaders who suffered for the better cause. The action did not change; the moral outlook of the American majority has shifted.

[Both photographs from Wikimedia commons - permissions free or copyright expired]

German athletes at the 1936 Olympics raised their hands giving the Nazi salute upon accepting their medals. They were not condemned. Their medals were not in question. Other nations gave their national salute too.

This line of argument was used by defenders of Smith and Carlos to members of the Olympic committee. The committee's response was that the Nazi salute was deemed a national gesture representing all Germans and was therefore appropriate. The gloved fist represented a political movement only and reflected the aspirations of only a segment of the American public, and was therefore disallowed.

In other words, it is assumed that every German could vicariously claim victory whenever an athlete identified as "German-Nazi" won an event, but not every American could vicariously identify with the salute made by Smith and Carlos. Nationalism must be all-pervasive. The athletes must be seen to represent their entire herd (nation) and not just a segment of it. Had Smith and Carlos conquered their group politically and made their salute universal within their nation, it presumably would have been accepted also at the Olympics.

Two approaches to our social spheres
God/Country/Family/Job

Family life is governed by the emotional standard articulated by Karl Marx, "From each according to his abilities, to each according to his needs ."[16] This is a tidy summation of our Moral Mind 1 outlook. In a family, the older and stronger kids get more chores to do and greater responsibility toward looking after the younger and weaker ones. But in the family, we all share in the gains and losses; we take care first of the smallest and weakest. The baby often has his way.

When we leave the family, we pass into the herd and establish loyalties, friends and competitors, and attain social positions governed more by the sentiment "survival of the fittest,"[17] a phrase better describing our Moral Mind 2 outlook. Individually, we bounce back-and-forth around and between these moral potentialities.

Though we call Moral Outlook 1, "family morality," it is not limited to morality within families, though it is most clearly understood in that social setting. And while we named Outlook 2 "social morality," it makes itself felt within families as well, since there are positions within families that are occupied by superiors who deserve higher honor and respect. The study of our moral patterns and their application in either family of social settings is the firmest foundation upon which sociology, psychology, and our philosophy rest.

Dual moralism

Mind 1	Mind 2
From each according to his abilities, to each according to his needs	Survival of the (socially/physically/mentally) fittest

If we recall our illustration of the moral cycle, we remember that our moral outlooks differ not only in kind and objective but also in force of application. Each of us is capable of reacting in any way and at any location around this chart. But most of us find a range of moral activity where we are comfortable, either on the liberal or conservative side of things. Culture represents the collective average of the moral position of the people who comprise it. Over time our culture has been growing safer and more productive and moving leftward in response.

Figure 2-2

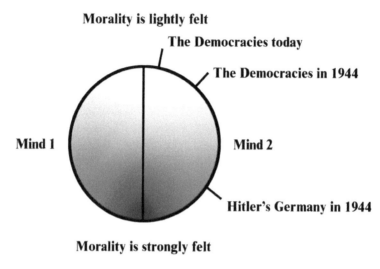

Herds and sub-herds

At the turn of the last century, writers like the Polish sociologist Ludwig Gumplowicz[18] devoted a lot of effort trying to imagine how large societies develop. They envisioned smaller groups growing ever larger through the merger of tiny clans and tribes. They imagined leaders like a Biblical Moses rising up to merge the twelve tribes of Israel into one big clan, or people like Sam Adams and George Washington attaining social power and using themselves as focal points around which separate states unite into one big nation.

Such mergers depend upon the leader's skill in convincing everyone that the similarities between these small social units outweighed their differences. The great leader breaches gaps in differences. The newly merged larger group is defined by some common cause, by pledging an allegiance to these common things and people. Otto von Bismarck uniting the German states is a good example. But the leader cannot lead unless he is mated up with followers designed to follow. Humans must be capable of both leading and following.

To accomplish such things requires a herding animal amenable to such talk and such concepts. Notions of who we are and what we believe are malleable. Important thinkers have suggested that all human concepts are plastic and moldable by the forceful personalities of others. Albert Einstein suggested that the average person is incapable of independent thought.

> Few people are capable of expressing with equanimity opinions which differ from the prejudices of their social environment. Most people are even incapable of forming such opinions.[19]

Einstein seems to state the obvious. We have all felt this way when the group seems to be moving in a direction we personally do not prefer. By pointing it out, he suggests he is not one of these people. But how can we know? Is a minority opinion always more original than a majority opinion? Most of us are well versed in only a few areas. When asked to give our opinion in matters outside these few areas, we usually look for the most informed person around us, with whom we might agree and support.

Einstein's lament restates sentiments we have heard from Rousseau and many others, that the state was made for man, not man for the state. He saw examples of both modes of action around him. From his position he preferred the one and hated the other. Einstein was a Mind 1 feeler.

Mind 1	Mind 2
The state was made for man.	Man was made for the state.

In reality, Einstein and all the rest of us are always both. When we look at subgroups, we find the same loyalties and attachment that we see expressed for nations. The members of the Hell's Angels live for their group and expect their motorcycle gang to come to their aid if possible. Loyalty and honor mean something to them. It does not matter if we call our group the Mormon Church, the Boy Scouts, males, or our employers; we identify with them and we expect to sometimes stand up for them; but we also expect them to stand by us if possible. We apply our two moral minds to all social situations.

We are inventive, decisive, and unique in narrow areas, followers in most others. Einstein wrote in the shadow of World War II when he complained that too many had followed like sheep the leaders he felt intuitively to be misguided. Neither Einstein nor Gumplowicz or many after them fully addressed the impact of the ongoing creation of sub-herds and subcultures within the culture.

Conclusion

Human herding is a dynamic process the complexity of which reflects the difference in brain size between us and our animal relatives. We share with them a dual morality, hyper-expressed in human beings, more complex and difficult to understand. A morality bisected by the urge to put the needs of the individual ahead of the group, or to put the needs of the group ahead of the individual.

In conclusion, we follow intuitively, consciously, and subconsciously. We try to lead when we can by purposefully deviating from accepted norms through the use of outlandish styles of dress (saggy pants) and by trying to convince others that our styles of music or movie preferences are best. When others follow our lead, we gain status. The farther from our group others are perceived, the more tolerance we have for their suffering. For ourselves and our group, we avoid suffering and seek prosperity by relying on two modes of judgment: Mind 1 and Mind 2. The first of these comes into play when we are safe and times are good; the second when there is danger and want. In easier times, we tend to organize sardine-style and eclectically dress, talk, or act as we please or as those immediately around us are doing. In harder times, we structure ourselves vertically and follow leaders and pre-established rules and customs that assure our safety.

Dual morality gives us the moral flexibility to see right and wrong in more than one way; to see good and evil in whatever way is necessary to ensure the survival primarily of the herd, secondarily of any individual in it. But no matter which type of socio-moral organization is in place, every group is made up of individuals - and it is to the level of the individual that we turn now.

Notes

1. William Godwin, *Enquiry Concerning Political Justice* Vol. 1 (London: G.G.J. Robinson, 1798) xxiii.

2. William Kitchner, *The Cook's Oracle* (Edinburgh: A. Constable, 1822) 34. Retrieved 2016-12-13
< https://archive.org/details/cooksoracleconta00kitc >

3. Plato, *The Republic*, trans. Benjamin Jowett, in *The Great Books of the Western World* (UK: Encyclopedia Britannica), 7: 320.

4. Herbert Spencer, *The Principles of Sociology, in Three Volumes* (New York: D. Appleton and Company, 1898) 1: 557, 563, 568. Retrieved 2016-12-13. <http://oll.libertyfund.org/titles/2634>

5. C. Wright Mills, *The Sociological Imagination* (New York: Oxford University Press, 1959) 132-133.

6. E. O. Wilson, *The Social Conquest of Earth* (New York: W. W. Norton Inc, 2012) 54.

7. Pliny the Younger, *As the Romans Did*, trans. Jo-Ann Shelton (New York: Oxford University Press, 1998) 342.

8. Aristotle, *Politics*, trans. Benjamin Jowett, in *The Great Books of the Western World* (UK: Encyclopedia Britannica), 9: 446.

9. Aristotle, *Nicomachean Ethics*, Book II, trans. W. D. Ross, in *The Great Books of the Western World* (UK: Encyclopedia Britannica), 9: 348-355.

10. Thomas Aquinas, "Treatise on Fortitude and Temperance," in *The Summa Theologica*, trans. Fathers of the English Dominican Province (Benziger Bros. ed., 1947) II-II, Q 141-143. Retrieved 2016-12-14. < https://www.ccel.org/a/aquinas/summa/SS.html >

11. Reported in Mark Walter, *Courtship in the Animal Kingdom* (New York: Anchor Books Doubleday, 1988) 105.

12. Henry L. Mencken, *Minority Report* (Baltimore: John Hopkins University Press, 1997) 39.

13. Adolph Hitler, *Mein Kamph*, Ford translation (Elite Minds Inc., 2009-2010) 212-213.

14. Ibid., 173.

15. Ibid., 170.

16. Karl Marx, "Critique of the Gotha Program," in *Marx/Engles Selected Works*, Vol. III (Moscow: Progress Publishers, 1970) Part 1. [Online] [Retrieved Dec. 12, 2016.] < https://www.marxists.org/archive/marx/works/download/Marx_Critque_of_the_Gotha_Programme.pdf >

17. This phrase was originally coined by Herbert Spencer in his *Principles of Biology* (University Press of the Pacific, 2002; originally published in 1864) I: 444.

18. Ludwig Gumplowicz, *The Outlines of Sociology* (Philadelphia: American Academy of Political and Social Sciences, 1899).

19. Albert Einstein, *Ideas and Opinions* (New York: Bonanza Books, 1954) 28.

Chapter 3
The Individual

WHAT IS INDIVIDUALITY?

If a flock of geese flew over our heads, we would know it was comprised of numerically individual animals, but to us, one would be exactly like the next. If you have seen one goose, you have seen them all. If we are in the army fighting an enemy we call the "terrorists," we attack them indiscriminately. Terrorists and geese may have individual identities among themselves, but to us, one is just about like another; and during war or hunting season, we are happy to shoot any one of them on sight.

If we are separating all fifth graders from sixth graders in the school cafeteria, each is an individual in some context, but for this purpose they are simply one of a group, and anyone in the group called "fifth graders" moves to the left, and anyone in the group called "sixth graders" is moved to the right. How they differ in other ways does not matter for the purpose of our effort. What matters for this effort is only how they are the same in the one category we care about now.

We socialize with others in two basic ways. We classify them as parts of groups in which all the members are treated alike; or we treat them as individuals requiring personalized consideration. Functioning properly with others demands we see things both ways. We are just one of a certain category of things, such as males, Americans, or pilots. And we are also individual people with specific names and personalities.

For most creatures, individuality is usually limited to the relationships among them and other members of their species. To us, a penguin is a penguin, a worm is a worm, and a mouse is a mouse. Unless we have a personal relationship with one of these creatures, we look at them as all pretty much alike.

In the lives of these animals, mating, parenthood, and their place in a local pecking order describes the relationships wherein they may be recognized as unique individuals. Outside of these considerations, one penguin is like another, even to other penguins. Unless they are your parent, your cub, or your mate, a tiger is a tiger, even to other tigers. One may guard a particular territory or be the mother of certain cubs, but in these few considerations alone do we distinguish individuality among tigers. The more socially complex the creature, the more likely individuals are identified as somehow distinct and recognizable by others of their group.

Among a group of chimpanzees or dolphins, individual members are recognized and acknowledged outside of the parental or mating relationship. Some minor trait or characteristic is discerned, allowing them to distinguish one individual from others. The species itself is advanced enough to observe and acknowledge such nuances. Of all creatures with such capabilities, none are as advanced as humans.

We have an enhanced capacity to recognize individuality among members of our group and among the things with which we come into contact. To a hawk, one mouse is as tasty as the next; but we can hold mice as pets, caring for and finding one far more worthy than another. A tiny white patch on his head allows us to distinguish our pet mouse from all others. Onto him we project affection and consideration. We might have been equally attached to any pet mouse we cared for, but since we happen to have chosen this particular one, we give its life added value.

As the most complex social creatures, we have both multiplied the number of categories and classes through which we distinguish others – farmers, Mexicans, blondes, Red Sox fans, etc. – as well as recognized the number of unique individuals within any of these classes. Our minds are enhanced devices for recognizing individuality, as well as being advanced devices for recognizing patterns, classes, and categories into which to lump things in order to quickly ascertain what we can expect of them by the herds/classes/species/groups they belong to.

The two outlooks of our dual morality assist us, as each handles individuality and grouping in different ways. In Mind 1, we try to see everything and everyone as being part of one big group whenever we can. In this mind, the individual nuances of habit and personality are used as acceptable distinguishing features. Fred prefers to play tennis and Sally prefers to go bowling. These are both acceptable ways to pass the time and they also allow us further ways to distinguish Fred from Sally. We are, each of us, unique in a number of ways, but since all these differences are acceptable, we are equally worthy members of our one big family. In a Mind 1 situation, we are distinguished by our individual personalities and preferences. A person is defined and distinguished horizontally relative to his or her own habits and desires.

In Mind 2, we categorize vertically. Individuals are measured by the groups with which they identify, or the level and status they command. Individuals are recognized by how well or how poorly they display shared qualities. And some of these qualities are superior to others. Fred is also the mayor, and in this position he commands greater respect than Sally, who works as a baker's assistant at the donut shop. Fred is equal in some way to Sally; Fred is superior in some way to Sally.

Mind 1	Mind 2
Everyone is an equal part of one universal group.	Each of us can be distinguished by the groups, classes and categories we belong to or the loyalties we express.
Each is uniquely identifiable by personality.	Each is identifiable by looking at his associations, function, status, and character.
Our actions are determined by our own wants and needs.	Our place and our duty are determined by our relationship to others.

Personal preferences are moral choices too

Each of us develops a repertoire of habits, hobbies and obligations that define our lives. Which of these are judged as socially significant and which are categorized as socially insignificant vary with circumstance. I might be a white pharmacy worker who eats sausage pizza and plays poker with a group of black and white men and women every Wednesday night. All of these behaviors can take on a moral component.

To a couple of my acquaintances who happen to be unreconstructed racists, my association with blacks at the game seems distasteful. Before I had a girlfriend, I gave no thought to the fact that a few of my poker buddies were women. Now, my girlfriend tells me that she feels uncomfortable every time I go to play poker because there are single women there. She would prefer I find a game that was "male only." My girlfriend is also a vegetarian who thinks eating meat is a bit wrong. She has never directly criticized my pizza choices, but her moral distaste runs against my sausage. My boss at the pharmacy is also a deacon at our church, but he never took much notice of my private life. Now that he has found out I am living with my girlfriend, he is putting pressure on me to marry her – to "do the right thing."

The hobbies, habits and petty choices we make tell others something about ourselves relative to them. Among the guys and gals at the poker house, pizza toppings and girlfriends were considered in a Mind 1 fashion: one was as good as the next and all were acceptable. To my girlfriend, pizza toppings had a moral component: some were better than others. A person did "better" choosing one topping and they did "worse" choosing another. Exactly which of our casual personal choices we approach from a Mind 1 perspective and which we view in a Mind 2 fashion depend on how we and others perceive the action in terms of threat or advantage. All choices are potentially moral choices; what changes is the moral category through which we perceive them.

Because we are a herd, we can be individuals

The advantages of being part of a herd are obvious. We are fed without being farmers, clothed without being tailors and housed without being carpenters. Even the weakest among us survives with the ever-present help of the stronger. We do not have to prove ourselves worthy; born into our herd, our worth is assumed. For herding creatures, keeping alive the wounded, the weak, the idiot and the eccentric is a possibility.

In non-herding creatures, this is not just unlikely; it is impossible. Lone members of non-herding species have little concept of an obligation to others of their kind. In non-herding animals, the incapable soon die. Outside of the temporary relations of sex or motherhood, non-herding animals remain hardly aware of the existence of others of their species, and if they run across them, they are likely to view them as a threat. The lone individual with a disability, a behavioral variation or a weakness soon perishes.

Among non-herding animals, the death of any one goes unnoticed. With the social creatures, the death of one will not be allowed if it can be helped. Among herding creatures, having others around is vital. Neighbors benefit each other. Humans, as the preeminent herding animal, have institutionalized pecking orders, methods of sharing, and means of cooperative protection. Morality is the intuitive set of behaviors by which these things happen. By having others around, by being part of a herd, I can specialize in only one thing and do everything else poorly, and still do well. Morality has evolved within us to regulate behavior toward each other.

Keeping others around, being helped, and helping them defines morality.

Because we are a herd, we can be individuals. The single-celled organism or the lone creature survives only if every aspect of it functions properly. Any serious defect in any part means death. The multi-celled creature can afford the loss of a few cells and go on. In the multi-celled animal, imperfect parts can often be abandoned; the loss of a few cells does not threaten the entire animal. Similarly, for a herd, the loss of a few members does not end its existence. This is the dichotomy of herding. Each is an individual, yet each is part of the group.

Every individual is valuable and deserves protection, but the loss of any one or even a few does not spell the end of the group. The group goes on, though individuals perish. By contributing to the welfare of the group, individuals achieve some type of immortality. Their contribution, the improvement of the herd, lives on after them.

Sometimes it is even necessary, for the preservation of the group, to sacrifice some of its individuals. Like the lizard who voluntarily loses part of its tail to a predator, or the lobster giving up a claw to save the rest of its body, herds sometimes find it necessary to sacrifice a few of its more dispensable members so that its more vital parts are protected. Young male baboons sit and watch for carnivores at the edge of the group. They occupy the most dangerous parts, with the females and higher-ranking males at the center enjoying the most protection. Humans accomplish the same ends with far more sophisticated means.

Mind 1	Mind 2
Individuals are paramount, since our group cannot exist without them.	The group is paramount, since the individual cannot exist without it.

Biological Individuality

Individually, we could not achieve individuality. Higher animals have at least two types of individuals: males and females; insects like bees expand individuality to three: queens, workers and drones. Creatures like termites have four types of adults: queens, workers, soldiers, and drones. Each type of termite or bee looks and behaves differently. This is true of ants too.

Because bees, termites and ants are a herd, they can be individuals. With herding creatures, the specialized type of individual can only exist if another type exists alongside it, which compensates for its shortcomings. Once specialization occurs in the herd, a second, third, or forth type of specialization *must* occur to ensure all necessary functions are performed for the group.

The queen bee or queen termite not only looks different from others in her group, she also functions in a different way. This means she possesses distinct urges and impulses to carry out her specialized duties. The queen can neither feed nor defend herself. To be provided for and protected, a worker caste and a soldier caste have developed alongside her, which sacrifice themselves to provide and protect her. The queen, worker, and soldier function together as a unit. For the queen's, worker's, or soldier's physical specialization to be of use, a psychological specialization and interdependence must have developed concurrently within them and among them.

Individuality has existed for tens of millions of years among the insects. It has existed long enough to develop a number of unique physical and physiological individuals. Among the warm-blooded animals, the only form of biological individuality that has existed long enough to produce supporting physical distinguishability within a species is sex – maleness and femaleness. The larger animals have not yet developed physical features that distinguish personality or functions within a herd beyond this.

Among the primates, the different roles performed by the two sexes were complemented by changes in appearance, attitudes and preferences. Differences were manifested not only by changes in the physique of males and females, but in emotional patterns as well. Emotional urges differed between the sexes, but within one sex or the other, they were largely the same. What one male baboon wanted to do was pretty much what any male baboon wished to do. Some monkeys were nearer the top of the social order, and others nearer the bottom. Some led the hunt, others followed. When leaders died, followers could change their thinking and take over. Individuality, where it might occur, is more an attitudinal thing, a slight mental or physical advantage that was fleeting. Individuality, where it has occurred among the mammals, is understood by behavior and place in the group. For us, how we act and what our place is in the group, and not how we look, has become who we are as individuals.

The human division of labor, which has resulted from our expanded mental ability to pursue options different from those of our neighbors, has accentuated individuality. This is a recent thing in evolutionary terms. It has not persisted long enough (and been so unchanging) as to establish a physical form that coincides with a particular skill. Humans do not give birth to overly large muscular males who reliably will desire to join the military or play football alongside a second phenotype of eggheads with extra good eyesight to read with and curved backbones to assist them in bending over their laptops or sitting in chairs to read books.

Herd advantages and the creation of differences

The deficiencies of any one member of a herd can be compensated for by others. The near-sighted or deaf zebra can avoid the lion about as well as his perfectly sighted and well-hearing brethren do, as long as he runs when his pals run and stops when they stop. The half-blind or deaf zebra never has to see the lion at all. Among zebras, some can be near-sighted, some far-sighted, some can have a keener sense of smell than the others and some a keener sense of hearing. If the individuals rely on each other and work together, the advantages of one can be put to use by all. The disadvantages suffered by some can be mitigated.

Zebras can be individuals. They may differ one from the other and still do well. In fact, individual differences may benefit everyone. A zebra born in the group with a larger than average number of brain cells devoted to distinguishing the scent of predators aids his herd disproportionately in that narrow way. Even if this surplus in smelling power was gained by a deficiency in cells for vision, he can still be an asset. By relying upon others to compensate for his sight deficiency, while providing the group the benefits of his scent superiority, this different zebra – the unique individual – can benefit the herd. In fact, the herd consisting of a number of unique individuals is probably superior to one comprised only of uniform and undifferentiated individuals. Within the confines of a herd, individuality itself can be an asset.

Individuality is distinguishability. Among humans, individuality is understood to be an aspect, not merely of appearance, but of personality and character. Individuality is the peculiar set of interests, skills or habits possessed and pursued (while others are absent or ignored), in a different combination from those of our neighbors.

Individual personalities are only possible when we are surrounded by others who accomplish all the necessary things we choose to neglect. Individuality is an aspect of herd behavior. Only herds can have individuals. And the more integrated the herd, the more unique the members can be. This poses a new challenge for morality: If we all start doing different things, how can we know what is right?

THE ORIGINS OF DUAL MORALITY

We look around us and see that animals organize in two general patterns: horizontally like the starlings, where one takes its cues from its neighbor; or vertically, like chimps following the lead and instructions of superiors. Morality, defined as doing rightly, is acting in a way recognized as best and proper under the circumstances we face. But as inseparable members of a group, this means two different things. We can be moral and do right relative to ourselves, or we can be moral and do right relative to others. Sometimes these two choices are at odds with each other. Doing right for me might mean hurting others in some way. Or, if I do for others, I might have to sacrifice myself.

Both moral views are present within each of us. But they are not blended; they are distinct. We feel things one way, and then we can also feel them another way. We speculate here: Where do these moral feelings come from? Why is it that we can feel in a Mind 1 horizontal fashion and then at other times feel in a Mind 2 vertical way? Morality, that is, doing rightly, has been divided in two ways from time immemorial. But the two methods of right action have not always been present in the single individual. For most creatures, right action has always been two potentially different things, depending on what our role was relative to others. That is, it depended upon whether we were born female or male. Which of these types of herd members we were defined the pattern of our correct behavior.

When all boys grew up to hunt and fight and all girls grew up to raise babies, correct behavior for each was clearly distinguishable, and the difference was determined by our gender. Right and wrong actions existed in one way only for each of the sexes. Among primates, and we can presume it applies to early humans, the duties of the males applied to all males; the duties of the females applied to all females. When another group of strangers approached our herd's territory, the males advanced to confront them. It did not matter which males were present; any and all males were expected to act in this way. This action was right for males. Females, when confronted by a group of strange males, retreated with their babies to a position of safety: this was right. The reaction for each sex was determined by what was best for the group. Both did the morally right thing for their condition. Under identical conditions, right action for the male was not the same as right action for the female. Moral correctness needed to be two different things.

Our gender determined the actions that were right for us. Other members of our group need only identify us by our sex to understand how we will feel and act. We did what was right for our group by doing what was right for our sex, and we were probably stressed when others did not act reliably in accordance with theirs. At this pre-human era, individuals could not exist in the way we understand them now. What uniqueness they had was concentrated around gender. Males acted differently from females, but pretty much like all other males. Females were different from males, but virtually interchangeable with any other female. Like chickens, we were divided into roosters and hens, and like chickens, one rooster was like another, and a hen was a hen. If you had seen one human of each sex, you had seen them all.

The good of the individual or the good of the group

Looking at the larger monkeys and apes, our closest relatives, we find that maleness and femaleness mean a great deal. As a pet or as a zoo exhibit, a male monkey might do about as well as a female. In those settings, the differences between the sexes are negligible. How the male pet monkey acts toward its owner might be identical to how the female pet monkey acts towards its owner. But put those same monkeys into a troop, and being a male means an entirely different thing from being a female. How the monkey reacts to other monkeys in a social situation tells us about monkey morality. Being a "good" monkey means doing what is expected of you when you are around others of your kind.

For the vertically-oriented males, strength and boldness earn him the most respect and move him up the pecking order of males, allowing him access to more mating opportunities with females. To gain such a position, displays of open aggression and a willingness to take risks are necessary. His most significant contribution will be to fight and acquire, taking from other groups, and other males in his own group where necessary. For the female, these behaviors make little sense. Her position is secure and unchallengeable. She will be in charge of her own family group, and any risk to her is a greater danger to the baby who will be clinging to her. For her, sharing and not competing are almost always right. There is no need to contest with others for greatness when you are indisputably the decider. Every mom is the greatest mom in her own nuclear family.

He fights off other males and protects his group from predators. By routinely and voluntarily putting himself at risk, he puts the good of the group before his own good. She intuitively avoids such conflicts. Neither she nor her offspring can survive if the males do not do their jobs and bring her to feeding areas in safety. She links her own personal safety to the protection of her offspring. In her view, it is right that the group sacrifice for her and her babies. He lives for the group; the group lives for her.

From the point of view of the female primate, right is the group sacrificing for the individual, the stronger protecting and sharing with the weaker. From the male point of view, right is the individual sacrificing for the group, and the weaker giving way to the stronger.

The female obviously displays what we have referred to as Mind 1 moral feelings and actions. She prioritizes provision, she prefers to equally distribute resources to her family, she promotes sharing with others, and she tolerates divergent behaviors within her immediate clan. The male displays Mind 2 moral preferences. He views his place in terms of position, duty, risk, sacrifice, with some getting more and others getting less of both social respect and the sexual and material benefits that accompany them. With the female and her brood, all need to have; with the males, some can have and others might not get any.

Mind 1	Mind 2
Our primary concern should be for the wellbeing of the individual.	Or primary concern should be for the wellbeing of the group.
The group exists to protect us individually.	We exist individually to protect the group.

If both sexes wanted the same things, they would do the same things. To get them to do different things, nature has them desire different things. The separate biological roles played by men and women in the group could only be accomplished with a change in the way each of them felt, then thought, then acted.

The distinguishing characteristic of the primate male comes from social leadership; for the primate female, it is from control within her family. Doing right for the male was doing male things, like fighting other males and guarding females in breeding condition. Doing right for the female had been ensuring her offspring were safe, providing them with enough food, and mating with the best males available. As long as males were the troop leaders and group guardians and females were the family's focus and caregivers, their patterns of action, of doing right, could remain distinct and sexually based. One's duties, feelings, social and personal responsibilities were tied to one's gender.

From mothers and men to women and fathers

Prior to the creation of lifelong bonds between males and females, the group was everybody and protecting and providing for it was an incidental and often-circumstantial responsibility of the males. Families, and protecting and providing for them, was the job of the females.

When every male had to hunt and fight, what distinguished one from another was their relative capacity to do these things. The differences between them were measured in terms of greatness. The superior male was the great warrior, the legend, the leader. These were the ideals all men strove for.   In the world of women, eating, mating, and child rearing consumed almost her every thought. She need not be concerned with battling males she had no chance of defeating. Her role was to protect her offspring. And each child was worthy of consideration. No child was inherently superior to another, and each needed to cooperate and share with siblings who were guaranteed to be younger or older, more or less objectively capable. Doing what was right for all equally, regardless of objective measures of ability, was to be doing good. It was not greatness that counted, not a separation and superiority, but cooperation in doing what was best for all. Within the family, when we all did what we were supposed to, we were good.

Our superior mental capabilities were built upon a previous and more primitive template of moral understanding. For tens of thousands of pre-human years, there had been two distinct moral codes to follow, two ways in which to act that could be right – the female way or the male way, the family way or the social way, the search after cooperative goodness or the thirst for competitive greatness.

Variability had been more of a male thing
Predictability more a female thing

Until recent centuries, the need to bear and rear children guaranteed women had to be family members first, societal members second. Men had it the other way round. Having to work outside the home 60 hours a week, males were likely to be members of their social group first, husbands and fathers second. This was right. We had no choice.

This situation must have been true and right for the better part of the past 50,000 years: women as masters in the home, men as masters of everything outside it. Within all modern cultures, the males are still likely to be more socially diverse and unique among themselves than its females, as numerous studies have shown.[1] Having less of their time and interests biologically directed toward the singular activity of preparing a child to join its group, males can be more eclectic in their interests. Her interests are still likely to be focused on children and grandchildren.

Small children require specialized care. Experimentation and a willingness to try something new on infants are dangerous. In lean times, a mother who tried to feed and dress her infant in ways that other mothers around her and before her had never done was not likely looked upon as an innovator so much as a selfish lunatic who risked the life of her baby. The successful mother is remarkably similar to most other mothers.

Parenting can be looked upon as a craft. As with soldiers or jockeys, one experienced practitioner can be exchanged for the next, with reasonable confidence they can carry out their responsibilities. One mom, like one dad, or one soldier, is much like another. Within the trades, one barber is like another, one tailor like another too. But whereas being a mother was most likely what a woman would be asked/expected to do to best contribute to her herd, being a father was only part of what a male was expected to do, and maybe only a small part.

Half of the human race had to be dedicated to the one single task of mothering, with everything else being of secondary concern, while the other half, the males, could be dedicated to pretty much everything else. Females as a sex needed to be capable of focusing attention on developing individuals and the small details that ensure their survival. Her cultural role has remained, until recently, biologically predetermined. She and all others of her gender would be required to keep alive a small being that began life helplessly and would need everything done for it. Every female of every generation from time immemorial could be anticipated to have this demand placed upon her. Before the development of production, trade and agriculture, males were similarly handcuffed. The responsibilities of every male would be to forage, hunt, compete for sex and protect the group. This was every male's job description. With the development of production and trade, the opportunities to diversify behaviors beyond those that had previously remained unchanged for a million years became available to both sexes, but this diversity was circumstantially more available to males than to females.

The herd cannot afford women to be failures. The future depends on them successfully raising children to adulthood. We can miss a meal or two, but we cannot miss a generation. Most women have to get it right every single time. This reality shaped our moral Mind 1 outlook, and all future aspects of Moral Mind 1 understanding emanate from this reality. The children must survive and must be raised to take their place in the group. Cooperation and sharing resources within the family ensured the survival of every member.

The male, freer to do any number of things, lives life as the disposable partner in the relationship; he could take more risks. If he succeeded in finding some new social innovation, the group as a whole could benefit. But if he failed, the group was hardly any worse off than it had been before. Males could risk and males could fail. In fact, the group probably benefitted most by having males that risked and didn't fear failure. Producing males who sought out risk and who tolerated high levels of danger was likely a social advantage. Individuality then, from the group's point of view, could be a male thing more safely than a female thing.

Risk

The very notions of risk and failure were evaluated differently by each moral outlook.

Moral Mind 1 The Individual and Familial Mind	Moral Mind 2 The Group and Herding Mind
Everyone must make it.	Some are dispensable.
Risks need to be limited or eliminated.	Risk is to be sought out.
When everyone has to make it, and when we are all of equal value, success or failure has less meaning.	The successful survive, prosper, and are to be emulated. They are superior to the failures.
We are all equal.	Some are better than others.
Cooperation is the highest social ideal, displaying the moral traits necessary in the family environment.	Competition helps identify the best among us, determining the traits necessary to succeed in the social environment.

THE BIRTH OF CULTURE: THE IMMORTALIZATION OF INDIVIDUAL INSIGHT
Man becomes human and creates history

We have speculated about life 50,000 years ago when the ancestors of modern humans lived side-by-side with Neanderthals. The two great apes were hunters who mastered fire, buried their dead, and carved simple killing tools like spearpoints and stone skinning blades. Both species existed together for thousands of years, generation upon dreary generation, century upon repetitious century, daughters doing what their mothers had done, sons following the example of the adult males in their group. Humans and Neanderthals were stuck in time. As with lions or giraffes, there was no change, and *with no change, there was no history* for any species: all the females raised children and all the males killed game and fought among themselves for dominance.

For most of human history, being a wife and a mother was always going to be demanded of the female; working outside the home was a secondary function. Weeding the garden could wait; feeding the baby could not. If the woman did those few things well and without fault, her family benefitted. The male role in the family was less significant. Men had to be second-best moms, ready to step in if necessary. His role in the home was contingent, hers a necessity. But outside the home, he had to be ready to do almost anything. The male never knew in what century, or to what land, he would be born in. His culture might need him to be a sailor or a shoemaker, a warrior or a saint – there was no way to tell. For the woman, it mattered less into what century she was born or to what community. She could know in advance that her first and most vital duty, right up until yesterday, was to be a mother. She was the specialist, he the generalist.

We can assume that for primitive humans, like most animals, the herd consisted of permanent females around which males came and went. Males more expendable, females far less so, the hive buzzes around their queen. Any one worker or drone is expendable, but lose the queen and all is lost. Female lions define the pride; dominant males come and go, occupying a place in it for only a few years before they are superseded by younger and stronger rivals. Are things so different for humans?

What brought the males into the family and brought the females out of it was the one thing that distinguishes us most dramatically from other creatures. So what was the event (or combination of events) that led to males being more closely incorporated into families and females more active outside of them? I think we can conclude that it involved the expansion of tool use and trading, combined with the alterations of social organization that had to accompany it.

Tool use alone did not change us. As long as everyone used the same tools in the same ways, we all remained nearly identical people, with each doing about the same things as everyone else. When all males made spears and all females roasted woodchucks for their babies, males and females could retain their own distinct moral code, which guided their own patterns of behavior. Tool use by itself would not change that. Other animals use tools. Otters and seagulls crack oysters on stones; chimps roll noisy cans. Tool use changed us when some of us began using some tools while others did things differently.

There were once only two kinds of humans: the male type and the female type. Both used the same tools in the same ways. Everything changed when some people began using one type of tool while someone else used another, and when we figured out how to exploit and promote these differences.

There was a time, we presume, when all males hunted, all males made spears, and all males wore hides. Then individual variety happened. Individuals had always emerged who could make a better spearpoint than others. His spears would be sharper, stronger or made more quickly. This individual prospered in two ways. Firstly, he gained by employing a superior weapon, and secondly, he benefitted from the increase in social status he achieved as the other members of his group first admired and then tried to copy his methods. He and his group shared in recognizing his enhanced reputation, but his spearpoints were his own; each person still made and used his own creations.

Another member of the group may have been better at skinning and tanning hides. This individual may have prospered and may have moved up the social hierarchy, as his superiority in a task done by all others was apparent. As their status increased, the better spear maker or hide skinner would have had access to more females and can be imagined as likely to produce more offspring. If so, whatever was going on in their heads that gave them the ability to do these tasks a bit better than their peers may have been passed down to their children. In this way, slowly, very slowly, and reproductively, their small herd may have genetically benefitted from their individual prowess. The members of their group, generation upon generation, might carry more of the habits or genes expressed by these more capable individuals. But this was a multi-generational process. It is fundamentally the same process of biological evolution used by birds, buffalo, and every other creature. Then a leap occurred.

At some point, the minds of our ancestors expanded to conceive of how everyone might benefit directly from the superior spearpoint maker and the better hide skinner. At some long-ago critical juncture in human evolution, our ancestors grasped that, if the guy who made the best spearpoints made everyone's spearpoints, everyone could benefit. And when everyone gained individually, the group as a whole gained as well. But how could one man put off hunting to make all spearpoints? Others would have to do his hunting for him. He made spearpoints, and in turn the others thatched his roof or shared their meat, and everyone gained.

This was the birth of culture: when the idea or invention that originates in the individual mind gains immortality by being adopted as part of the practices of the group. Everyone can now wear the best skins tanned by the one guy who does it best. When this leap in mental ability, in social ability, occurred, it meant we no longer had to live as hunter-gatherers, and could move into villages and larger communities. Production and trade became possible. *Cultural individuality* was born, taking its place alongside sexual individuality, and modern society became feasible.

This change must have been exponentially more difficult than we imagine now. For a million years we understood that all males did this and all females did that. Our strongest inner-feelings of right and wrong demanded we reward such right and punish all wrong. Right and wrong was the same for everybody, yesterday, today, and forever. Now some of us were doing some things while others were occupied doing different things. How could we have recognized this as right also? How could we judge right and wrong in a group where everyone was doing something different?

Males were not tied down to a single time-consuming and all-important task like child rearing. Males, having the time, must have found it easier to focus on production and trade. Fatherhood takes a few minutes of passion and a few minutes of play every day. Motherhood requires more rapt attention all day long when a baby is small, and caring for offspring demands almost a lifetime. A division of labor and trade may have evolved socially between males concerning hides and spears, but every mom still had to give birth and care for her own offspring. Motherhood was not fungible.

Some males might eventually farm lettuce and others herd cows, but their wives needed to retain a biological calling that could not be so easily shared and traded. One woman in the village could not birth and raise everyone's children. Individuality, in practice, potentially meant less for the females than the males.

The creation of history

Production and trade created something new: cultural individuality. What one person was doing could be, for the first time, something completely different from what the others were doing, or what others had ever done – and this could be right also. Our views on correct and incorrect behavior had to become more flexible.

The expanding production that accompanied specialization and individuation allows us to exist in much larger herds. There was more and more stuff for everybody. We were no longer relegated to being nomadic hunter-gatherers who stripped a location bare of food and moved on. We settled into communities to farm, raise animals, and manufacture. Populations grew; towns came into existence. Our tribes were tens; they became herds of hundreds and then thousands. All the old urges, instincts and moral goals were adapted to the expanding opportunities our dual morality supported.

Leadership had once meant only the top position of the entire group, but now it became the upper position in any number of narrow subcultures within the main herd. Everyone was a leader in his own house or atop the craft in which he worked. Our subgroups expanded. Opportunities to be social, as well as familial, multiplied.

Just why individuality came so strongly and suddenly to humans is debatable. But it happened. Some people began to do things differently from others while still being able to cooperate within the same group. Our morality accommodated the change;

and it changed everything. For the first time in the lifetime of the species, one generation of its creatures did things differently from the last! When individuality happened, history happened.

It was not so much that each of us individually were doing so many more things – each of us might still be doing only one or two things – but the group collectively did more things as each of its members did something different from the others. We did not all become better artists, farmers and spear makers, but we all developed the ability to recognize and exploit these differences in the few who did. We specialized, cooperated, traded and grew richer and safer than any animal species ever dreamed. We had the mental and physical ability to change our world to meet our needs, and by changing our patterns of social organization, we learned to best use them.

Once our ancestors developed the ability to differentiate and trade, every year witnessed something happening that had never happened before. Change piled upon change. Every Neanderthal was probably about as good at making spearpoints and at keeping himself warm and dry as any other Neanderthal. If he was not, he died. But this was not true among humans; some of us stunk at these things but could find other ways to be valuable – and more of us survived.

Tool production and trade

At the dawn of history, some of us became herders, others hunters and others farmers. This development of individual skills was undoubtedly a difficult challenge because it required a whole new way to understand right and wrong. For the first time in the history of our species, labor was not just divided into two kinds, the male kind and the female kind. Suddenly, one's labor might be any one of a number of different things. Within the sexes, one male could be doing something different from other males and still must be looked upon as doing right. A female could be doing things different from what other females were doing and she also needed to be seen as doing right. How do we know what is right when everyone is doing his or her own thing? Morality expanded in complexity as the notion of individuality and community became more sophisticated. Before we could do different things, the idea that different things could be done needed to be accepted.

At some point in pre-history, the roles of the sexes became less distinct. Males and females began to share their social and personal responsibilities. Females were expected to participate in what the males were doing and the males contributed more directly to the females' efforts. Each had always retained some innate potential of feeling right in the way the other sex felt it, but it had always been unnecessary. Now things were different. When the male brought what he did into the family, and when the female merged her family with the activities of the male, each had to be able to contribute to the efforts of the other. *By merging our social roles, we have had to combine our moral feelings.*

Neanderthals probably remained one like any other, with not much more individuality than is expressed by tigers. If you had seen one, you had seen them all. Homo sapiens became individuals. Knowing a sailor was different from knowing a farmer. As the mind expanded, it compartmentalized, and the acts that our big-brained ancestors performed became compartmentalized too. Modern science tells us that about 12,000 years ago, human encampments became more complex. Spearpoints became stylized; cave art more detailed; jewelry, ornamentation, and burial more reflective and expressive. Between then and now, not even the sky has been the limit.

Parents of multiple children discover quickly that their kids may look alike, but they do not act alike. Striving for individuality has become an aspect of human behavior. For a second child wanting attention and noting that his older brother is a better reader, he focuses on drawing. A third child may attract attention through joking and gags. Each will try to find a way to distinguish himself or herself from the crowd.

The defining characteristic of humanity is not just tool making, but *the expansion of individuality* within the confines of a greater group. Just how much of this is biological and how much is cultural is unclear. It is even unclear how much these terms mean. Can a thing be cultural without it being biological? Certainly, like the skin's ability to tan, burn or freckle, our particular ability in these areas is not obvious until we are exposed to sunlight. The brain's ability to create individuality seems to be a complex response to environmental factors early in life. Just how, and in which direction, cannot be predicted. Just how much of an individual any one of us can be is not known until we are put in environments conducive to behavioral variation.

NEAR MONOGAMY CREATED THE POSSIBILITY OF TRUE SUBGROUPS

Individuality multiplied and the capacity for a dual moral perspective expanded within each of us

A remarkable change was going on, not just in trade, but in relationships as well. What it meant to be a male could not change until what it meant to be a female changed with it. A change in the relationship between women and men had to occur to make the changes in production and trade feasible. *Modern humanity – and modern morality – only became possible when the two roles began to converge.* Men could not change and become craftsman and fathers without an equally revolutionary change taking place with women.

For centuries beyond number, every male competed with every other male, vying to mate with every female. Everyone was born knowing the game: every female was *potentially* available to any male who achieved a socially superior position. Males earned mating opportunities by competing with other males for social status in narrow ways. For every male, this is what had to matter most. From a biological point of view, there was only one career every male wanted to participate in – herd leadership. The guys at the top got the gals. But this had to change or production and trade could never have been possible.

There had been only one measure of status that mattered: group leadership. This outlook had to be modified in the minds of the females before modern society became possible. If mating was only assured through one activity, it made sense to focus as much as possible on that one thing. But if mating became possible as a result of other factors, then focusing on these other factors could also make biological sense. The cultural forces changing the males were changing females too. Both sexes acquired the ability to recognize social contribution through creation and trade. As we gained the ability to bestow social status on a wider range of activities, the rewards for achieving such status began to be spread throughout a wider segment of the group.

With the development of production and trade, males within the same group began doing *dis*similar things. Females acquired the ability to recognize the advantages of these other skills. Status began to be acquired not just through group leadership, but also by excelling in some technical specialty. The superior spear maker who traded spearpoints for game was recognized by the other males through an enhanced bestowal of status, and by females as a viable and desirable mate. So too was the group's best cave artist or sandal maker. As goods accumulated around the males with superior skills, females gathered around them too. As subgroups of spear makers, tanners and medicine men evolved, mating with the males at the top of these subgroups satisfied the female requirement to breed with superior types.

Modern social life, and cultures running into the millions, would hardly have been possible unless there had been a reasonable prospect of most males mating. It took the development of near-monogamy to allow production and trade to pass from a possibility to a reality. Individually skilled producers, and not just the herd's martial leaders, also had to get the girls.

At some point long before history, females began to trade their invaluable attentions for the valuable assets of males who possessed more than just status; they held material wealth, the wealth that ensured the survival of the female and her offspring. With an expanded mental capacity to create and trade, and the monogamy that allowed it to be biologically feasible, survival could now be assured for hundreds, thousands or millions. The population of any producing and trading group was potentially limitless. The formerly almighty dominant male at the top of the pecking order simply could not command the attention of the growing number of females. It was neither in his interest to hoard them, nor in their interest to be so exclusive.

Production and trade may have been a human potential for generations, but until a move by the females occurred that created the near-monogamy we now enjoy, males would not venture too far down that road. Males give up wealth for women; they seldom give up women for wealth. Once the females were on board – mates who rewarded productive males with their attentions – society as we know it was inevitable. Once the women were more exclusively the partners of productive males, they could focus their time on assisting his efforts. Productive life became linked to family life. She could share his concerns and he began sharing hers. Right and wrong, alongside proper behavior, began to drift. Masculinity and femininity grew less distinct.

Almost monogamous

Monogamy is not uncommon among birds, but in other species it is less frequently observed. It is usually accompanied by low sexual dimorphism. That is, in monogamous species, the males pretty much look just like the females. Swans, geese, and penguins are monogamous, and we cannot readily tell the male from the female. Both sexes look alike. Ducks do not mate for life; the male duck looks different from the female. Among primates, none bond exclusively with just one mate for life – none of the larger apes are monogamous, not even us humans; we know this by looking at ourselves. Look around.

Among the mammals that are not monogamous, a high level of sexual dimorphism is common. The boys are clearly distinguishable from the girls. Sexual differences are often expressed in scent, but size and weight are common factors as well. In species that do not mate for life, males tend to be larger than females, more aggressive, and carry distinct secondary sexual characteristics. Sexing the animals that do not mate for life is usually an easier task then telling males from females in monogamous species:

Flamingos are monogamous and appear almost indistinguishable.

[source Freeimages.com]
Gorillas travel in families where a dominant male silverback guards two or more
females.

Human males are still easily distinguishable from females and our looks betray our less monogamous past. Our habits of dress often develop to satisfy our innate urges to distinguish males from females. In some cases, as with Japanese geishas, differences are exaggerated.

Monogamy may be as recent as advanced tool production; otherwise men and women might look more alike. We are probably still moving in that direction – toward a more secure mating for life and even greater physical androgyny. In spite of the fact that, as we move toward a more comprehensive Mind 1 culture, traditional forms of social institutions like "marriage" fade, long-term dedication to a single spouse may continue to grow. Such alterations of instinct undoubtedly take hundreds of generations. But it is possible that, even though there is less and less social pressure to stay with only one mate, we will find ourselves doing so anyway. Assuming this monogamous pattern continues, we can guess how humans might look in twenty thousand years. Males without facial hair, women with reduced breast size, men and women appearing indistinguishable from a distance.

The move to monogamy may have marked the point where humans diverged from Neanderthals and other proto-human-like relatives. It is possible that we survived and other near-human species became extinct because our near-monogamy was conducive to social situations that favored survival. Competing with Homo sapiens families, which benefitted by having a second adult to help with the children and a second set of hands to help with production, Neanderthals could not keep pace. Lacking dedicated husbands and wives, Neanderthal tribes had to remain much smaller, and these competing large apes never enjoyed the reproductive advantages that our over-producing extended families guaranteed. Perpetual estrus now accompanies perpetual production.

Our men are still clearly distinguishable from our women and children. Yet we are a near monogamous species. Maybe not enough time has passed for our physiology to catch up with our psychology. We have moved from being one type of creature toward being the other type. We have moved from a past where our ancestors were probably much like the chimps or gorillas, and where no permanent mating bonds occurred, into a present where near-permanent bonding has created the two-parent family with males taking an active part in child care and females contributing to tool production. Acting differently requires feeling differently. To be a successfully monogamous creature, morality had to adjust.

With the onset of near monogamy, with the closer cooperation and interchange of behavior between the sexes, the separation of roles was eliminated: *our morality merged but did not blend*. We became creatures with two ways to see the world. Each of us now enjoys (or is tormented by) two ways to judge right and wrong action.

When each male acquired his own female, and every female had her own male bound to her to help provide and protect, they needed to grow in tune and in touch with their now expanded social responsibilities. Being a woman became more than being a mother, and fatherhood was born. Where before family meant mother and children and society meant adult male-to-male relationships, and both family and society each had its own set of moral rules, now family and society became closer things. Society became the interplay of families and individuals.

Right and wrong came to be understood as a carrying out of our duties in accord with both our "personal" responsibilities as family members and our "social" responsibilities as members of the group. We, male and female, took care of our family and we took care of our group. Sharing and competing came to be seen in broader ways to be applied at different times. We became more adept and flexible about when it was right to share and when it was right to compete. Sometimes sharing was done with everyone socially; then again, in leaner times, it was right to only share with the tiny clan that was our own family. At times we competed only with people outside our herd, and cooperated with everyone within it. And in tougher times, we even competed with others in our own herd for limited resources. What was right and what was wrong became more varied and complicated

Our transition to near-monogamy enhanced our ability to see family things in social ways and social things in family ways. We expanded our notions of what could be right and wrong in both social spheres. Each of us became capable of desiring co-equal goodness as well as superior greatness. Today, female or male, we want to do what is right for all, and also, we wish to be seen as superior in some way. Male or female, we want to be good and we want to be great.

Because the demands of a diverse society beyond the family are more broadly varied than the demands of child rearing within the family, the proto-monogamous and more *socially oriented human males* were more likely to be distinguishable among themselves than the proto-monogamous *family-oriented human females*. With expanded production, we do more varied and different things for society than we do for our family. Having the bulk of the responsibility to deal with the non-human world of snakes and crocodiles, or finding water holes, or making spearpoints or fishing hooks, along with dealing with other males from within and without the group, the social male likely had to be a more flexible creature than the family female. With the advent of near-monogamy and the creation of extended parenthood, fathers entered the family and mothers moved outside it, and the roles of both expanded.

Anything you can do I can do better

There is no trainable skill done by one sex that the other sex cannot accomplish, though maybe through more effort. Certainly boys seem more inclined to some activities than girls. Most 21st century feminists seem to have come to terms with this. If we watch television or examine social media sites, we are far more likely to see young males drawing attention to themselves by riding their bicycles off roofs, or challenging each other to hot pepper eating contests. And we find females posting pictures of themselves sporting a new hairdo or promoting some healthy eating plan.

Humans gained advantage "above" other animals with the development of complicated tool use and exchange. Both sexes emerged capable of complex thought, tool creation and use, but along with these expanding abilities we retained the earlier vestiges of a more narrow sexual individuality. When we act as farmers, bankers, or carpenters, our sex may not matter at all; the male banker is no different from the female. But regardless of what craft we practice, we remain men or women. Identifying ourselves and others by gender still tells us much and probably most of what there is to know about us individually.

Looking more closely at traditional gender roles, we discover they match up with the herd organizational models described earlier. Females acting as mothers organize their group – themselves and their children – horizontally. That is, where possible, each of her children is loved and cared for equally. She distributes resources equally between her children. As the central character of her tiny group, the mother (if she gets involved) usually finds it morally right to look to the smallest and weakest first, and focuses her attentions there before others. She will often go hungry to feed her brood. She is the focal point of her group, but she is not the superior whom the others have to serve; she may direct their activities, but it is for the good of all. She lives for them; they need not sacrifice for her.

Males, on the other hand, tend to organize their activities vertically, with leaders and subordinates. Male-dominated social organizations, like the military, business corporations, bass fishing clubs and criminal gangs, have leaders, lieutenants, and low or unranked trainees. Male-oriented social structures are usually organized vertically, where the group looks upward first, or backward to written procedures, customs and rules, to chart their course of action. This ability to organize both horizontally and vertically has come to define complex human social structure.

Right and wrong continued to evolve along two parallel streams. Both males and females could see the world in two ways. Having two moral guidelines gives us more options in every situation. We judge a thing as right or wrong depending on which moral mode we are operating in at the moment, and feel (almost) completely justified in doing so.

Mind 1	Mind 2
Sharing is right; the smallest come first.	Competition is right; the biggest, strongest, fastest should get the most rewards.
Family and those within the home are most vital; those outside it are secondary considerations.	Society and those who lead it are most vital; the average person or family is of secondary importance.

Being creatures with a dual moral outlook, we look at all social arrangements in two ways: the horizontal or the vertical. We imagine that one butcher is about the same as another butcher, but then again, we can imagine one butcher is better than others. Blessed with this dual morality, we find no contradiction in holding both views simultaneously; one meat cutter is like another, and one rises above the others. A butcher is a butcher, but the head butcher gets more respect and earns the attention of more customers and potential mates than his young assistant. The basic moral pattern of mating with the superior performer has been retained with our females and has expanded to incorporate our new-fangled capabilities.

As we developed these subgroups of weavers and painters, it was imperative to retain an affinity for continuing loyalty to the larger group. A weaver could only succeed by trading his goods with others who did things besides weave. We have had to develop the ability to identify more closely with some than others, like those in our craft, while retaining an overarching grand loyalty to our herd. These traits continue to be expressed by us today. Our expanded mental capabilities have allowed for a hyperinflation of the variety of social subgroups, subcultures and ideologies, all operating under the umbrella of larger social groupings.

We may all be Americans, but some of us are also Baptists, communists, bowlers, or electricians. Within the shared larger group we call our own, exist others who are distinctly not of these types, people who identify themselves as Catholics, Republicans, and gamblers. Morality has expanded to include not only the ability to see each of these groups as right and proper, within their own sphere, but also to see them as cooperative or competing within our circumstance. The growth of mental ability, the production and trade it produced, and the doubling of our morality has allowed for the exponential multiplication of our behavioral possibilities.

Mind 1 Horizontal Morality	Mind 2 Vertical Morality
One trade is as good as another.	Some trades are socially superior to others.
One worker within a trade is as good as another.	Some workers within the same trade can be better than others.

INDIVIDUALITY TODAY
The meaning of life

Joe is a barber and Ted is a tailor. Joe spends his time doing one thing; Ted spends his time doing another; Joe talks about what he knows at length, Ted yaks about something else. But they are also both American males. They are both different, and yet the same. Possessing a dual morality allows us to feel ourselves and others as both different and the same at the very same time. How much Joe the barber differs from other barbers or Ted the tailor differs from other tailors becomes a separate question from how barbers as a group are treated within the larger herd relative to tailors. Not only do people compete with others of their craft, but the crafts themselves also jostle for recognition within the group. Within the crafts, the Joes and Teds compete with others of their interests for hierarchy, status and success.

So when we ask what the meaning of Joe's or Ted's life is, we begin to get a picture of a dual purpose of personal and public. In some way, the question of the meaning and purpose of Joe's life is answered in part by his craft as a barber and his relationships with women and offspring; but Joe also imagines himself as part of a greater herd beyond family and within and outside his craft.

Tautologically, the more diverse the society, the more individuality exists within it. Diversity and individuality are two ways of saying about the same thing. Modern democracies are full of bizarre and unique individuals of assorted abilities, beliefs and practices. Democracy is an opportunity to influence more than our family or our gild, but our herd also. When we accept that the meaning of life comes through the things that give life meaning, and what our life has meant is described by the freedom to develop our interests and be recognized for our unique achievements, then lives lived by Homo sapiens who have so many opportunities mean more than the lives of tigers or ants who do less. Pleasure and happiness are linked to personal and social successes. Having the opportunity to experience more diverse pleasures and having a broader understanding of happiness mean that "the meaning of life" for human beings is a broader and deeper thing too.

Pleasure satisfies us individually in the present. Exactly what pleases me may not be what pleases you. Happiness is an evaluation of our activities over time and in relation to standards beyond ourselves. Here too we find another example of how the dual nature of our moral understanding has led to two distinct terms being used to describe similar things. If we believe we have lived up to what was expected of us, carried out our duties toward others and they towards us, than we believe we are happy. Our pleasures are more personal and individual, our happiness more a communal thing. So when we wonder if pleasure and happiness can be different for different people, the answer seems twofold: both yes and no. Our pleasures are unique to us and can vary greatly from those of our neighbors or our spouses, but our happiness is more a shared thing. Where I find my pleasure may be vastly different from where you find your pleasures, but my happiness and yours are likely to be discovered in about the same ways: in carrying out our sociobiological responsibilities and being recognized for doing so; by being good parents, good citizens, people of faith, caring neighbors and reliable coworkers.

Personality and character
Pleasure and happiness

Equipped with two moral patterns, the internal emotional conditions described in one mind vary a bit from how we perceive things in our other moral mind. The emotional goals and achievements are weighed and measured, then compared, in accordance to the moral standard of each outlook. When in Mind 1, the focus is on the individual and the smaller or weaker in any social relationship. In this mind, the proper social outlook is one where priority is given to assisting the individual. In Mind 1, we see right as valuing and addressing the needs of each member of the group equally. In Mind 1, the time horizon for action is now, as the need is seen to be in the present. In Mind 1, we look inward, into ourselves, for motivation. We are hungry; we must eat. Satisfaction in the now is called "pleasure," and reward in the present is a key aspect of our Mind 1 outlook. Being "present oriented" and beginning with the supposition that each one of us is equal to everyone else, our differences are not used against us. In Mind 1, our habits and preferences are chalked up to a thing we call "personality," and anyone's personality is accepted as being about as worthy as another's. We may concede that we prefer people of a certain personality type to others – but there is no suggestion that one personality is inherently superior to another. A preference does not imply superiority. In Mind 1, we are creatures seeking pleasures and avoiding pains, living in the now, and just how we go about our lives is a matter of our particular personality and the preferences that it entails. But in Mind 1, there is also an aspect of "ultimate right" and happiness.

Happiness in a Mind 1 outlook is conceptualized as the entire group being cared for, where we are all understood to be equally worthy. The elimination of oppression, violence, and social inferiority are key aspects of the Mind 1 vision of happiness. Propriety in Mind 1 is the group in the service of the individual, with an overall aim to accomplish these goals.

In Mind 2, the emphasis is on the individual in the service of the group. In Mind 2, we focus on our obligations to others. We do this by upholding laws, customs and traditions. The identity of our group is not only known by what it consists of at the present moment, but, more importantly, by what it has been and where it might go. Our individual outlook is narrow and tiny when we see with only our own eyes, but by upholding the traditions and practices of the past, we gain the wisdom of a hundred generations. Our group embodies the collective traditions, habits, and social patterns of the people like us who lived before.

In Mind 2, the Mind 1 focus on *personality* is replaced by a focus on *character*. Where *personality* is seen to reflect an individual's preferences and habits, which are about as good as any other individual's as long as no one gets hurt, *character* is a reflection of upholding what is understood as "right" by our culture and traditions – it is performing our duty by the group. When we speak of personality, we think in terms of pleasing ourselves; matters of character involve living up to our social obligations as transmitted to us by past or present superiors. Some people may sing and dance, while others play chess. These are matters of personality. But a person's trustworthiness, honesty and reliability are matters of character.

When we speak of an individual's "personality," we usually mean their preferences, habits, and mannerisms, which identify them as individuals. Every individual has a unique set of personality traits. He might be the type who tells a lot of jokes or maybe the type that never seems to understand a joke when it is told. When describing a "personality," we might say she loved the theater or hated it, played tennis or bowled. But no matter how we describe another's "personality," it is presumed to reflect the individual's own choices and preferences. There is an equality about personalities; you may not like mine, but this is my personality and no one's personality is inherently better than another's. There is no "standard" of a "good personality" that is established for everyone.

Character, on the other hand, is not determined by the individual. Character is a matter of cultivating virtues and avoiding vices. A good character is a standard that applies to everyone in society, and does not vary from individual to individual. The virtues of honor, courage, temperance and honesty are standards that everyone is supposed to strive for. While personality focuses on who I am as an individual, character focuses on how I ought to behave as a member of a group.

If we say, "He is a person of questionable character," or that someone "lacks character," we are implying a deficiency in his or her social reliability. To comment on someone's character is to pass judgment on how they behaved relative to those around them, to which they owed something. When we speak of honesty, loyalty, or integrity, we are talking in terms of character, not an enlivened personality. A lack of personality is an individual's own concern; but a lack of character might be his neighbors', who have to lock their doors and guard their wallets.

Personality is something we are born with and that shapes our actions with a focus on what we prefer; character is something we develop as we shape our actions in light of what our group prefers, and what others expect from us.

Personality and character can be differentiated in terms of emotional expression. Personality, as an aspect of our family-style morality, is a matter of individual expression. Your emotional preferences tell us who you are as a unique individual. In a Mind 1 pattern, the type and intensity of emotional expression we display are determined by us – we can act out; we may seek fun or we may be more morose than others; maybe we cry easily or laugh loudly. It doesn't matter. All forms of emotional expression in Mind 1 are acceptable and good, as long as there are no negative consequences for others.

We fall back on Mind 2 "character" in more serious or formal social circumstances, where frivolity or individual expression have no place. In such circumstances, we emotionally react as others traditionally have done in these same circumstances. A person "of character" is often visualized as a serious and grave individual, not easily moved to excess emotion in any form. Emotional outbursts could be construed as signs of weakness. People of character have their emotions under control.

It is important to distinguish the *emotional control* that is attributed to Mind 2 character from the emotional *restraint* that characterizes the shy, reserved personality type. Character is not the product of personality, and emotional control is not exclusive to the reserved personality. Emotional control is more like "emotional management/supervision" – it involves ensuring that one's emotions are either displayed or restrained in accordance with custom and tradition, that is, in conformity with what is expected by the group and appropriate to the formality of the situation. Indeed, in Mind 2, there are circumstances and occasions – weddings, civic celebrations, ceremonies, etc. – where a failure to display the appropriate emotions is suspect.

Armed with two moral outlooks, we can see our relationship to others in two lights, each aiming to allow us to best handle the situation at hand:

- We can understand "proper action" in the terms laid out by our Mind 1 family morality. In this moral outlook we try to value people and their preferences as equally valuable as our own. And our differences are chalked up to mere matters of opinion and our own unique "personalities."

- We can also understand "proper action" in the terms established by Mind 2 social morality. In this outlook we try to ascertain more important from least important, more valuable from less so; more educated or informed from less educated or informed, etc. Individuals are evaluated in terms of "character," that is, in terms of how they conform to a preexisting standard that we hold.

Both are vital, both are us, but they are not the same thing. Operating within a herd, we find occasions to react to our circumstances by expressing individually determined pleasures and pains, while at other times we find it best to express behaviors according to traditional patterns of actions, which the group has predetermined will lead to our happiness. Invariably we interact with some people who seem to focus on short-term pleasures and pains, while others we run into act as if their focus was on a plan for long-term happiness.

MORAL MIND 1 Horizontal/Family Mind	MORAL MIND 2 Vertical/Social Mind
Individual identity recognized in terms of: **PERSONALITY**	Individual identity recognized in terms of: **CHARACTER**
Moral target that guides action: **EQUALITY**	Moral target that guides action: **MERIT**
The focus of activity: **THE INDIVIDUAL AND HIS SELF-DETERMINED PREFERENCES – pursued in terms of pleasures**	The focus of activity: **THE GROUP AND ITS PREDETERMINED PREFERENCES – pursued in terms of happiness**
The group's needs are: **SUBORDINATED TO THE NEEDS OF THE INDIVIDUAL**	The individual's needs are: **SUBORDINATED TO THE GOOD OF THE GROUP**
Doing right is determined as a circumstance of: **THE HERE AND NOW**	Doing right is determined as a circumstance of: **PAST TRADITION**
PERSONALITY: The diverse and unique habits or practices preferred by the individual, and which distinguish him from other individuals	**CHARACTER:** Measured against a common standard and based on how the individual supports existing social structures that have protected the group in the past – customs/tradition/manners.

MORAL MIND 1 Horizontal/Family Mind	MORAL MIND 2 Vertical/Social Mind
DIFFERENT BUT EQUAL Promotes the self: "As good as anybody else"	**BETTER THAN OR WORSE THAN** Promotes some practices (and the people who display them) as preferable to others
PERSONALITY: Encourages the expression of emotions	**CHARACTER:** Discourages the spontaneous expression of emotions
Institutions such as marriage should be based on personalities, on the compatibility of personal tastes and preferences. We marry for personal needs.	Institutions such as marriage exist firstly for the good of the group, and secondly for the benefit of the individuals involved. Marriage can be prearranged, matching social position to social position. Retaining position overshadows individual preferences. We marry for group needs.
Marriages, divorces, abortions, and other social relations exist for the good of the individual as determined by individuals.	Divorces, contraception, child bearing and abortions are all rightfully controlled for the good of the group and might be determined by the group.
Flaws are merely quirks of individuality some may dislike. We all have them. We write "tell all" books. As we are all equal, we cannot rise or fall relative to others in a horizontal society.	Flaws are things to be hidden, apologized for and corrected; otherwise we risk losing social position in a vertical society. We hide our flaws.

Are we compatible as individuals?
Mate selection

Females choosing males

Over the centuries, there has been no way to determine in advance what the male might be required to do. Circumstances may demand he be a farmer or a soldier, a fisherman or a fiddler. From the female's point of view, any decent looking male might do, as long as he is socially accepted. One male is interchangeable with another. Culture assists her in making her choice easier.

Biologically speaking, it matters little to mother and baby if dad is a competent plumber, landscaper, or lawyer, so long as he can provide for and protect his family. Looks and social status tell her quickly all she needs to know about him. The woman need not be an expert in carpentry, landscaping or law to determine his relative value as a mate; society does that for her. His social standing informs her of his worth as determined by the group. Success and popularity mean something; a thousand heads are better than one. If everyone else thinks he is great, she supposes he is too. For most females, looks and status combine to create an irresistible aphrodisiac. He may be an unromantic brute, a dullard or a wife beater. But for most of history these concerns were private and personal. As long as he carried out his social duties toward his family, society need be no further involved in their relationship.

Males selecting females

His criteria for an adequate mate are as narrow as hers: looks and loyalty. With no social standing possible for the female throughout most of human history, he did not evolve to look for it in her. He needed only to determine if she was healthy and could be presumed to be fertile. This is done based on looks. We all know a pretty girl when we see one. She is young and healthy and we find her attractive. We unthinkingly presume she possesses the maternal skills necessary to do her job. If she is pretty and not promiscuous, she was all that could be asked for. He needed training to attain a place in his group; she did not. She became capable upon entering puberty and attaining desirability. She might be a scold, become a drunk, and keep a messy house, but those were private matters. If she took reasonable care of her husband and children, society need not get further involved in the matter.

This seems to be an unromantic account of mating. Here, especially in our free and easy democratic era, we want to believe individuality matters. We like to think our mates are somehow superior to most others, or that they are somehow a better fit for us. I think this is unsupportable. Had we never met our current mates, I suspect we would have found another and been about as satisfied.

Mating is among our strongest social impulses. And in youth it is irresistible. Then, almost any available male or female will do. We will rationally create reasons why we needed to be involved with this or that person. Some variation of the sweet church-going girl who runs off with the member of the motorcycle gang, or the nerdy history-reading tropical fish raising guy who takes up with the tattooed stripper are common enough to all. Many times even these seemingly mismatched individuals stay together for years, raising children and taking care of their own needs. What they require from each other are not the things that make them individuals; what they need, and what they usually can get from each other, are all the things that make us all the same.

Do we raise individuals or near replicas of ourselves?

Laughing at his own son, who got his mother, and by his mother's means, his father also, to indulge him, he told him that he had the most power of anyone in Greece: "For the Athenians command the rest of Greece, I command the Athenians, your mother commands me, and you command your mother."

-Plutarch, Life of Themistocles[2]

When I was young, it was the rage among couples to raise their children androgynously. Boys were to be given little dolls and tea sets and girls given trucks and plastic snakes. Sexism was proclaimed a nasty holdover from darker cretin times when boys were raised to be one thing and girls taught to be something different. And it was up to the brightest among us to do our part in eliminating sexism from the lives of our kids, beginning with eliminating it in the nursery. After all, did we want our daughters to be denied anything available to our sons? If sexism were eliminated first in the nursery and preschool and later in adolescence, it would, of its own accord, later vanish from adult society.

As best I can tell, our little girls walked away from the toy guns and strolled across the nursery to pick up their brothers' dolls. Our little boys grew up slightly more likely to drive real trucks and a little keener to raise actual anacondas. Teaching children to suppress their own urges and other influences so as to conform only to our own ideas of proper sexuality has limits. As herding creatures, we do not raise our children in a vacuum. Our sons and daughters become who they are, not only under our influence, but also under the guidance of everyone they meet.

Talk to almost any little four-year-old boy or girl and they will not only know they are boys or girls, but they will usually be happy they are of that sex. They will tell you that people of their sex have the most fun and, on the whole, are to be preferred. Shortly after we learn to speak in sentences, we can say, "I'm a girl." And more than this: we understand clearly that girls seem to do different things from boys. Little kids want to sexually self-identify; little boys tend to enjoy dressing and acting like adult males, and little girls feel good dressing and acting much like adult women. They are born to seek out and participate in the areas that make us sexually distinct and individual. A boy is not a girl, and in spite of our best efforts, they seem to figure it out at a very early age.

I have often asked little boys, "If you could die and come back as one of these two things, which would you choose – a boy turtle or a girl human?" All so far have chosen the boy turtle. I would then go on to give them other choices – a boy frog or a female human? Again sex was given priority over species, and the boys choose the boy frog. This pattern of question and answers became predictable in both sexes. Sexual identity seems stronger than species identity, at least until puberty.

I watched an older man joking with his seven-year-old grandson. The child was proclaiming rather forcefully that boys were better than girls and that, as best he could tell, girls did not do anything that was any fun:

Old Man to grandson: So, you don't like girls?
Grandson: Not really.
Old Man: When you grow up, what would you rather do, marry a girl or a platypus?
Grandson: I'd rather marry a platypus
Old Man: If you marry a platypus, will it be a girl platypus or a boy platypus?
Grandson: A girl platypus of course... I'm not weird!

There are a significant number of boys and girls who do not (psychologically) identify with the sex they were born with (their "biological" sex), but instead identify with the other sex (their "gender" role). They use the term "sex" to refer to their biological identity and "gender" to refer to their psychological identity. If in fact there was no differentiation between boys and girls except a physical one, then it would make no sense for a boy whose biological sex is male to claim that he "feels like" a girl (or for a biological female to claim that she "feels like" a boy), since "feeling like" is a psychological phenomenon. In other words, if there were no psychological differentiation between boys and girls, then there would be no difference between "feeling like a girl" and "feeling like a boy," and transgender identity would make no sense.

In spite of tremendous cultural pressures to androgynize, the females in the developed democracies still act quite differently from the males. The great division in human individuality is not between rich and poor, or farmer and technocrat, or urban and rural; it is still between the male and the female. My wife is an avid magazine subscriber. In every room, you can find copies of *Woman's Day*, *Good Housekeeping*, *Readers Digest*, *People*, and others of a similar type. The publications catering to women are easy to spot. The issues are filled with advice on having sex, being sexy, remaining healthy, looking good, caring for children, housekeeping, cooking, and the common doings of entertainment celebrities; such interests are more common in women than men.

Magazines tell us who we are by identifying what we care about. Both sexes crave information on the activities that interest them. Females buy more magazines with formats centered on family or relationships; males are more focused on group activities beyond and outside of the family — publications focusing on activities like hunting, rock climbing, politics, science, cars, sports or history. The language and emotional content of the publications differ too.

Stroking, congratulatory phrases are common in women's publications, less common in men's. In hers, headlines include phrases like, "Now it's Time for You" or

"You Do So Much for Others, Now Do for Yourself" and "The Secrets He Won't Tell You." Headlines on the cover of his magazines are less likely to be so personal. For the male, the liner notes read more like, "Skateboarding for Fun and Profit" or "The Wildest Moose Hunt Ever" or "Obama's Show Trials."

Our wealthy and free society is growing ever more capable of providing specific information and entertainment molded to niche audiences. Culture is fragmenting and re-fragmenting, as every urge or habit can be catered to. This is allowing ever more distinct and fine-tuned entertainment to develop. The most successful television shows are watched by both men and women, but entertainment, like our clothing styles and deodorants, are increasingly being tailored to one sex or the other. We all know a "chic-flick" when we see it.

Our airwaves are overflowing with shows where young girls dance and diet, while on the other channel young boys risk jumping motorcycles or setting world records for swallowing the greatest number of hardboiled eggs. We are still scrambling to figure out how it all fits together. It is not clear how much these differences are culturally based.

Magazines targeting women focus on many of the same topics they did 150 years ago: matriarchal power, human relationships, femininity, sexuality and health. Her periodicals cover a broad range of topics, but most center on the home, family or personal improvement. For the past two centuries, many feminists have imagined that, as women left the home for the workforce, acquired social power and wealth of their own, their tastes would start to mirror their males' more closely. This has not always proven to be the case. Women do work more outside the home and earn more money than ever, but their interests and their incomes are still largely devoted to causes they've championed for centuries.

For the boys, there is a disproportionate attraction to risk, competitive games and violence. The older man still enjoys these things vicariously, through war movies or by watching the sports he is no longer fit to play. She retains, into old age, a keener interest in her looks and her children. It is grandma who will remember the grandchild's birthdays and keep baby pictures of her own kids hanging on her walls right next to granddad's dusty old mounted bass.

Individuality is becoming more varied for everyone
But for most of us, it still begins with male and female

The weekend after Thanksgiving, the store will be packed with women shopping for Christmas, while their males are sitting at home watching football games. Not all the shoppers will be female and not all the football watchers will be male. But the numerical differences are too large to ignore or pretend these things do not tell us something about femininity and masculinity.

It is easy to see how biological necessity molded women into creatures specializing in detail-oriented personal relationships, with their mates focusing on more general public interactions. It was the first and most primitive division of labor. We still exhibit these ancient psychological outlooks. Females vicariously crave situations charged with person-to-person drama. Males seek the emotions generated by group-to-group drama and are drawn to war movies and war documentaries. Nature has molded us to be drawn to the activities and emotional expression we will need to exhibit in order to succeed. As a group, women want to know how to resolve conflicts between people and within the family, males to resolve conflicts outside it and between groups. Males are also more drawn to non-human investigations of nature and animals. A documentary on the reproductive behavior of elk or earthworms is likely to have an overwhelmingly male audience.

Daytime soap operas attract a viewership that is predominantly but not exclusively female. War stories and history documentaries appeal overwhelmingly to men. As herding creatures, we are capable of experiencing emotions vicariously through the actions of others. We seek out the kinds of emotional stimulation we were made to maneuver in.

Soap opera plots are repetitive and predictable; they focus on the creation and resolution of personal relationship problems. Women, far more than men, gravitate to them. Men unfamiliar with adult females often dismiss these shows as meaningless emotional psychodrama. They are far more than this. The men in these shows are usually two-dimensional incomplete characters with vague occupations and ill-defined hobbies. Soap opera men serve as the sexy and capable boyfriend, lover or husband. If he is a social success or a daredevil who overcomes great odds, he qualifies as a mate, especially if he is rich and handsome.

The details of female-oriented entertainment revolve around solving his and her relationship dilemmas. The grubby, socially incapable male is dismissed. He may be dangerous or he might be no threat at all, but one way or the other, the low-life male is not likely to be a love interest. His social problems do not concern the female, who has chosen her mates wisely. In the typical relationship drama, romantic comedy or soap opera, what exactly the guys do for a living is unimportant; as long as they are reasonably attractive and socially adequate, they are acceptable. If they are ugly, poor or violent, they are unwelcome. She needs to be pretty and healthy; and she needs to be smart about relationship issues. If she is all of these things, she will likely consider her own life to be a success. Her entertainment interests are likely to be sexually specific. She wants to know what other women are doing or have done.

The shows that appeal to men are likely to be activity or group oriented. They are just as repetitive and predictable as the dramas that attract women, but the conflicts are different. Unlike the personal conflict-resolution dramas, which keep the female's attention, his are usually not between individual people who know each other; males are drawn to conflict at the group level. He watches sports teams compete in games, nations compete in wars, and scientists in a battle of the brains with aliens. One baseball game looks pretty much like another, but he wants to watch them all. Competition between individuals interests him; boxing, tennis and golf are popular. But the struggle is for physical mastery over an opponent; it does not directly involve interpersonal emotional tension.

With him, police shows are entertaining. They feature the superior authority representing righteousness, chasing excitedly after a miscreant; and with minor variations they are watched again and again, one story hardly differing much from the last or the next. War documentaries are popular. One aerial bombing conducted from 40,000 feet may look much like the next one to his wife, but the husband sits and watches them all. The siege of Constantinople, the fall of Fort Sumter, the German defeat at Stalingrad, then the baseball game and the Bass-Masters Classic are all viewed with the same slack-jawed gaze as the one gracing the faces of the children as they watch cartoons. Sexual differentiation is not so strict that we never come across men who watch soaps or women who are entertained by war documentaries, but experience teaches us that our entertainments are as sexually dimorphic as our bodies. Maleness or femaleness is still the greater part of our individuality. And how men choose the best way to occupy their time will differ from how women choose. This difference can be seen as right for them.

What one sex wants from the other is general: she wants a male to seek her, to provide a nice living for her, and to protect her. The entertainment that appeals to each of the sexes makes the actor who represents the opposite sex appear personally superior. Actors representing unappealing aspects of the opposite sex usually do not entertain. Unrepentant promiscuous females do not capture the sympathetic attention of most males; and incapable or socially buffoonish males (like the three stooges) are not found to be entertaining by most females.

The morality that likely has its roots with our distinct sexual roles is merged within each of us now. Every man and every woman is both a Mind 1 and a Mind 2 being.

Mind 1 Morality	Mind 2 Morality
Conflict resolution, which focuses on personal relationships, family life, females, the weak and children, most easily captures our attention.	Conflict resolution between groups, or competitive contests between males, gets the most attention.

Mind 1 Morality	Mind 2 Morality
Wrongdoers are often looked at sympathetically as those who need to be corrected, not eliminated.	Wrongdoers or competitors outside the group may need to be overcome, defeated, or even destroyed.
Risky behavior is not particularly entertaining.	Risky behavior is very entertaining.
Conflicts and struggles taking place now are most important.	The conflicts and competitions that went on in the world yesterday are almost as important as what is going on today.

Today we live in a culture striving for androgyny in all things. What interests a woman can interest a man, and anything a man does, women do also. But culture has not yet superseded a biology that still keeps us distinct and sexually individual. Most do not believe, and most cannot be convinced, that males take care of children or will nurture ailing grandparents as well as females. Here is a scenario and a question every experienced person can be relied upon to answer correctly:

Imagine you are a parent of three preschool children. You and your mate work 40 hours a week and your three young kids must be dropped off at a daycare center every weekday from 9AM to 5PM. In your town are two identical daycare centers. Both seem equally well equipped and maintained. It will cost an identical amount of money to send the kids to either one of them. The only difference between the two facilities is that one is staffed in every position by men, the other staffed completely by women. To which facility do you entrust the care of your three small children?

Any adult will choose what they know instinctively to be the correct answer. The girls can be trusted to best watch the kids.

The other task that every generation of humans must be prepared to handle is the male specialty: confronting and killing anything that threatens us. Males retain our superior trust to handle difficult social situations; females we believe best handle matters of family. Modern Homo sapiens displays the widest spectrum for individuality created anywhere in nature. But as unique as each of us are, our similarities still far outweigh our differences. Meet almost any man or any woman from the present day or from recorded history, and simply knowing the single fact that they are a man or a woman tells us most of what we will ever need to know to get along with them; it will tell us what is likely to please them, and what they look forward to in life. *We are individuals, like everyone else.*

The males are drawn beyond the family to fight enemies and are curious about nature. Males hunt and fish and fight. They are born to it and no generation lacks for male members itching to get at it. One clue that these things are a-rationally imprinted prenatally in our brains is that these activities are looked upon more as play than as work. Little boys fight battles against imaginary foes and grow up to look upon catching fish and shooting deer as recreation. That it might be a mere manifestation of pre-human urges is inconsequential. The boys dream of fighting and winning, hunting and exploring. We have evolved to see our biological duties as our everyday pleasures. Our emotions have been tailored so that we gain immediate pleasure in performing what is in our long-term best interest. Sex is fun; it is not work. It leads to children, which provides opportunities to sacrifice for others and gain happiness over time. Pursuing the proper short-term pleasures leads eventually to long-term happiness. Nature has ensured that what is necessary as "work" is enjoyable as "play."

Moms want to eat and they want to lose weight. We trust that if we went back 2000 years and bumped into Cleopatra, she could tell us a lot about Roman politics, but she would also tell us about her latest diet plan. Being prettier and richer than the other girls counts for something. To look good is something that has real meaning to most females; it gives them confidence when interacting with both men and other women. Both sexes strive to be admired by the group at large, and especially by those of their own sex, whose opinions they value most.

What type of individual am I?

Humans have always tried to categorize themselves in some form of "personality type." Our modern emphasis on the importance of Mind 1 "personality" over Mind 2 "character" has deeply influenced the works of psychologists like Carl Jung. Jung coined the term "individuation" to describe the process of creating the individual personality in the midst of the collective character of the group or the species. An important part of Jung's work were the concepts of the individual unconscious and the collective unconscious, the individual unconscious being the accumulation of memories and feelings piled up in the recesses of one mind, and the collective unconscious being the patterns and archetypes of feelings and emotions we share with the group.[3]

The concept of the collective unconscious is not unlike Plato's Theory of Forms, where there is the presumption that the individual mind is born with conceptual structures within it; that we are preset to fear, to worship, to anger and to recognize friends etc.; and that the individual becomes just a current and circumstantial variant on the preset pattern. Researchers inspired by Jung have concluded that the patterns of aptitudes within each of us are not infinite, that there is a limited number of personality types, and that these types can be identified. Knowing the type of person you are, employers and others might be able to predict how you might fit into their workplace.

Like the ancient attempts to identify personality types as being of earth, air, fire or water, the modern efforts at personality-typing is a more up-to-date version of the ancient belief that people are complex but knowable, and that they come in a limited number of varieties. Human types are not as limited as with the insects, queen/worker/warrior/drone, but there is not an over-abundance of types either. The recognition that there are these types and the efforts to delineate, describe, and enumerate them is at least as old as recorded history. The typing is imprecise, and we still debate the merit of the process.

Isabel Myers and Katherine Briggs, working in the early 20th century, developed personality tests based on what they referred to as "personality indicators."[4] These attempted to predict interests, workplace aptitudes, and vocational abilities. In their method, there are 16 basic personality types. At my daughter's insistence, I took an online computerized version based on the Myers-Briggs personality tests. It proposed to give me real insight into my own personality type after answering only 72 yes-or-no questions. So I took the test.

I was computed to be an I-N-T-J type of individual. The description of this personality type was detailed and included the following:

> INTJs live in a world of ideas and strategic planning… INTJs are driven to come to conclusions about ideas… an INTJ … gives a gift to society by putting their ideas into a useful form for others to follow. The INTJ is driven to translate their ideas into a plan or system that is usually readily explainable… They value clarity and efficiency, and will put enormous amounts of energy and time into consolidating their insights into constructive patterns.

[www.personalitypage.com]

Considering that I was in the middle of writing an 900 page philosophical treatise explaining the scope and reach of human moral enterprise, I thought the observation either quite insightful, or a very lucky guess.

Damn statistics

We are a group; that allows us to be individuals. But we as individuals still largely do what everyone else is doing. The social circumstances that make some of us choose X can easily make most of us choose X if they persist.

Poverty means we are living closer to the edge of survival. Destitution makes individual relationships more vital, as we can hardly afford to do everything ourselves. Penury pushes us to a vertical Mind 2 moral outlook, where people must be prioritized and public duty must often take precedence over personal pleasure. In poorer times, social structure becomes less varied and more defined; in such times, women invariably fall beneath men in the verticalized public pecking order, in circumstances where they are seen less and less in public because their duties do not allow it.

Among themselves, men struggle to appear capable and independent. Emotional control is a demonstration of strength of character. In a society where there is not enough to go round, and where the better people must get the larger share, it does not pay to show faults or weaknesses. Big boys don't cry.

As wealth grows, we become more independent of each other. In the wealthiest of circumstances, everyone can make it and no one is left behind. Welfare and impersonal social assistance programs become practical because they become feasible. But just because we can help the poorer among us does not mean we ever would. We do not institute such programs until we "feel" the wealth of our group should be spread around. Our circumstances change how we feel. Morality can be sharing, but it has often had to be hoarding. Doing right is a reaction to circumstances.

Concomitantly, the more that is available and spread around, and the more the wealthy are inclined to spread it around, the more the needy among us should be emotionally compelled to accept it. Our feeling of right and acceptable behavior needs to change to best react to this new prosperity. Where before, in harsher times, to show need and weakness may have revealed a fault within us and needed to be hidden, in wealthier times, displaying need can be an advantage. When not facing immediate threat, those in need can be helped.

In modern times, there is more wealth to go around than there used to be. But our cultural attitudes change more slowly than our material circumstances. In former times, our old Mind 2 attitudes of personal independence needed to prevail. In earlier times, being on welfare was, and needed to be, a shameful thing, a sign of weakness. It indicated a measure of inability and identified someone as less worthy. In vertical times, we needed to know who was better and who was dispensable. This has changed.

In times of continued wealth creation, the Mind 2 morality of vertical social place is being superseded by a Mind 1 moral outlook of equality, horizontalism, and non-judgementalism. We hardly care what anyone else thinks, and my neighbor's money is in some way mine anyway. Sharing is right. Collecting and redistributing wealth becomes the most moral and right thing to do. Accepting the wealth redistribution is no longer shameful, but a just payment for finding oneself below where we all need to be – or should be.

As wealth grows, all measures of social bonds begin to break down. We do not view the world in the deep Mind 2 manner of duty, honor, social responsibility, pride and self-respect. What we owe others is not our primary concern. We move to a more Mind 1 view of self-satisfaction, personal pleasures, wealth redistribution, and the encouragement of open and public emotional expression. The effects of broad-based and widely dispersed wealth and ongoing personal security become felt in all our social relationships. We no longer keep jobs and homes for our entire lives, but move freely to chase hobbies, money or boyfriends. The old notion of growing up beside childhood friends or living our lives in the same neighborhood as one's parents had done becomes a thing of the past.

We may lament that people do not stay in the neighborhood in which they were born, or that people no longer stay at their job their entire life and then retire; and we may fret over rising divorce rates; but we personally do not miss the opportunity to move to the better house, or change job, or leave the relationship that has become emotionally untenable. With safety and plenty, our morality shifts to accept a wider range of choices as equally acceptable.

The effects can be seen in our climbing divorce rates. As Americans grew richer and safer, social interdependence deteriorated, and what it meant to be a couple changed. Personal commitment used to be defined through a social institution called marriage, and it lasted for life. Marriage was an institution that established a relationship between a couple and their society.

In the sixteenth century, King Henry VIII had to ask the pope for a divorce. Marriage and divorce were too important to be left to individuals, even to kings. As recently as the lifetime of Andrew Jackson, a person from Tennessee had to petition the state legislature to grant a divorce. Times have changed. We have grown richer, and relationships are more often seen as personal rather than social things. Marriage is now a commitment between individuals; it is no longer a relationship between two people and their society. And when the individuals involved no longer want to be married, they split up. Mind 1 morality, the moral outlook of plenty and safety, now affirms that society need have nothing to say about it, as it is no longer a threat to anyone but the individuals involved. This is easily demonstrated by our growing divorce rates:

Year	Divorces per 1000 marriages[5]
1860	1.2
1880	2.2
1900	4.0
1920	8.7
1956	9.3

During the Great Depression of the 1930s and 1940s, rising poverty and personal insecurity stopped the trend for a while; then it resumed in the 1950s. Since the 1960s, the phrase "divorce rate" has come to be less of an ominous statistic. Lots of people get divorced now, but most seem to do all right. Society has not fallen apart just because many of its families have. We are rich.

Now, being a couple is no longer defined by being married. In fact, because people marry later, and often not at all, divorce rates may be coming down. Cohabitation before marriage and people choosing never to marry at all give these statistics less relevance. We are no longer just married or divorced. Now people speak in terms of "serious relationships," and can have many of them in a lifetime. Marriage-the-public-and-social-institution has become marriage-the-personal-relationship.

If wealth continues to grow, marriage itself will become a quaint custom of only ceremonial value. We are almost there. But this change in custom hardly affects how deeply disintegrating relationships can affect us. Crying over lost love or wondering why our children will have to grow up in a broken home devastates us. Our Mind 2 morality tells us we are doing wrong somehow. We have let others down. We are not living up to the standards of social expectation set by custom and our betters. There is also the on-going desire to raise our kids in an environment sheltered from personal anguish. Is divorce still failure? Can we really be expected to stay with only one person forever because we wear a metal band on a finger? Can we accept that lacking this ring and this ceremony we are free to jump into as many beds as possible?

The reality that mommies and daddies do not stay together forever still seems like a hard pill for a kid to swallow; and we do not want our children to have to swallow it. Are children better off being sheltered from the new morality evolving around them? Should we prepare them to live in modern society by teaching them that a relationship should last a lifetime, or is it wiser to prepare them for the increasingly more likely event that their relationships will last only a few years? What is right? What should the modern parent do?

The ends of our morality do not change. Our dual morality exists to ensure our survival and the prosperity of our group. We do this in two ways: by protecting the individual at the expense of the group, or by protecting the group at the expense of the individual. Which of these outlooks is at play at any time is decided by circumstances. What is right and what is wrong in their detail are variable things.

Moral Mind 1 The personal and private matter most	Moral Mind 2 The social and public matter most
Individual lives are invaluable.	Individual lives are expendable if their loss promotes the greater good.
Share and share alike – ideally we should all have the same.	Some often deserve to get more than others – Ideally the best get the most.
Look down to the least among us for clues on how to act, distribute resources and do right.	Look up to the greatest among us for clues on how to act, distribute resources and do right.
The minimum wage should be a floor beneath which no one should be allowed to fall, which provides a minimum standard of living. Your pay should reflect your intrinsic worth as a human being.	The minimum wage (which probably should not exist at all) is simply an entry-level wage. Its meagerness provides the impetus for the worker to learn more and do better. Your pay should reflect what you are capable of doing for others.

Sometimes we are confused by the specific applications of morality. What society once deemed as moral or immoral changed over time. What was known to be unacceptable yesterday can be accepted today. What was wrong can be right. When what was wrong before is right today, we often have a hard time understanding it.

In 1904, a New York City policeman arrested a woman for smoking a cigarette in an automobile, telling her, "You can't do that on Fifth Avenue!"[6] A woman smoking in public was a display of her lack of concern for customary decency, which demanded that public need take precedence over private pleasure. By placing her own self-satisfaction above the superior example she should have been setting for others, she ran afoul of her era's Mind 2 moral practices. She had an obligation to set the example – and she set a bad one. What men and women could do in public in 1904 was determined by standards of what the individual owed to the group.

Women smoking in public would not remain immoral for long. Women smoking in public could not remain a "bad" thing because increasing safety and security allowed changes to take place in custom and how we viewed what was or was not risky, and therefore questionable behavior. In our own richer times, what men or women do in public is largely determined in Mind 1 ways, by what they owe to themselves, not in Mind 2 ways, by what they owe to the group as determined by custom and tradition.

Either moral outlook may be in play to condemn smoking or support it, depending on how the argument is framed. For a Mind 1 egalitarian, if men are smoking freely, then it should certainly be acceptable for women to smoke as well. But, then again, if protecting the health and wellbeing of others is the emotional aim, a Mind 1 oriented outlook may condemn smoking for everyone – men and women alike. In either case, as long as the rules are the same for everybody, a Mind 1 oriented outlook may support smoking in one decade while condemning it in the next.

The same is the case for a Mind 2 outlook. If smoking is an activity that has traditionally been practiced by only one sex, then Mind 2 supports this kind of arrangement. If it has become the custom for both sexes to smoke (or that neither of them does, as is the case with marijuana), then a Mind 2 outlook will favor whatever option custom and tradition dictate.

CONCLUSION

We are individuals and we are members of a group. We are never only one or the other. As we have grown more complex in our individuality, our institutions and grouping patterns have become more sophisticated as well. Our dual morality undoubtedly originated in an ancient primitive prehistory when our roles and whatever was meant by individuality were at first primarily sexually based. We once had two more clearly distinct grouping patterns: the family pattern and the social pattern. There was a time when we were usually either family-group humans, that is, females and offspring, or we were social-group humans called adult males. Recent human evolution witnessed the explosion of fantastic productive capability. It was probably enhanced by a growth in an intellectual imaginative ability that allowed for both the creation of tools and their trading. This was accompanied by a social move toward monogamy, which facilitated it. Males and females began to act together more closely in all endeavors.

Near monogamy and the perpetual estrus of the female has allowed both sexes to help the other satisfy all biological urges with unprecedented assurance. This has allowed for the expansion in the size of our groups to unheralded numbers of producers and traders. Family changed to include fathers; society changed to include women. We all became parents, producers and protectors.

In the next chapter we will look more deeply into the concept of morality itself, and how it is expressed in an epistemological sense – what it means to think and feel. Morality is first a mental process before it becomes a physical act. Its existence in a dual form, and what it means for our notions of right and wrong, is where we turn next.

Notes

1. See a review of some of these studies by Sean Stevens and Jonathan Haidt, "The Greater Male Variability Hypothesis – An addendum to Our Post on the Google Memo," [Online] *Heterodox Academy*, Sept. 4, 2017 < https://heterodoxacademy.org/the-greater-male-variability-hypothesis/ > [Retrieved Sept. 10, 2018.]

2. Plutarch, *Life of Themistocles*, Dryden translation, in *The Great Books of the Western World* (UK: Encyclopedia Britannica, 1952, 1990) 14: 96.

3. Carl G. Jung, *The Archetypes and the Collective Unconscious*, trans. R. F. C. Hill (Princeton: Princeton University Press, 1977)

4. Katherine C. Briggs and Isabel Briggs Myers, *The Myers-Briggs Type Indicator* (Palo Alto, CA: Consulting Psychologists Press, 2015).

5. Bernard Berelson and Gary A. Steiner, *Human Behavior* (New York: Harcourt, Brace and World, Inc., 1964) 311.

6. John A. Mayer, "The Cigarette Century," *American Heritage Magazine*, December 1992.

Chapter 4
The Two Sides of Truth

Or

Individuals ⟷ Groups

Mind 1 and Mind 2 are our two versions of "truth." If there is enough for everyone to survive, we think it right to act in ways that ensure they will. If there may not be enough for everyone to survive, we must feel it right to act in ways that ensure the most vital among us can. With two distinct moral patterns available to each of us, and with the possibility of each pattern being applied heavily or lightly, the number of nuanced moral outlooks available is enormous. This wide range of moral outlooks makes itself felt as "moral flexibility," and allows us to maximize the number of possible "correct" choices we might make in any circumstance.

Being members of a herd, this flexibility does not need to be displayed identically in each individual. Some of us can staunchly hold onto one outlook, some of us the other, with many more feeling somewhere in-between. In 1940, some Americans thought we should get involved in fighting the war against Nazism. Others felt we needed to stay out of that war. Both sides believed they were "right." Many Americans came down somewhere between these positions, feeling that we should help the allies with food and materials and everything short of committing troops. In response to the bombing at Pearl Harbor, most Americans shifted their opinions and came to believe that joining the war wholeheartedly was the "right" thing to do.

WE NEED TO THINK IN DIFFERENT WAYS AT DIFFERENT TIMES

Wolves and foxes are born four to six in a litter. Both are canines and physiologically closely related. But socially they are quite different animals. Wolves, like dogs, are social. Foxes are not. This difference is profound, and consequently the two animals exhibit distinct behavioral differences right from birth.

Wolf cubs are destined to grow up and be part of a pack. Foxes will grow up to be loners. A study conducted at the University of Washington monitored both animals and reported that wolf litter-mates are born with assorted temperaments, including various levels of aggression. Some wolves are more dominant and others more passive right from the start. The red fox cubs, on the other hand, seem to be born more closely on a par with each other in terms of aggressive tendencies.[1]

It seems that nature has found a way to reduce internal aggression in social groups by ensuring greater diversity of temperaments in socially oriented species as compared to the more solitary ones, particularly with respect to levels of aggression. Limitations on the proportion of aggressive individuals born in any particular litter ensure that the number of fights for the top spot, and their severity, will be reduced. Not everyone will fight to be top dog. Recognizing who is dominant and who is passive right from the start minimizes conflict; who will lead and who will follow is recognized early and is established almost at birth. It would not be surprising to learn that all herding animals are born with similar genetically determined temperament variations, which ensures better future adult cooperation.

Among the people we know, it is easy to distinguish those with blatant leadership skills and those of a more passive nature. Leadership ability is sometimes born with us and does not always have to be made. Being a "natural born leader" has a biological component.

With humans, the most emotionally diverse of the animals, leadership involves much more than just a higher level of aggression. A superiority of compassion and the ability to gain the confidence of others are needed too. When political candidates seek office, they spend a great deal of time trying to convince us that they understand and empathize with our problems, they are concerned that making a living isn't easy, and that most of us will not have saved enough to send our kids to college. They assure us that by voting for them, these problems will become easier to manage.

Political Leaders decide how collective resources will be distributed, usually making decision no more consequential than which roads will be paved first or which changes to zoning rules will be approved. But, at the extreme, leaders also decide who lives and who dies, who gets more and who gets less.

In times of stress, when there are more applicants than jobs to employ them, or when there are more bellies to fill than food to fill them, it is not always the strong or most aggressive that get the most; it could be the accommodating or the shrewdest who prove themselves most sagacious and thereby most fit. But by whatever means advantage is attained, we tolerate inequalities easier in times of stress. In times of ease, we encourage sharing and a more equal distribution of resources. Each of us can see things in these two right ways. Which of our Moral Minds we apply to the situation depends on how we assess the circumstances we are in right now.

The two sides of truth:

MORALITY IS ACTING PROPERLY, SO HOW IS IT DETERMINED?

Is there enough for all?
Can we all make it?

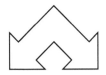

If Yes	If No
Mind 1	**Mind 2**

Horizontal – Personal – Family Morality	Vertical – Social – Public Morality
Sharing equally is the foundational outlook.	Allocating resources by merit is the foundational outlook.
Pleasure and pain describe what to seek and what to avoid.	Virtue and vice describe what to seek and what to avoid.
We must look down and around for our cues on who to take care of.	We must look up to leaders, superiors and professionals for guidance and example.
Our concerns are about adjusting to the present circumstance and making improvements to ensure a better future.	Our concerns are about carrying on past customs and traditions to ensure a prosperous future.
The group sacrifices for the individual.	The individual sacrifices for the group.

Acting properly is acting morally. We understand why political group dynamics are so complicated when we realize that the herd benefits most when we are not all operating in just one moral mode. We do best when there is always some social pressure to share alongside others urging us to do more to protect. We do best when there are always some of us warning against threats from inequalities within the group as well as others arguing that the danger lies most from threats originating from outside it. In short, *we are prepared, flexible, and safest when we are socially conflicted.*

OUR FIRST SIDE OF TRUTH
PROTECTING AND PROVIDING EQUALLY
Moral Mind 1 equalizes us because we all can survive

Aristotle advised his most famous student Alexander the Great to treat the Hellenes as a leader and the barbarians as a master.[2] The great philosopher urged the great general to consider the Greeks as family and others as strangers. Everyone understands the sentiment and the difference. Applying the right morality at the proper time ensures success.

The first of these we have called Method 1, which makes us see everyone as worthy, everyone as valuable, and pushes us to make sure everyone has an equal share. But for most of history, Homo sapiens have not enjoyed the luxury of exercising this outlook beyond the immediate family. Outside the sheltering acceptance of home, want and fear awaited everybody. Necessity fostered competition for a share of limited resources. To succeed socially beyond the home, one displayed the requisite Mind 2 outlook. We treated our families as family, and outsiders more like strangers.

Our Mind 1 view, our "familyish" view, does more than protect us in times of plenty, ensuring we all get a fair share. Mind 1 allows for greater tolerance for variations in the behaviors of those around us. A Mind 1 environment signals us to let our hair down, to play, to have fun – we are safe. In Mind 1, we can let our faults show. We can pursue the things we want individually, with less concern for how we look to others. We are secure and well provided for.

Mind 1 morality is becoming the cultural outlook of all modern societies experiencing wealth beyond any scale they had known before. Operating in this mode, we are called liberal, open minded, accommodating, bleeding hearts, sometimes childish, and ultra-modern. It focuses us on the present; it encourages the direction of cultural resources to those around us and beneath us, and especially toward the "have-nots." Though both liberal and conservative are relative terms, we can look around and easily discover that Western culture is far more liberal today than at any time in recorded history. When we are safe, secure and in the midst of material abundance, our herding mind emotionally leans toward our family morality. This is the first of our two sides of truth. Each is intuitive and subjective.

Moral Truth Outlook 1 THE LIBERAL OPEN MINDED AND ACCOMMODATING ASPECT Horizontal social structure We strive to be "good" and to have "fun"
We feel the group should make sacrifices for the individual.
We believe the individual is the bedrock of society – ALL FOR ONE (not one for all, as in Mind 2).
We are compelled to learn the habits, languages, and customs of our group as they appear before us now. Modern songs, modern gestures, modern dress are most right and best.
The present contains the most valuable information we need to know.
Right and wrong are judged as aspects of pleasure and pain.
Values of the present (not virtues of the past) are most important, and they are locally variable and exist as a unique part of every individual's outlook. I am the best judge of me.
In times of ease and plenty, when there are no threats immanent and no behavior seems to involve risk, we seek pleasures, and having fun can become our goal.
Personality (not character) is the defining aspect of an individual. It is a quirky and unique expression of self.
Criminality and social deviance are addressed in terms of reform and rehabilitation (everyone is valuable and should be saved). The death penalty is fundamentally wrong. Everyone should make it.

Responsibility for everything is shared:
  --When the student fails, the teacher and the system shares responsibility.
  --When a crime occurs, society must be partially to blame.

God is a generalized and depersonalized benevolent spirit that pervades everything. God is love.
What is best is but personal preference; there is no such thing as good or bad taste. We are all equally good judges. Who is anyone else to say what is right for me?

Moral Truth Outlook 1 THE LIBERAL OPEN MINDED AND ACCOMMODATING ASPECT Horizontal social structure We strive to be "good" and to have "fun"
Social acclaim is viewed in terms of fame (not glory). Fame is current and now; it does not transcend time.
Equality is the ultimate political aim; after all, we are all fundamentally of equal value.
A social androgyny of dress and attitude sets in. For example, everyone is a lady and everyone is a gentleman; or to be more precise, these are terms of distinction that make no sense at all and eventually should fall from use. No one is a lady and there are no gentlemen.
Pleasures can be attended to before duty. Our attitudes can change, whereby we put ourselves and our families before social responsibilities. We may take on the attitude that "the first bill you should pay is to yourself."
We are all equally valuable; there are no superior types of people.
Democratic political equality takes hold as cultural structures built upon Mind 2 verticality move toward Mind 1 coequal horizontalism. -- Leadership is temporary and rotated. -- It bubbles up from the group.
The present counts most. Culture is whatever is happening now, and referred to as "society."
The biggest threat comes from misappropriation of resources within the group. The individually rich or powerful from within the group bear watching.
Society is described as best represented through concepts like "the people," "the public," "the masses."
The leader follows the group – sardine organizational style.
Production is viewed in terms of cooperative efforts of coworkers – equality of productive value.
A classless society is the social aim – equality of social position.

Moral Truth Outlook 1 THE LIBERAL OPEN MINDED AND ACCOMMODATING ASPECT Horizontal social structure We strive to be "good" and to have "fun"
An outlook of universal humanity pervades. Spirituality and an equality of all faiths and creeds are seen as the morally superior position – equality of faith.
Since everyone is equal, it makes sense that majorities (not the superior individuals) should rule.
Pleasure is the *sine qua non*, providing it is available to everyone. Emotional expression of every type is rightly encouraged. Feelings should be expressed and enhanced.
Sexy and youthful are ultimate goals and highest compliments. We should emulate the young. Society looks around and down for guidance.
Family is often a horizontal grouping where everyone matters equally. At the extreme, moms and dads, like our gods and our leaders, can be exchanged and rotated to find which one best suits us now.
We primarily follow the example of those around us.

From each according to his abilities, to each according to his needs.
  --Being able to do more does not mean you are more valuable than those who are able to do less.
  --Needing more does not make you less valuable than those who require less.

Everyone's voice matters equally.
We must do right as we determine it to be with those around us now. The past is hardly known.
Personality is a reaction to the events of the present (not the examples of the past).
Personality focuses on the self and promotes the self "as good as anybody else" – different but equal.
Marriage, like all social bonds, is based on personality and current taste or preferences. We marry for personal needs. Marriage and divorce are based on personal whim. We marry for love and personal motives; not for any obligation we have to others or to society.

Moral Truth Outlook 1 THE LIBERAL OPEN MINDED AND ACCOMMODATING ASPECT Horizontal social structure We strive to be "good" and to have "fun"
Marriages, divorces, abortions and other social relations exist for the good of the individual as determined by the individual. All relationships, friendships and even the responsibilities of parenthood are experienced on demand, and depend on our fancies at the moment.
Our flaws are largely personal peccadilloes others dislike. Flaws are not defects, just differences.
Ultimate equality can even include the world at large or animals. We learn about other nations, other lands and other creatures to shield and share with them if they have less than we do.
We write "tell all" books. Since we are all flawed, we cannot rise or fall relative to others in a horizontal society. Express yourself! Current fame, not reputation, is what matters most.
Homosexuality, heterosexuality, or any sexuality is as good as another. Who is to say it isn't?
Violence is the only real and ultimate evil.

Mind 1 is the morality of luxury and security. It is the moral outlook that comes over us in times of plenty and motivates us to push for democracy. Equality creates democracy; it is not the other way around. Representative governments arise in times of wealth. We call this outlook "liberal" and even "permissive." Sometimes we use terms like "progressive." They are all words that distinguish this view as a morality of the present rather than the established past.

Actions are mapped out by reason and motivated by emotion. And it was Aristotle who said it is not in the nature of desires to remain satisfied. The great problem facing morality and moral philosophy is the question, *What is it that we should want?* What is it that we should desire? What is the proper emotion we should be feeling right now?

If we want rightly and desire properly, then we and our group will do well. When we want the wrong things, we and our group suffer; wanting the wrong things is bad. But how is it possible to want the wrong things? If we want it, isn't it in some way right? If we want it, isn't something inside of us telling us that it is right, at the moment? We discover right and wrong in conflict.

When we want to eat ice cream but mom tells us we need to eat our vegetables instead, a right vs. wrong conflict is created. To get our way, we often argue with mom, telling her that ice cream is as good as vegetables, or that we have eaten plenty of vegetables and now it is time for ice cream. In other words, we try to establish a Mind 1 condition. We say that it is merely opinion or personal preference that vegetables are to be eaten now and so our preference is as good as mom's. Mom doesn't often buy that argument. She imposes her will upon us as the superior in the situation, and she commands us, her underlings, to do as we are told.

We determine right by debating it through conflict, through trials within ourselves or with others. We can want what others would have us not want; others can want what we would have them not want. We have the ability to see right differently from how others are seeing it. Often our moral outlook does not match our neighbors'. We might see the application of a Mind 1 value as right in the moment, while they see the need for a Mind 2 virtue to be applied.

We can also be internally torn. Our dual morality allows us to see some things as both right and wrong at the same time. Our conscience bothers us. That means that whatever mind prevailed, the other still nags us to reconsider.

OUR SECOND SIDE OF TRUTH
PROTECTING AND PROVIDING UNEQUALLY – REWARDING BY MERIT
Mind 2 prioritizes everything, because we may not all be able to survive

Our other moral outlook, Mind 2, protects the group from dangers emanating from outside it. People who see the world illuminated in this light are labeled "conservative," by nature as well as by politics, and rightly so. When we are in this mode, we are self-conscious about the impressions we make. We seem a bit inhibited and a bit old-fashioned.

In Mind 2, we look to distinguish ourselves from the rabble that exists, at least psychologically, all around us. In this mind, we recognize better and worse, favor some things over others, and look to learn from the past. Our betters need to be emulated.

Our Mind 2 suggests that others have known better and we need to find out who they were and what they knew. This is the moral outlook that overtakes us in times of stress and danger. This method dominates us whenever a threat to our self, our family, our country, or our ultimate good (i.e. god) occurs. When there is not enough to go around and not everyone can survive, this mind is likely to take control of our feelings. It recognizes that this attitude is also likely to be shared by those around us. It prioritizes people and things and guides our best behavior when tough choices need be made. We do not want to be left behind.

Historically, human cultures have almost always operated in the stress of want, need, and fear. It is only in the most recent centuries that large nations emerged from the constant shadow of these dangers. Consequently, Moral Mind 2, our conservative and "group-protecting" mindset, has dominated everywhere throughout almost all of human history – in every tribe and on every continent.

Our ancestors were, and had to be, right wingers – at least at the social level. This cultural perspective describes the predominant moral order of every nation from classical China and ancient Egypt to the modern Middle East. It dominates in tribes still living in hand-to-mouth primitive conditions. Members approach life from the point of view that their nation is best, citizenship is a privilege, their institutions should be preserved, the gods of old should be revered, and outsiders cannot be trusted to feel as they, the members, do. In conservative groups, human relationships are governed with an eye for social good. Children should honor parents. The better people control emotions and direct them to the public good. The best men rise to the top by leading the group (with the threat of war or violence) to safety and prosperity. The best women become the wives of the highest men by controlling their sexuality and dedicating their loyalty to the family and the culture. Both sexes become safe-keepers of the moral order. Men retain control of social violence; women control private sexuality. We identify the lower orders of men as unnecessarily brutal and the lower orders of women as promiscuous.

A Mind 2 world is surrounded by threats. The best men are guardians of our physical safety; the worst men are cowards. This is the sociological outlook of the great characters in our history books. Courage and self-sacrifice are dominant concepts in a Mind 2 moral outlook. Some of us have to fight and even die, sacrificing ourselves so that the rest can survive. When circumstances are extreme, our morality becomes extreme. In dangerous times, our young men can be drafted and thrown into battle. This is needed for the group to survive, so this must be understood as right action. Without this capacity of thought, our herd would have perished or been absorbed into others long ago. Mind 2 morality, Mind 2 custom and Mind 2 tradition are what every culture understands as its own classical outlook. Like our other moral mind, Moral Mind 2 truth is internally consistent within itself. Right – right action – means what is correct right now. Often, what is correct right now means doing as we have always done in the past.

Moral Truth Outlook 2 THE CONSERVATIVE AND OLD-FASHIONED TYPE Vertical social structure We strive to do what's "right"
The individual sacrifices for the group – we all should do what we are supposed to do.
We believe it is the customs and traditions of our group that are the foundation of our culture – ONE FOR ALL.
The past contains valuable information to be learned and passed on.
Elders and experts should be properly respected and rightly followed.
Information about our group's hierarchy must be learned and understood. Memorizing the names of the presidents is a more valuable achievement than knowing the names of current movie stars.
Information about other groups and the natural world needs to be understood in order to better protect the group. Learning the capitals of foreign countries and the habits of gazelles is vital information for protecting and providing for the group.
Happiness is the ultimate goal in life. Happiness is achieved through the successful accomplishment of one's duties across time and relative to Mind 2 social expectations.
Virtues are paramount and knowable; they are already recognized by others and established in the group. Virtues are more important than individual preferences (personal values).
Character is the defining aspect of a person; character is what matters most (not personality). Character is defined as how well or how poorly you adhere to established norms of decency.
Criminality puts one outside the group; it is addressed in terms of banishment and punishment.
Individual responsibility and independence describe our proper relationship to others; we cannot be a burden, for we would weaken the group. Those doing most while demanding least are preferred. They are the superior types of people.
Social groups and subgroups are looked upon in terms of "us" and "them" – better and worse.

Moral Truth Outlook 2 THE CONSERVATIVE AND OLD-FASHIONED TYPE Vertical social structure We strive to do what's "right"
God, country, and family are objectified and often referred to existentially. They are often spoken of with similar wording as objects of duty, each deserving "loyalty" and having "honor." God/country/family are approached worshipfully and are presumed to be worthy entities, strengthened or weakened by our fidelity. God/country/family are things to "believe in."
Concepts like "good taste" and "bad taste," "better/worse taste" make sense. Good taste can be acquired. The preferences of the better, socially superior people define better taste.
Glory (not fame) is the object of public service attained by personal sacrifice and, like happiness, transcends time and place. You can take glory with you when it's your time to go.
Ladies and gentleman exist; they are the better people, and differ from base individuals.
Doing one's duty (not having fun) is the ultimate good.
Social hierarchy stretches from the ultimate leader, god or good, through a king or a dictator, an aristocracy, a peasantry, castes, even down to slaves and untouchables. People are prioritized.
Lessons from the past teach us much and are highly valued. These define our culture, which protects and preserves us. What worked yesterday teaches us what will work today. Following tradition protects the social order from destructive disruption.
The biggest threat comes from things outside the culture or rule breakers who thwart cultural norms and laws.
Individuals are rightly sacrificed to profit and preserve the many; those who fall for the group are heroes. Nobility and ignobility exist. Conscription is proper and noble.
Religion, the state, the military, the home, our jobs and all society are viewed in hierarchal terms with leaders, tiers of followers and non-members.
The group follows the leader – chimpanzee style.
Management and unions are opposing things that may have different aims.

Moral Truth Outlook 2 THE CONSERVATIVE AND OLD-FASHIONED TYPE Vertical social structure We strive to do what's "right"
Social classes struggle to protect positions for themselves and their offspring – place matters. The compartmentalization of people and their actions is seen as necessary.
Our country, our faith, and everything of ours are to be preferred over other people, other nations and other faiths. Our culture protects us; their culture protects them. This is right.
Aristocrats, the best people and past heroes know more and should be emulated. The amateur, the young, the inexperienced and the lower classes are not to be followed if one is to prosper. We should look up for guidance.
Stoicism is praised. Emotions show vulnerability and are to be hidden or controlled.
It is acceptable that some be allowed to do or get things that are different from what others might do or have. Different people can have different rights and various privileges. Needs/rights/privileges vary according to the environmental stresses and demands being put on the group.
Character is based on how the individual stoically supports existing and established social structures. Those who support them most have the best character.
Character is displayed when the individual puts the group before his or her own needs or desires. He does this by following rules and traditions.
Marriage may be forever and divorce anathema, depending on the custom; conducted in light of what is best for society. It can even be forced upon us as an aspect of personal sacrifice for the good of society.
Marriage, divorce, contraception, child bearing and abortion are all rightfully controlled for the good of the group, and their lawfulness is rightly determined by group leadership at the top.
Flaws are things to be hidden, apologized for and corrected; otherwise we risk losing social position in a vertical society. We rightly and properly hide our shortcomings. We don't air our dirty laundry or those of our friends or family in public.
Dishonor is the ultimate evil.

In a harsh Mind 2 world, neither men nor women find it objectionable that one sex might prevail in some areas hardly known to the other. When trees needed to be felled by hand axes and babies played in every home, those most fit to work in these areas specialized there. There was less room for error. In a Mind 2 world, different things can be expected from different people. In hard times, the labors and hardships of the world are not distributed equally. If they were, we all might die.

In a Mind 2 environment, it is okay that men might swear and smoke while women shoulder the heavier burden not to. We are not safe and wealthy enough to make *equality* the ultimate good; knowing one's place and doing one's individual duty had to be what was right.

When the pack of wolves is at the door, dads were rightly expected to fight and maybe to die, while moms had to gather the kids and run to safety. There were no other choices; morality could demand we do different things. Classical morality dominates thought when we live in a world with few choices and most of them harsh.

THE PHILOSOPHICAL DEBATE
Mind 1 Utilitarianism vs. Mind 2 Deontology and Virtue Ethics

The distinction between Mind 1 and Mind 2 moral outlooks is reflected in the traditional philosophical debate between utilitarianism on the one hand and deontology and virtue ethics on the other. Philosophers have been unable to satisfactorily explain the development of society and the spectrum of human moral understanding because all were hampered in a search to find the one right way, the single moral code by which goodness can be gauged and understood. Clinging to the belief that there might be a single, logical and rational pattern by which we might explain ethical behavior, history chronicles a parade of thinkers struggling to cram all moral sentiment into one or the other of our two choices. Thinkers like Epicurus and Bentham came down in favor of a general Mind 1 outlook, and burnt the midnight oil attempting to show that right must be doing good by all more or less equally. Others, like Aristotle and Kant, favored a Mind 2 view, where standards of virtue and duty were the guideposts to follow in the search for proper behavior.

Mind 1
(Bentham 1747-1832)

The clearest and most comprehensive exposé on Mind 1 moral sentiment was put forth by Jeremy Bentham. In his work, titled *An Introduction to the Principle of Morals and Legislation*, he outlines what he believes is the underlying bedrock of all morality. Bentham does not identify this with "family" morality as we have, and instead tries to make it the single universal pattern of all private and public moral action. He calls this "the principle of utility." The standard, he claims, is to always try to do the greatest good for the individual, and the greatest good for the greatest number when thinking in terms of a group. From this point of view, number supersedes merit, honor, accomplishment, or any other factor of moral consideration and moral reward. We are all equally part of the undifferentiated "number" whose good is to be considered. Here is Bentham:

I.   Nature has placed mankind under the governance of two sovereign masters, pain and pleasure. It is for them alone to point out what we ought to do, as well as to determine what we shall do…The principle of utility recognizes this subjection, and assumes it for the foundation of that system, the object of which is to rear the fabric of felicity by the hands of reason and of law. Systems which attempt to question it, deal in sounds instead of sense, in caprice instead of reason, in darkness instead of light.

II.   …By the principle of utility is meant that principle which approves or disapproves of every action whatsoever according to the tendency it appears to have to augment or diminish the happiness of the party whose interest is in question: or, what is the same thing in other words to promote or to oppose that happiness. I say of every action whatsoever, and therefore not only of every action of a private individual, but of every measure of government.

III.   By utility is meant that property in any object, whereby it tends to produce benefit, advantage, pleasure, good, or happiness, (all this in the present case comes to the same thing) or (what comes again to the same thing) to prevent the happening of mischief, pain, evil, or unhappiness to the party whose interest is considered: if that party be the

> community in general, then the happiness of the
> community: if a particular individual, then the happiness of
> that individual.
>
> VI.   An action then may be said to be conformable to the
> principle of utility, or, for shortness sake, to utility
> (meaning with respect to the community at large) when the
> tendency it has to augment the happiness of the community
> is greater than any it has to diminish it.[3]

In the eighth volume of his masterwork, *A History of Philosophy*, Frederick Copleston notes that many thinkers formulated similar moral principles before Bentham:

> Bentham himself remarks that the principle of utility, as so
> interpreted, occurred to him when he was reading the *Essay
> on Government* (1768) by Joseph Priestly (1733-1804) who
> stated roundly that the happiness of the majority of the
> members of any State was the standard by which all the
> affairs of the State should be judged. But Hutcheson, when
> treating of ethics, had previously asserted that that action is
> best which conduces to the greatest happiness of the
> greatest number. Again, in the preface to his famous
> treatise on crimes and punishment (*Dei delitti e delle pene*,
> 1764), Cesare Beccaria (1738-94) had spoken of the
> greatest happiness divided among the greatest possible
> number. There were utilitarian elements in the philosophy
> of Hume, who declared, for example, that 'public utility is
> the sole origin of justice'. And Helvétius … In other words,
> Bentham did not invent the principle of utility: what he did
> was to expound and apply it explicitly and universally as
> the basic principle of both morals and legislation.[4]

Mind 2
Kant (1724-1804) and Aristotle (384-322 BC)

Mind 2 morality is common and also recognized intuitively by all. It is the morality of tradition, of commandments, of proclamations. Something is right because it is recognized to be so, felt to be so, and understood to be so *a priori*. This aspect of our moral nature is exemplified in things like the Ten Commandments, the Bill of Rights, the Christian classification of the "seven deadly sins," and other historic traditions that attempt to ground morality in absolute and universal rules of conduct traditionally recognized by those better or brighter than we are.

Kant's deontology is an example of the Mind 2 orientation to morality. Both utilitarianism and deontology focus their attention on the question of right and wrong *actions*. But while Bentham argued that the morality of an action can only be determined by an analysis of its consequences, Kant argued that the morality of an action can be rationally derived from contemplating the act itself. Like the chemical elements or the laws of physics, the laws of morality can be discovered. They are not made by man, nor are they only for man. Here is Copleston again, from *A History of Philosophy*:

> However, the main point which Kant wishes to make is that 'the basis of obligation must not be sought in human nature or in the circumstances of the world in which he (man) is placed, but *a priori* simply in the concepts of pure reason.[5]
>
> According to Kant, only those actions which are performed for the sake of duty have moral worth.[6]
>
> In practice we all act in accordance with what Kant calls maxims. That is to say, we all have subjective principles of volition. Now, a finite will cannot be good unless it is motivated by respect or reverence for a universal law. In order, therefore, that our wills may be morally good, we must ask ourselves whether we can will that our maxims, our subjective principles of volition, should become universal laws.[7]

Aristotle's virtue ethics[8] is another example of Mind 2 morality. Virtue ethics is distinct from both utilitarianism and deontology in that, rather than focusing on the morality of *actions*, it focuses on the morality of the *person*. Rather than asking, "What makes an action right?" it asks, "What makes a person good?" In virtue ethics, it is the quality of a person's character (his virtues) that determines morality. Virtues are those qualities of character that are traditionally upheld and transmitted by the culture and acquired through habit and practice. Good actions are performed by a virtuous person, and a virtuous person will perform good actions.

It is not surprising that there is no concept of "the good person" in Mind 1 that corresponds to the Mind 2 orientation to "character." In Mind 1, everyone is equal, so it makes no sense to talk about "good people" and "bad people," or to rank people in terms of "better" and "worse." Mind 2 "character," as we have seen, has been replaced by Mind 1 "personality," and one personality is no better or worse than any other. In Mind 1, only *actions* are subject to moral judgment, not *people*; we judge the crime, not the criminal.

The debates between the utilitarians on the one hand and the deontologists and proponents of virtue ethics on the other hand are often referred to as arguments between consequentialism and non-consequentialism. The dispute boils down to the question of whether something is good because it has been traditionally recognized as good absolutely and for its own sake, or whether it is good because it results in positive benefits.

THE RANGE OF MORAL SENTIMENT

Until now we have been using parallel tables to separate and describe the detailed nature of our two moralities.

Figure 4-1 illustrates our two moral patterns. Our two sides of truth can be illustrated by placing them side-by-side to form a continuous circle. On the left is Mind 1 morality, and on the right is Mind 2. The top and bottom points of the compass represent the extremes of a continuum along which our dual moral urges can be plotted, from the most strongly felt at the bottom to the most weakly felt at the top. A variation of this diagram is what will be used in most instances from this point forward. Both variations of subjective truth reside within us, and we are pushed back and forth to various points around this circle by circumstance. Not only can we individually be placed at different points around this circle, but collectively, our culture can be represented as occupying one general area of this universal dual human moral outlook. Figure 4-1 represents the range of moral sentiment within each of us, and it can also be used to express the range of collective moral sentiment in the group. At the top, either of these outlooks is expressed weakly; at the bottom, our emotions run strong and deep. We will discover that moral cultural history can be mapped by moving around this diagram.

Figure 4-1

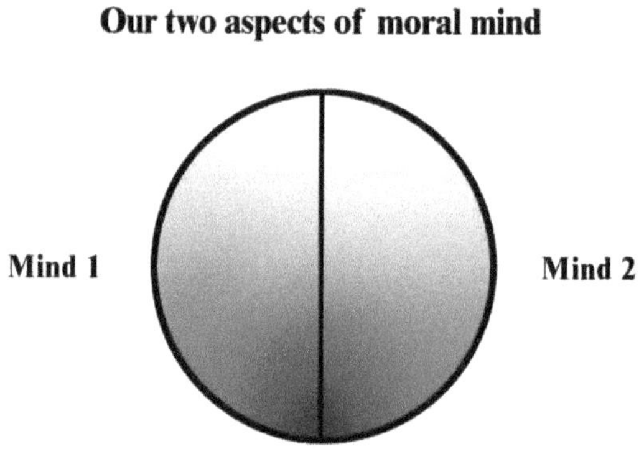

Our two aspects of moral mind

Mind 1   Mind 2

Conscience is not reason

Having multiple moral outlooks on the world has proven an enormous advantage. Each represents a different angle on reality and each guides us differently in our effort to imagine what is proper and meaningful. We have two systems of moral understanding and two ways in which we judge right from wrong. Humanity, its individuals and its groups, might at any point be guided by two moral patterns, but the physical universe, the non-human world, is not. The world of rivers, volcanoes, sunburns and snakebites is unaffected by our wishes; it is ruled by physical laws beyond the reach of our hopes and unmoved by our needs. To understand the world that exists outside of humanity, we had to develop the capacity to suppress both our moral value systems and understand reality without the taint of human need.

Necessity demands we interact with a world beyond people, a world of lions, tigers, bears, thorns, and communicable diseases; a world where death really happens. This world takes no account of human moral judgment. The mosquito bites and transmits malaria as quickly to the president as the beggar. Human morality seldom accounts for the goals of the mosquito. When it is biting us, we swat it. The biological imperative of dandelions may be to multiply in our yards, but we take no account of it and we kill them.

Morality sets our goals and guides our path, but morality can never be enough to survive in the world. We also need a way of recognizing and dealing with a universe outside of the human herd, beyond the reach of sympathetic human feeling. Alongside our dual morality, we have the ability to recognize the non-human world, and to relate to it rationally, not just emotionally. This rational ability is what we call our logical mind and it is represented at the top of our moral compass. In a rational outlook, no moral emotions are necessary and none are needed or wanted. Emotions can actually get in the way and hinder our survival. If a valuable object rolls off a high cliff, we must accept that it is gone. Gravity works on humans as well as objects and if we jump off the cliff to retrieve the object, we will die. It does not matter how much the object meant to us or how much we want it. Emotions must be suppressed to recognize danger and preserve life. Outside reality must often trump internal desires.

Human morality has no place outside humanity and in the world of sheer rationality. One plus one equals two; and $1 + 1 = 2$ even if we do not want it to. One plus one is always two, regardless of how we feel about it.

The answer is "2" for everybody, good or bad. It matters not who does the adding or how deserving they might be. No matter how much we love our little children, if they say $1 + 1 = 3$, or 4, or 5, or anything other than 2, they are wrong. The rational world operates in the same way for the sadist as it does for the saint, for Americans as much as for Nazis. In the rational non-human world, right and wrong do not apply. Understanding the world beyond humanity, we do not deal in right and wrong, only in facts or fictions.

We accomplish this ability to see the world logically by suppressing (as much as we can) our two moral impulses. *We suppress the urge to feel right and wrong in order to more clearly see fact or fiction.* This suppression of purpose and our ability to ignore human meanings in actions allow us to discover what seems like a third way of understanding the world. We can see things in terms of Mind 1 truth or Mind 2 truth; we can also see things amorally, in terms of no truth at all.

We are capable of a limited amoral view of the world. We understand that rivers can flow, species go extinct, and the earth can cool without a direct relationship to human beings. It is often a struggle to see things this way, but we have the capacity. This outlook is examined more closely in the following chapter.

QUAD-REALISM
Science and knowledge
Religion and belief

Once we account for moral intensity, our dual moralism naturally changes to a sort of quad-realism. We have been focusing almost exclusively on Method 1 and Method 2 morality as our two sides of truth; but just as importantly, and more importantly when speaking of science, mathematics and anything external to us, we step outside our moral minds and recognize that events occur outside human agency or consequence. And though we can never move completely away from our morality, there are occasions when our moral outlook is weakened. We can understand and explain things, not just in terms of human purpose and meaning, but also using words like "cause and effect." Using the illustration introduced earlier, we can visualize how, by minimizing both our Mind 1 and Mind 2 moral urges, we free ourselves to see the world without a human moral component.

Figure 4-2

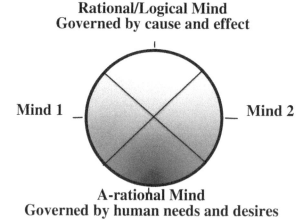

At the other extreme, we can also minimize the impact of our senses and internalize our understanding so that all we focus on is what we want and what we need – what we wish to be true. When we suppress the external world, we free our own internal imagination to view the world solely in terms of its conformity to some human moral outlook. When morality is weakest, the mind is free to contemplate science; when morality is strongest, we understand reality in relation to internal subjective beliefs. When we add intensity to dual morality, we achieve quad-realism:

Real life happens between extreme a-rationality and subjectivity at the bottom of the cycle (where only human desires count) and pure rationality and objectivity at the top (where human needs do not). We are always subjects viewing or acting upon objects. *Reality for each of us is the point where subjectivity meets objectivity.*

This ability to see things as objective and unemotional or purely subjective and emotional, along with either a Mind 1 or a Mind 2 outlook, creates the four zones of moral understanding I call "quad-realism." Institutions and complex social structures have emerged to cater to the needs and satisfy the desires of each of our four emotional possibilities. Near the top of our moral compass, and when we are acting unemotionally, we express the sciences. On the left, institutions of family and social welfare are created. On the right, corporate verticality and military institutions of a hierarchal type are formed. Near the bottom, and to satisfy the emotive needs of our extreme human-focused subjectivity, we create our religions.

Our day-to-day lives are ruled by two moral outlooks, and in addition to these, life wobbles back and forth between two poles of rational/a-rational extreme: pure morality at the bottom and amorality at the top. When we are feeling like all that matters is what is good for human beings, we are acting close to the bottom of the illustration. At other times when we feel what humans want doesn't really matter, we are acting more toward the top of the diagram.

The ethical contradictions of history from slavery to liberty, the divine right of kings to modern democratic equality are all moral positions that can be plotted out on the chart above. All of these can be understood as right and best. All have been right and best at one time or another. Using the chart, we can plot every aspect of human moral history.

It will allow us to explain how – and more importantly *why* – humans variously distinguish good from evil, and call something right today where tomorrow that same thing will be condemned as wrong. From all these possible vantages in our moral cycle, all the moral codes will become decipherable.

When suppressing internal desires and seeing the world with our emotions turned off, we believe in cause and effect, and in this mindset we can develop science. Acting at the other extreme, when we turn our gaze completely inward and turn off the influence of external experience and cause and effect, we easily imagine that what we want and need is all that matters. In this mode, prayers work and miracles happen; we magically get what we want. We like to have it both ways. We operate at both the top and bottom of the circle. Also, we jump left and right. At one time, we may be quite sure everyone is equal (on the left), and then again, there are occasions when we believe some people and things are more important than others (on the right). We can believe these things strongly or mildly.

Equipped with our capacity to see the world in terms of this quad-realism, we have conquered it. By adjusting our feelings about things to however we need to see them at the moment, and by creating social institutions that help us satisfy the wide range of moral urges in the human moral spectrum, we have become the most creative and complex creatures that ever lived.

We see pictured at the southern point of our moral compass the institutions we create to satisfy the needs and wants generated when our emotions are most intense. In Mind 1, when we are feeling safe in close familial association, we create the cultural tools of fun and sharing, like musical events, playgrounds and welfare agencies. In Mind 2, our need to feel protected is met by police forces, fire fighters and the army. When all human morality is suppressed, our urge to understand the outside world is met through the institutions of science and technology. And, at the bottom of our compass, where both moral outlooks come together at the extreme, we create religions to provide us a path to ultimate safety, security, and infinite moral right.

Figure 4-3

The Institutions we create to meet the emotional demands of our morality

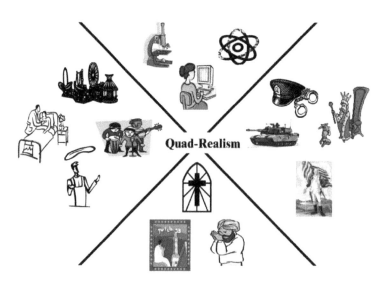

Quad-Realism

ANCIENT EXPLANATIONS FOR OUR MULTIPLE MINDS

Our dual morality and quad-realism have been apparent to perceptive thinkers since time immemorial. Two thousand years before Confucius, the Chinese attempted to understand and explain the dual nature in human character and human social organization. One effort was compiled in a book called the *I Ching*, where it was proposed that opposite forces were at work within us. Sages told us these forces complement each other and, if correctly understood, will work together to help us achieve our goals.

The binary nature of man's moral understanding was recognized; explaining *why* morality should be expressed in two ways has been the challenge. In his book, *The Complete I Ching,* Taoist Master Alfred Huang explains how the ancient Tao illuminates the dual aspect of man's nature.

Figure 4-4

Many westerners know the I Ching, but they do not know the Tao of I. Of the numerous treasures in the I Ching, I value the Tao of I the most...The Tao of I also discloses that when situations proceed beyond their extremes, they alternate to their opposites. It is a reminder to accept necessary change and be ready to transform, warning that one should adjust one's efforts according to changes in time and situation. The Tao of I also says: In a favorable time and situation, never neglect the unfavorable potential. In an unfavorable time and situation, never act abruptly and blindly. And in adverse circumstances, never become depressed and dispair.[9]

Chinese elements and stages of change outline man's moral condition

We in the West are familiar with the writings of Plato, Aristotle, the Epicureans and the Stoics. All founded schools purporting to explain the physical as well as the human world. Ancient Chinese thinkers also tried to explain what we find in ourselves and others. They asked the same questions we do. Are people equal or are some better than others? What does it mean to be a superior person? Why do we change, sometimes believing one thing, and then at other times choosing to believe another? What is most right?

Long before Carl Jung or the Myers-Briggs personality test, the ancient Chinese concluded the universe was made up of knowable elements (Hsing) and that the arrangements of these elements told us something about physical phenomena and something about ourselves. In the West, people spoke of four humors or astrological signs. In the East, they came to recognizably similar conclusions. Lacking the modern scientific method, the ancient Chinese, like the ancient Europeans, Indians and Egyptians, were left to look inward to the souls of men for their answers.

For most of history, in the East as well as the West, times were tough. Mind 2 morality was the outlook that dominated all society. In this mind, some of us are recognized as better than others. Culture was composed of superiors and inferiors, and doing right might differ among people, depending on the place one occupied. In the East as well as the West, rationality was used to systematize what we irrationally concluded. The mind is a slave to the heart.

We find an example of this in the Chinese Hsing. Through combination, everything in the universe is composed of wood, fire, earth, metal, and water. All the world, and people included, is made up of different combinations of these things. And, as in all struggling cultures, the combinations are arranged in a vertical form, from least to best.

Today we speak of temperaments being affected by deficiencies in minerals or an imbalance of hormones. The ancient Chinese used a similar rationale, suggesting that temperaments could be understood as relationships and balances of the Hsing within us. Who you are is understood by which aspect of Hsing you match:

- *Wood*: rising, developing impulse and expansion
- *Fire*: the embodiment and definition of action and active design
- *Earth*: change and flux
- *Metal*: sinking, contraction and decline
- *Water*: contemplation, calmness and reflection

The five Hsing correspond to the five dimensions, five steps of evolution, and five stages of human development, which, in classical cultures, were always viewed vertically. Here we see the effects of Hsing acting upon us and revealing how we might be described from lowest to highest:

1. *The Common Man*	Sleep	Rock
2. *The Worthy Man*	Dreaming	Vegetable
3. *The Superior Man*	Reflection	Animal

4. The Called Man	Walking	Human
5. The Holy Sage	Awareness	Tao/Godly

The aim of man at each stage of development is different, with the higher and better person being understood as the man having the highest and best aims:

1. *The Common Man* looks for material goods. This is the position of the vast majority of the world – everyone striving for more things.
2. *The Worthy Man* looks beyond the material and strives for growth and education.
3. *The Superior Man* makes sense of life when he unites TAO and TE, intention and motivation.
4. *The Called Man*, with the task, "Ming," from heaven, will change the political situation.
5. *The Holy Sage*, the highest human calling, is in tune with heaven, earth and the TAO. His mere existence makes him a living pillar around which a culture might grow.[10]

Moralists East or West always suggest there are more important things in life than money. Both intuitively condemn as an inferior aspect of the common man the seeking of material goods, while the superior person and the called man try to change the world for the benefit of others. The same themes repeat themselves again and again everywhere in our human dialogue. We note also how the ancient Eastern thinkers used both equality and hierarchy to describe human morality and social structure.

No matter where or when we look, in every culture around the world and throughout time, we find our philosophers concluding that we are creatures with a dual moral understanding. The ancient and modern thinkers of both East and West generalize moral right, social structure, and social good, as ideally arranged in one or the other of these two possibilities:

- Correct feeling and behavior is the protection and provision of the group through the recognition of a universal equality, with the central leadership directing the sharing of all wealth. This outlook suggests all goods are owned by everyone. Democratically, our land, loves and loot should be common commodities. Wealth and social authority are owned equally by all.

  Or

- Correct feeling and behavior is protecting and providing for the group through the recognition and rewarding of the best first and those of lesser ability later. In this moral outlook, wealth and social authority are commanded and controlled by aristocratic individuals below the level of the top leadership and are made available for the good of the group as directed by social leaders and individuals close to but outside leadership.

No matter how we look at the production and control of wealth, it is only valuable when it is put to the right purpose. Wealth for wealth's sake is always bad. Greed is a sin everywhere.

In ancient times, poor cultures existed in circumstances where few could gain while many others had to lose. There were simply not enough resources for everyone to live well. Consequently, every classical writer reflecting on morality, including the ancient Chinese sages, presupposed a vertical structure was most right when describing the proper moral outlook. The best need to be nurtured and given first priority, while the worst must be improved or marginalized. Proper morality was understanding that this social and material inequality was right.

Family, government and religion did well the more they turned us into better people by raising us up morally. Naturally, some made it and many could not. Some were simply going to be superior to others. This was the way of the world, and nothing much could be done about it.

Plato, like other ancient Western thinkers, danced around a concept of a general equality for all, but in the difficult world of ancient Greece, he still fell back on the idea that some of the people might need to be told they were made of iron, others silver and the best of gold. In his version of utopia, his perfect society, outlined in his book, *The Republic*,[11] and given a facelift in his later work, *Laws*,[12] some still needed to be understood as superior to others. The great thinkers living in harsher times simply saw no way around it.

Understanding the individual and the group
Psychology, sociology, and moral terminology

We will discover that our dual morality guides and shapes the larger structures of life. Just as the six-sided snowflake is created because of the nature of the six-sided water molecule that composes it, so our social structures take on a dualistic or quad-realistic nature because they are based on the divided outlook within us.

Modern thinkers like Swiss psychologist Carl Jung (1875-1961) developed theories of personality suggesting human psychology is religious by its nature, inventing terms like "individuation" to explain how the conflicting aspects of mind were integrated into the individual personality.

The scientific disciplines of psychology and psychiatry investigate what we mean by terms like "personality" or "character" as they apply to individuals. For modern researchers, "personality" has superseded character as the more vital aspect of the psyche, central to understanding the goals and motivations of human beings today.

Though psychology was not a field of study in the Middle Ages, priests and philosophers attempted to explain and correct human behavioral deficiencies in the terms that meant something to them. In modern times, success in life is seen as an aspect of personal satisfaction. In former harder times, success was seen as doing well in relation to others in the group.

We no longer focus on improving the characteristics that determined success in more vertically oriented times. In the past, things like courage, cowardice, slovenliness, or gluttony were the concerns of educated priests and counselors trying to better understand and advise us for improvement. The emphasis now is on discovering the attributes prized in our commercial democracies, which focus on the individual first, like personal interests, hobbies and habits, and technical aptitude. Today we believe that it is through satisfying individual desires that the community is benefitted. In the past we believed in the promotion of the old virtues, which focused on satisfying community needs, and by doing this, the individual might be best rewarded. We were a Mind 2 culture; we are transitioning to a Mind 1 world.

What are valued most these days is not social virtue (Do we even know what that is?), but personal production, sexual expression, punctuality, and individual feelings of security or anxiety. With names like "archetypes" and "self-actualization," Carl Jung tried to explain why we do what we do; Freud told us it was largely about sex drives, with terms like "agoraphobia" and "anticathexis." Today we speak of "personality types" and "personality traits." Gone are ideas of the seven deadly sins, which apply equally to all. In the realm of social psychology, it is our individuality that matters now.

How we act is who we are. Who we are is determined by what we do. In our modern production-based (as opposed to social-position-based) culture, the type of person you are is now often defined by what type of job you have. It is no longer all that important to be firm about what type of family atmosphere you supported, or how courageous you were in battle, or even how devoutly you supported your religion. Now what matters most and defines each of us most clearly is our production.

We concern ourselves very little with conversations about men and women as moral agents; we now refer to them in the terms that affect us most: as producers and consumers. We no longer ask if Johnny had been sent to church each week. Now we want to know if Johnny has a decent pair of shoes and a coat to wear. We do not define good as helping Johnny save his soul. We define it as helping him acquire a skill and get a job. Modern opportunities for production have shifted our focus from the things that were important in poor societies (Mind 2 customs and virtues) to those that are important in factories and on assembly lines, which are amoral and physical. The moral attribute that allows us to succeed in this modern condition is the suppression of both our Mind 1 and Mind 2 emotions, which enhances our ability to deal with the external non-human reality of levers, gears, temperatures and numbers.

IMPROVING MAN
Are we most improved when we
do more for ourselves and our families
or when we do more for others?

Ancient medical men and modern psychologists address deficiencies of character and personality in the terms important in their own culture. Prior to the renaissance, Moral Mind 2 conditions prevailed throughout the world. Creating the superior person was understood in Mind 2 terms:

- Enhance those qualities appreciated in a Mind 2 world and you have enhanced the individual.

A person was especially improved if he or she were made the better person *culturally*. The qualities appreciated in our social dealings with others outside the home were the qualities that deserved our greatest attention. A person might be improved in their personal dealings too, made a better wife or husband, but this was largely the role of the church and outside the scope of government and moral philosophers.

In a Mind 2 environment, improving man was the highest role of politics, philosophers and churchmen. Making people more moral was defined as social progress. Unlike today, where social progress is determined by Gross National Product and equalizing pay rates, in former Mind 2 times, improving everyone's Mind 2 social awareness was the goal promoted by all cultural institutions. The kingdom that produced the most people who expressed themselves best in Mind 2 terms, like the bravest men and the most sexually chaste women, was the superior culture. (These are still the standards understood in Middle-Eastern cultures today.)

Mental health and moral understanding were acknowledged by one and all to be conditions that conformed to this Mind 2 moral perspective. Smart people saw things in these Mind 2 ways. Fools and hedonists saw things differently, but they were the bad elements in society. In the past 1,000 years, we have been moving steadily leftward from this Mind 2 moral outlook toward a society where our Mind 1 feelings are better represented. And what is fueling this move toward a Mind 1 outlook of ease and fun is the accumulation of wealth and the increase in safety and security that wealth engenders.

Using the circular diagram introduced earlier, we can chart the movement of our culture's predominant moral outlook through the ages. Recalling that the left side of the diagram illustrates our Mind 1 values, while the right side of our illustration depicts Mind 2 virtues, the place occupied by any culture at any point in time might be picked out. Recall also that toward the top of the diagram, both moral patterns are weak, while at the bottom, both are strong. Thus the moral positions of our societies can be arranged and plotted.

What we discover is that, with the occasional setback, western society has been moving steadily leftward for the past 500 years – from an earlier cultural condition where the individual existed for the good of the group (Mind 2) on the far right of our circular diagram, which reached its pinnacle in the early Middle Ages, toward the social understanding where the group, the herd, the culture, exists for the good of the individual (Mind 1):

Figure 4-5

The drift leftwards

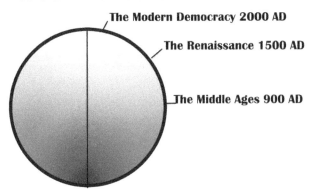

Things have changed, and the mechanism of that change has been production and trade. As society has grown wealthier and safer, we, individually and collectively, are biologically pushed to drift toward a Moral Mind 1 outlook of sharing and equality. We have less to fear from forces outside the herd and more to fear from the improper distribution of the plenty that is around us. In our moral Mind 1 outlook, it is not self-control but self-expression that is valued. Individuality, personal vitality and a tolerant outlook become the focus of all our attentions and even take over the focus of our politicians, churchmen and our mental health providers.

The creation of people who see everyone equally is the goal of good moral practice and political order. Industrialization and hyper-production continue to move culture leftward. The instrumental role played by production will be investigated in the chapters ahead. For now, we acknowledge that circumstances of plenty (another way of saying great production) are more than merely conducive – they are in fact vital and necessary – to the leftward movement in the moral cycle. We discover, from a cultural point of view, that *how much we make defines who we are*. How much we have defines how we feel.

Mind 1: We relax; we are at home
Mind 2: We are guarded and need be on our best behavior

Mind 1 is our personal and familial mind of right: We can relax in Mind 1; we are safe, and there is enough for all. We care about everybody and everybody cares about us. We can even be lazy or slovenly buffoons. We don't judge others and we don't expect to be judged ourselves. Times are easy, or we are at home and this should be how we feel about family. In times of want or stress, we operate in our other moral mind.

Mind 2 is our social mind of right: We are on our best behavior; we are in a more precarious position. We can judge others and we understand we will be judged. There is not enough for all, and we grasp it is right that we compete to get a share of limited resources. We do right to be seen as better than others.

Art, fashion, manners and everything else changes along with our changing moral outlook. Even the things we find humorous change. In our modern wealthy and safe time, automobile bumper stickers can laughingly show a child urinating on the American flag – nationalism is not to be taken too seriously. Or we might find it amusing to dangle imitation testicles hanging from plastic scrotums off the bumper at the rear of our pick-up truck – sexual expression is to be enjoyed, not discouraged. A century ago, these depictions would not have been seen as humorous (at least not openly so). Urinating on the flag and imitation testicles would have been considered beyond vulgar, indeed as openly offensive and obscene. Years ago, still in the midst of a Mind 2 culture, emotional control concerning matters of sexuality and nationalism would have been demanded. A dedication to the traditions of our culture, including its flag, would have been understood as right and would have been demanded before and above any amusement gained by an individual. No one would have been allowed to display such things publically, with a sneer or a smile. If a representative of the law did not make us remove them, a well-placed rock through our windshield would let us know we were violating community standards. This is no longer true. In a Mind 1 world, the individual, not the community, sets the standards. Emotional expression is encouraged, and what can be expressed is defined by what is good for the individual, as determined by the individual personally. Shame is now a thing of the past. It is a Mind 2 concept and has little place.

Mind 2 morality, as the dominant social force behind our morality, is passing. A different moral shadow is starting to loom over us now. We can urinate on flags or advertise our sexuality, but that doesn't mean we can do anything we please. Moral Mind 1 is still a limiting morality. Outlook 1 still corrals us. But we are restrained in a different direction. We have not abandoned moral prejudice. We have merely shifted our prejudices to fight against new foes.

We can pee on the flag; that might be acceptable and even funny. We can hang an imitation scrotum from the rear of our trucks and laugh. But modern sensibilities would never recognize the humor in a bumper sticker that read:

REAL MEN BEAT THEIR WIVES AND KIDS
ONLY WHEN THEY REALLY DESERVE IT

Why not? Why is this not funny? There is a reason. There is a reason this went out of style:

THE ONLY GOOD INDIAN IS A DEAD INDIAN

Today violence against anyone within the group is condemned and discouraged. A universal concept of equality permeates what is right. We can no more condone slapping children than we can beating dogs, evicting Indian tribes or segregating public swimming pools. All may have once been right. Now all must be acknowledged as wrong. Political correctness is the application of the correct moral mind to the circumstances of the moment. We are expected to share whichever moral prejudice enjoys overwhelming social support at the moment. Customs and practices developed in a Mind 2 outlook, where some could be seen as better than others and violence and exclusion were often necessary, are now transitioning to a place where everyone can and should make it and no one should be considered less in any way than another.

Truth, in a Mind 1 moral environment, is understood in terms of individuals and families, not in terms of groups and strangers. Personal expression is encouraged. Fun is the watchword every day. Urinating is a comical event. Flags are passé. It is people, not groups or nations that matter. It's wrong to even see things in terms of groups. Grouping is bad because it excludes some and includes others. Most importantly of all, in a Mind 1 environment, violence is intolerable. We all can and should do well.

In reality, the first bumper sticker (above) would be in poor taste in either moral mind. In Mind 2, our feelings, particularly those towards our families, are usually not matters of public discussion. In a Mind 2 outlook, the better people would not display bumper stickers. The second sticker, if it concerned a condemnation of people outside the group, might be more acceptable in a difficult Mind 2 environment. In extreme circumstances it could be morally right. Like all overt displays of emotion, bumper stickers would find their way onto the cars only of persons of the lower type (or of the young, where emotional outbursts are more tolerated).

Today, a person driving down the street with the anti-Indian sticker above would be condemned. But if the word "Indian" were replaced by the word "terrorist," and the sticker read, "The only good terrorist is a dead terrorist," we would probably look the other way. The "Indians" threatened us yesterday, but it is the "terrorists" who threaten us today. So it is the "terrorists" who can be killed with social support and near impunity. However, as an overt emotional expression, we'd still expect to find such a sticker on the cars of rubes and hayseeds – typically of the meaner types of folks. Our ability to find enemies outside our group is shrinking, but it can never completely disappear; nor can we ever fully get past the concept that the control of excessive emotional expression is the hallmark of a superior person. We are all dual moral creatures.

In Moral Mind 1, flags, sex and bodily functions can be funny, but violence and inequality are not laughing matters. In Mind 2, degrading other groups outside our own can be righteous or even hilarious, but our own god/country/family are not things to be joked about. Right and wrong are not always the same things. Both depend on the moral mind we are operating in. Truth has two sides.

THE MEANING OF LIFE
What do we mean by "meaning"?

In a search for the meaning of life, we must first recognize what we are getting at with words like "meaning." Meaning is an aspect of thought. It is the relationship of one thing to another. Meaning is related to cause and effect as well as purpose; meaning links before to after. If a thing has meaning, it is understood to have a value outside itself – for, or in relation to, something else. If I ask someone, "What is the meaning of paint?" they might answer that it protects or that it beautifies something else. If we were to go around and ask people, "What is the meaning of life?" what might they say? What are its relations and what is its purpose?

Our answers waiver between the hackneyed and the banal. The waiter at the sushi restaurant says it's about loving one's family; my secretary claims it is about having fun; the politicians say it is about loving your country; and the minister claims it is about obeying God. Yet any one of them might concede the others were as correct as they are. What a coworker lists as the most meaningful thing in life one day might place second on his list a week later. Does the question make sense? Does life have any meaning at all? Can my life's meaning differ in any way from yours? Can I really determine what gives life meaning, or are there experts in this field?

We are stymied in discovering the meaning of life because we never consistently feel-think-act in only one way. Am I the judge or is somebody else? If we were but one moral entity seeking one goal, say a duck flying south, we'd have a narrow measure of success. We are not so one-dimensional. To succeed as a complex social creature, we must see success in ever-changing terms. Today success might mean acquiring money and sharing it with our mate. Tomorrow it could mean beating our friends out of their money at the poker game. Success is situational. What my actions "mean" depends on what my goals are, or what is right in the moment.

Being creatures of dual morality, we often find ourselves distressed by moving from one moral outlook to another. We vacillate between saving for tomorrow and spending today; between going to church with our parents and going fishing with our friends. We try to have it both ways and end up never completely sure how to answer the question, "What is right?"

This question, "What is the right thing to do now?" can be looked at in many ways. When taken to the extreme of absolute right, it can be imagined in terms of, "What is right for me to do always?" or, stated another way, "What is right is what I should be seeking to accomplish with all my actions together. What is my ultimate goal?"

Another way of saying this is, "What is the meaning of life?" What we discover, as creatures with a number of purposes and a dual morality, is that life has many meanings and some of them even contradict the others. We want to be stingy and generous at the same time. We want to be a Mind 1 creature of pleasure and so we dismiss our dalliance with the neighbor this week, while also being a Mind 2 creature and condemning our spouse for their dalliance with our other neighbor last week. We try to have it both ways. We maximize our advantages with our moral flexibility.

Even when alone, we are a group

Not long ago, I was on a long drive and my mind wandered. I was trying to decide what to get my wife for her birthday and I recalled she had mentioned needing a carpet shampooer. I passed the idea back and forth in my mind: Is a carpet shampooer an appropriate gift for a wife? It seems more like a mother's day gift, and she is not my mother. Part of me said it was not romantic enough. Another part said utility supersedes romance over time. What should I do? How do I decide?

I was so engrossed in my thoughts, I was surprised to look up and see my destination right in front of me. I had not even been aware how I had driven the last ten miles. It was as if my body was on autopilot. I know I drove the car, made the turns, and avoided the obstacles, but I could not remember doing it. Some part of my brain was driving, while the other part considered my dilemma. But debating it with whom? With myself?

If we are conscious, we are never alone. Neuroscientists tell us that our mind is really multiple minds working together in a single brain to accomplish the complexities of life. One part of my brain tells me a shampooer is a fine gift. Another part seems to be warning me not to get it. Part of my brain was driving my car, another part debating purchase options. Some part of me outside my consciousness was keeping my heart beating and another was storing memories. We hold conversations with ourselves in our own thoughts. As we drift to sleep we occasionally begin dreaming while still thinking of daily concerns – parallel thoughts. When all alone, we are a herd in our own minds; internally, in our own heads, we often do not agree with ourselves. If we often do not agree with ourselves, how likely is it that we will always agree with others?

Externally we exist among others who, we discover, are more than one personality too. Because we are one body and one voice, we present ourselves as one thing. We see others as single beings too, but this is not exactly the case.

Popular physiology

American writers like Robert Ornstein and British journalists like Rita Carter share a penchant for physical psychology and enjoy keeping interested amateurs like me informed of discoveries in brain research. Some medical findings are downright startling. Among the most mesmerizing aspects of this experimentation are the unexpected consequences of split-brain surgery.

Split-brain surgery is a procedure where the left portion of the brain is detached from the right. The resulting odd aftereffects of such surgery shed light on just how completely our brains can be more than just one "thinking and desiring" organ. This surgery, which severs the nerve connections between the two brain hemispheres, is sometimes employed as a treatment for epileptic seizures. The seizures diminish, but they are occasionally replaced with strange behavior, among the strangest of which is the phenomenon of alien hands.

When the brain is undamaged and unhindered by disease or surgery, the contrary impulses that take place within it are worked out below the level of consciousness. We hardly ever realize that our minds are at odds with themselves. Our behaviors and our emotions become predictable, as one set of mental processes tends to dominate. We act and feel in a generally uniform way. We know who we are, and other people do too.

We never imagine that, within our brains, little wars are being waged between various aspects struggling for dominance. The phenomenon of alien hands occasionally occurs, where a patient who has had such damage or has undergone split-brain surgery discovers that he is no longer consciously in control of both sides of his body; that one side of his body may in fact act to oppose what the other side is trying to do. The subconscious brain is not properly resolving its conflicts. Its struggles bubble up to the level of consciousness and even to the level of action. It has been observed in some split-brain patients that one hand wants to do something different from what the other has in mind. Here is an excerpt from Rita Carter's book, *Mapping the Mind*:

> ...M.P. was making good progress with an omelet when the left hand 'helped out' by throwing in, first, a couple of additional, uncracked eggs, then an unpeeled onion and a salt cellar into the frying pan. There were also times when the left hand deliberately stopped the right hand carrying out a task. In one instance I asked her to put her right hand through a small hole. "I can't – the other one's holding it," she said. I looked over and saw her left hand firmly gripping the right at the wrist.[13]

Numerous examples have been documented, including people who get dressed with one hand, while fighting the other that continues to undress them. One hand opens the door while the other slams it shut, and so on. Clearly the brain is a multi-functioning and multi-thinking organ. Whatever thought is, whatever emotion, motivation, imagination, and memory are, they function simultaneously in our brain. This obviously includes moral judgment and emotional perspective. It is not beyond peradventure to recognize that the brain might be clearly capable of coming to one moral judgment in one part of the organ while another sees things differently.

Modern science declares that we are not of one mind, but multiple mini-minds. This isn't a recent discovery. Investigators of our human condition have concluded this same thing for thousands of years.

Plutarch was a great thinker and prolific writer. He so impressed the Roman Emperor Trajan with his understanding of human reason that he gave the philosopher consular rank. In his multi-volume book, *Moralia,* written around 100 A.D., Plutarch repeatedly uses examples from common experience to explain to the Greeks and Romans of his day the very same things our modern scientists are telling us now – that is, that the human brain operates in a multi-faceted manner. Further, Plutarch suggests we divide human moral judgment along clearly demarcated lines.

Though Plutarch never illustrates moral understanding as concisely as we do here in this book, he certainly recognizes that within each of us lies a recognizable divide in our feelings, sometimes seeing things in terms of pleasures and pains, shunning the moral judgment of others (Mind 1), and at other times using a side of mind that puts right and wrong in terms of better and worse, where the judgment of people and things is necessary. In many ways, his understanding of human psychology seems as modern as anything written in our times, as when he speaks of the inability of pure reason to make any decisions at all if denied emotional guidance: "...if the passions could in reality be entirely done away with ... reason would be too inactive and dulled, like a pilot when the wind dies down." [14]

Reading Plutarch reminds us that most of our ruminations and metaphysics are as old as the hills. He tells us how Alexander of Macedon was disturbed by the discourse of Anaxarchus about the possibility of an infinite number of worlds. Subjectively, Plutarch, like our modern scientists, recognizes that each of us has within us a number of worlds in the mind. The dual nature of our morality is too obvious to have been missed by him:

> It is quite obvious then, that there is in the soul a perception of some such distinction and difference as regards the desires, as though some force were fighting against them and contradicting them. But we affirm that passion is not essentially different from reason, nor is there a quarrelling between the two ... but only a conversion of one and the same reason to its two aspects; this escapes our notice by reason of the suddenness and swiftness of the change...

> For no one ever perceives in himself a change from desiring to judging, not again a change from judging to desiring; nor does the lover cease loving when he reasons that he must restrain his love ... and neither through passion has he done away with reason, nor through reason is he rid of passion, but being born back and forth from one to the other he lies between them and participates in both.[15]

Plutarch recognizes, as we do, a distinction between our irrational selves, represented by our two moral minds, and a rational aspect of apprehension, which operates when both sides of our irrational selves are suppressed:

> ...when there is a struggle against reason on the part of the irrational ... straightaway the irrational splits the soul in two by its battling and makes the distinction between the two perfectly obvious.[16]

Plutarch, like Confucius, like the Tao Masters, like Freud and like modern neurologists, grasped that the aspect of the brain we call "the mind" is a multi-dimensional thing. Nevertheless, its various aspects are consistent and can be understood, including the manifestation of mental activity we call "morality."

HOW DIFFERENT CAN WE BE?

Skin cells vary slightly one from the other; some may tan easier than those next to it; if so, the person appears freckled. But freckled or not, the cell still performs other vital functions all skin cells perform, like protecting the body from bacteria. Tanning slightly easier than the skin cell next to it is not a dramatic variable, and so each of our cells may be mildly different, but they must all retain the ability to work together. When brain cell organization differs among portions of the brain, the heartbeat, the gait, the breathing, or the mind of the creature is affected. When the individual is born with an irregular heart or liver or lungs, an early death is likely to result. But variation in brain performance, particularly for a herding creature that can rely on his fellows for assistance, may be advantageous. The individual herd member born with a particularly efficient liver but suffering from an especially ineffective heart cannot count on other herd members to help out in the areas where he is weak. However, in many behavioral areas, devoting some extra mental capacity to one narrow range of behavior at the expense of another may actually benefit everyone. In large groups, it may be advantageous to have some members who possess an above average ability to reason while others are better capable of expressing desires (i.e. some to be better thinkers and others better feelers). Each brings to their group a talent that can be put to the service of others.

The "thinker" who finds it easy to set aside emotion and focus on facts devotes himself to science or mechanics. The extra-sensitive feeler is creative in artistic ways. Morally, the extra-xenophobic patriotic can do others a great service too. By being extra dutiful in watching for threats to established culture they are fist to warn of changes that might not be beneficial. The unusually sensitive "bleeding heart" is first to bring our attention to the plight of those who suffer material want. Each serves as a sort of "social leader" or "canary in the mine shaft," who calls attention to discoveries or dangers that he or she is especially attuned to and can recognize before the rest of us.

Like the cells in the body, each of us can be unique, but only mildly so. Most of us must retain the ability to perform a function within the herd to survive. We have hands with thumbs and fingers for grasping; at this gross level we are all alike. But examining the small details, we find we have unique fingerprints. Hands unite us; the fingerprints are too small to divide us. Though each face can be distinguished from a billion others in its details, they all contain eyes, noses and mouths. We can differ, but our differences cannot be as glaring and strident as to make us useless to others or have them be useless to us. Then we would be outcasts.

The brain, the personality, the psyche, the character are all understood similarly by us. At a detailed level, each individual's mind functions slightly differently and makes us unique, but at the level of gross generality, we must occupy our thoughts with very similar things as our companions do and solve our problems in similar ways; otherwise we would be unable to cooperate. But variance exists in the brain as well as the body and as variances become more extreme, so too does our thinking, for good or ill.

Normal and average in looks is not striking or beautiful. To be beautiful is to step away from the average, but step away too far and we become freakish, and the feature that could be recognized as desirable becomes anything but. A guy two inches taller than his peers seems more virile; a guy twenty inches taller is a monstrosity. Minor variations in thinking ability makes one a genius, but vary too much and we find savants, the mentally retarded or the socially isolated. We long to be individuals, but individuals accepted as part of a mass.

Individuality can make us too unique. If we become too distinguishingly individual in looks, thoughts or actions, we are suspect and shunned. Most of us achieve individuality by doing most things like everyone else, with only one or two things in a slightly more dedicated way.

Why do I do what I do?

A friend of mine was caught up in an adulterous affair. Temporarily captivated by a handy siren, he abandoned his wife and kids. After the thrill of new love/lust wore off, he felt guilty and returned home to mend his fences and reunite his family. The effort apparently worked and by all outward appearances, the couple resumed a semblance of their former lives.

I went to lunch with him and our conversation fell upon his struggle to return to normalcy with his wife. He told me that part of the healing process included sitting up with her many nights as she repeatedly asked him variations of the question, "Why did you do it?" to which he honestly and repeatedly answered with variations of "I don't know."

He assured me he did not know; something just came over him. He could not explain his actions any better than the rest of us could. Prior to meeting the sweetheart, he would never have imagined himself capable of such an affair, and now back with his wife, he thinks he will never do it again. The talking part of his brain was struggling to explain how some other portion of his mind commanded him to act. The talking portion of his mind was fumbling around for explanations, just as his wife and his friends were.

Maybe the talking portion of everyone's mind is no more aware of why we do things than our mates or our friends are. Sometimes it seems our partners, being more careful observers of our behavior than we are ourselves, tell us what we are going to choose before we know it. My wife seems to have a better grasp on what movie I will like, or what food I will prefer and what clothes I feel comfortable wearing than I do.

Are we taught interests or are we born with propensities toward them? Are we conceived with beautiful personalities preset or are we made that way by cultural pressure? In the creation of either a beautiful mind or a beautiful body, nature and nurture each count for something. We may share a common desire to be beautiful and brilliant, but we are not all beautiful or brilliant. Desire is not ability. Some people have skin that tans well and easily; others do not and must sit in the shade. Some minds retain information easily; others do not. We vary among ourselves, and our herd is composed of varieties of people.

As casual observers of the common man, we can come to no other conclusion than that a few people are brilliant in narrow areas, some are crazy in broad areas, and most lie in between. Most of us are remarkably unimpressive; we fail to outshine the average in looks, words, or deeds, either negatively or positively. We look around and see a world full of people like us in this way: most neither overly bright nor particularly dull; neither exceptionally good nor markedly evil; neither too selfish nor too generous; folks interested in a few common things, but almost none interested in too many things; and within any given culture, almost any one of them comfortably interchangeable with any other. Like the occasional zebra lost to the hungry lions, the loss of any one of us does not make much of a difference to the herd as a whole.

Thinking and feeling prepare us for speaking and acting

What do animals feel and what do animals think about? To move requires an inner impulse to go in one direction or another; to go after or move away from; to seek for comfort and safety, or retreat from fear and pain. To move at all requires inward direction. Satisfying the urges of existence is what everyday life amounts to, for both the snail and the saint. Ayn Rand said, "A desire presupposes the possibility of action to achieve it; action presupposes a goal which is worth achieving."[17]

We do not wish to eat steak when we are a month old or to enter foot races when we are eighty. Our urges come to correspond with our abilities. Social desires are generated within us corresponding to when our group needs us to have them. When we hear our homeland has been attacked, the group assumes we will feel threatened and angry, with our blood pressure rising alongside feelings of patriotism. They are seldom disappointed. We do not have to be taught to love our kids, our countries and our gods; we do it naturally.

Our internal urges and impulses are filtered through our senses and actions to achieve our goals. We feel desires and we devise strategies for their satisfaction. The process can be imagined as a turning inward and outward, of feeling first, followed by thinking and planning, followed again by feeling. We act and react until our desires are satisfied or until we recognize that under the current circumstances they cannot be. Thinking and feeling is the process by which we evaluate where we stand in the world. What we think about something is not the same as how we feel about it.

Figure 4-6

Nature decides which attributes are malleable by nurture

Satisfying urges is what it means to be alive. If we correctly interpret internal motivations and find ways to satisfy them, we win. Wanting, and acting in ways that satisfy those wants, settles the question of the meaning of life. *To live is to desire and to seek satisfaction for our desires.*

To live rightly is to desire properly and to satisfy those desires in the culturally appropriate way. The tiger gets hungry. This is need. Need serves no purpose unless it is accompanied by the possibility of satisfying it. Living well begins with desiring rightly, that is, satisfying only proper desires while suppressing or eliminating unworthy ones. This is true for the tiger and the man. If the only desire the tiger feels is to rest, he will soon die from hunger. If the tiger becomes hungry, but chooses only to fill his stomach with water, he will also starve. The animal must desire rightly, and for a tiger that means desiring meat. He must hunt properly too. He must look around and evaluate his opportunities (thinking) to get food. If he desires meat (feeling) and observes that food is available and that he must pursue it. He looks around, sniffs the air, observes his environment and what is available and decides where to go and how he might find food (thinking). He may come across a group of deer but if for some reason he cannot stalk this prey correctly (acting), he will also starve. He must desire (feel) rightly, think properly, and act correctly to survive.

The good/noble man struggles to desire rightly. He controls his urges to violence in peaceful times. He is a moral being. The psychopath shows no moral restraint. He gives in to urges to murder his neighbor. Proper feelings lead to proper thoughts and end with proper actions. This three-step pattern is reciprocal. We feel, we think about how to satisfy our feelings, we then act to carry out our plans. We then reflect on our past acts and evaluate how we "feel" about the consequences of our actions.

Proper feeling, proper thought, and proper action work together and define the successful individual. Morality is just another name for the plan that guides us to a successful life. It is a simple formula that gets complicated as we apply it to the myriad of circumstances in life.

Reality is where need meets opportunity

A wit once noted that the day they develop brain transplants, we should want to be the donor rather than the recipient. Personality and character – individuality – are only superficially things of the body; they are fundamentally aspects of the brain. Tigers don't enjoy the luxury of our enhanced individuality. Most tigers need to think, act and feel in about the same ways as all other tigers.

Tigers all share the same internal truths as they all face very similar external facts. Not so we humans. We may face external facts we cannot change; the sun rises and sets every day for us as it does for the Inuit or the primitive equatorial native islander. Yet we don't always share the same truths about them. For me the sun can be a star; for others it may be an astrological symbol, an evil being or even a god. Cultural factors influence how truths and meanings change from one place to the next.

The father of chemistry, Antoine Lavoisier, married a 14 year-old girl when he was in his thirties. The middle-aged poet Edgar Allen Poe did the same. No one around them objected. Today we wince at the thought. Should a man in his thirties marry a girl in her early teens? What is right? How do we know?

Humans, unlike tigers, do not enjoy identical truths, or even truths that remain static over time. Our facts are physical, our truths biocultural. Tigers do not have much culture; we do. We must be brought up into it. We must be told the things that are truths and how to tell them from lies. We must be told what to think of the sun, the moon, of Argentineans, and of heroin.

Before we can be told anything, we must be receptive to being taught. We cannot follow the commands of a superior unless we have within us the compulsion to look for guidance and follow it when it is found. We cannot, as a group, understand the concept of majorities unless we have within us the idea that what the group is doing is what we must individually do. We look to be guided.

The world is new and exciting when we are children. Everything is interesting. The brighter among us investigate with caution. The fear of Santa Claus is common among the young; when older, we forget how or why this could possibly be so – we are so accustomed to seeing him amiably.

While driving down the road one December, my four-year-old nephew squirmed when I suggested we stop at the shopping mall and see Santa Claus. I asked him why he was hesitant to visit the fat old elf. He responded in an unsure voice, "Where are his claws?"

We may be born with propensities, intuitions and a concept of Plato's forms, but facts and the truths concerning all of them are learned. Should a man called "Claws" be a matter of concern? We can see the fact of the sun, but what is the truth about it? Is it a star or a god? We all see the fact of Santa, but what is the truth behind him? Is he friend or foe?

What is a truth versus what is a fact, the subjective versus the objective: this has usually been the starting point and battleground on which philosophical castles were built and torn down. The proper definition of the sun as a god or as a star, the cause of the rain as emanating from prayer or atmospheric pressures, have usually been the focus of moral arguments and the start of moral theories. It pitted belief against reason, feeling against thinking. But starting from there, we get philosophies that are unclear and imprecise. The better method of understanding our moral nature is to first recognize the dual nature of our subjective truths. Once this is accomplished, we then can turn to the fact/fiction, truth/lie, and rational/irrational aspect of argumentation.

Now that we recognize the two sides of our truths, we will discover how rationality and a-rationality are merely conditions of the intensity of them. We will be better able to explain the variations in moral patterns and find out why we consistently create atheists as well as deists, scientists alongside priests, conservatives arguing with liberals. This chapter has been concerned with the dual nature and two sides of our truths. The next chapter focuses on what we mean by facts. It will contrast rationality with a-rationality and define the difference between truth and fact.

Notes

1. John Pfeiffer, *The Emergence of Man*, 2nd edition (New York: Harper & Row, 1972) 341.

2. Plutarch, *Moralia*, Vol. IV, in *Loeb Classical Library* (Cambridge: Harvard University Press, 2000), 397.

3. Jeremy Bentham, *An Introduction to the Principle of Morals and Legislation* (Kitchener, Ontario: Batoche Books, 2000), 14-15.

4. Frederick Copleston, *A History of Philosophy* (New York: Image Books Doubleday, 1966), 8: 4.

5. Ibid., 6: 312.

6. Ibid., 6: 316.

7. Ibid., 6: 320.

8. Aristotle, *Nicomachean Ethics*, Book II, trans. W. D. Ross, in *The Great Books of the Western World* (UK: Encyclopedia Britannica), Vol. 9.

9. Alfred Huang, *The Complete I Ching* (Rochester Vermont: Inner Traditions, 1998), xx.

10. Compiled from assorted online sources including:
   - http://www.ichingwisdom.com/hsing.html [Retrieved Dec. 12, 2016]
   - https://en.wikipedia.org/wiki/Wu_Xing [Retrieved Dec. 12, 2016]
   - http://www2.hawaii.edu/~freeman/courses/phil101 [Retrieved Dec. 12, 2016]
   - http://www.iep.utm.edu/wuxing/ [Retrieved Dec. 12, 2016]

11. Plato, *The Republic*, trans. Benjamin Jowett, in *The Great Books of the Western World* (UK: Encyclopedia Britannica), Vol. 7.

12. Plato, *Laws*, trans. Benjamin Jowett, in *The Great Books of the Western World* (UK: Encyclopedia Britannica) Vol. 7.

13. Rita Carter, *Mapping the Mind* (Berkley: University of California Press, 2010), 49.

14. Plutarch, *Moralia*, Vol. VI, in *Loeb Classical Library* (Cambridge: Harvard University Press, 2000), 83.

15. Ibid., 53-54.

16. Ibid., 63.

17. Ayn Rand, *Atlas Shrugged* Part 2, Ch. 1 (New York: Random House, 1956), 374.

Chapter 5
Truths and Facts

Facts

Truths

"A man was meant to be doubtful about himself, but undoubting about the truth..."
-G. K. Chesterton[1]

The intensity of our truths determines how amenable we will be to facts

We have two distinct and discernible moral codes within us; these we call our "truths." But this is not the limit of our flexibility. When feeling "right" in either of these moral ways, we also have the capacity of expressing them strongly or weakly as we feel our moral impulses irresistibly or imperceptibly. Our truths are not only left and right; they also can be staunch or slight. We can be diehard anti-abortionists, willing to bomb abortion clinics, or we might be just mildly against the practice, wishing it were outlawed but unwilling to do much about it ourselves. These two states can be viewed respectively as the subjective and the objective.

Figure 5-1

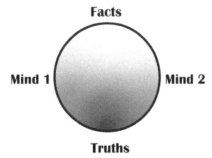

The intensity of our feeling for these emotional positions (our truths) can be illustrated with our familiar diagram of the moral compass. When we feel something strongly, we are nearer the bottom of the compass where our truths are experienced intensely. When we feel only slightly compelled by any emotional position, we are placed near the top of this diagram. We have shaded the colors of the diagram to illustrate the depth of our feelings. Near the bottom of the chart, the colors are strong and deep, while at the top they almost completely fade away. Logical positivists and empiricists give priority to facts, while the focus of metaphysics, the existentialists and the transcendentalists is on truths.

Our dedication to truths reveals our attitude toward facts. If we begin by stating that a truth is something we verify within ourselves and a fact is something that is verified by looking outside ourselves, their definitions seem rather straightforward. Scratch the surface though, and the problem discerning their relationship becomes apparent. Because truths are always our relationship and disposition to facts, and facts matter to us only in so far as our truths allow, we find that truths and facts are interdependent things.

Facts are something recognized by the mind, which, like truth itself, makes their recognition in some way a subjective phenomenon. Color-blind people see things differently from those who see all colors. For a color-blind person, there is no discernible difference between red and green. But for a person who can see color, the two are easily separated. Color-blind people understand that they are limited in this way and that others around them see things differently from them. So we might say that red and green exist for some by experience but for others only in theory. For the people who can see both red and green, these colors exist as a detectible fact. For those who cannot experience them with their senses, red and green only exist as a truth they have been told about. Can something be a fact for one person but only a truth for another? The study of truths and facts can get complicated right away.

TRUTHS GIVE MEANING TO FACTS
Facts are only as important as the truths they support

Truths or beliefs apply meaning to facts. For example, in my part of the country, it rains heavily in the spring. That is a fact. But ascertaining why we care, and what all this raining means to us, is a truth. Rain makes the crops grow, which makes us grow. Rain is good. We need rain. Goodness and need are truths. We live among tall trees and use them for building and burning to keep warm. Satisfying our needs for shelter and warmth are truths.

But being creatures able to interpret the world in multiple ways, we cannot help but see everything in a number of different lights. Even the rain and the trees are subject to our moral systems. Our moral minds assign meaning to forests, just as they apply meaning to everything else. However, if we suppress our truths, we can see the rain and the trees as things that exist outside our morality.

In Moral Mind 1 – our family morality and our inclusive morality, which favors equality – we can see everything as having near equal value. Trees and forests can be as important as people and pets. In a Mind 2 moral situation, where some things are better than others, people can be more important than trees. Then again, if a serf cuts down one of the king's trees, he might be rightfully hanged. The tree can be seen as more important than the serf. We can have it both ways. More than this, depending on the intensity of our truths, we can strongly believe these things, or only mildly hold to these positions. Maybe we are indifferent to both trees and people, seeing neither as more significant than the other. We are capable of all these emotional positions.

Figure 5-2

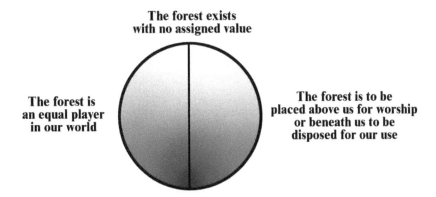

Armed with these variations of truth, we have the capacity to approach the world both superstitiously and scientifically. The more intense our beliefs, the more we operate at the lower portions of the illustration; the less attached we are to our human relationship with the situation, the more objectively and scientifically we see the situation.

Figure 5-3

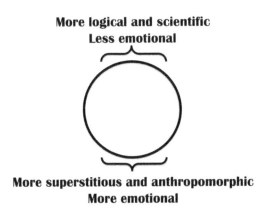

Things have meaning only in relation to what they mean to us. Applying subjective value (that is, "truth") to things has been vital to our survival. The same tree can be important or unimportant, necessary or expendable. Truths give meaning and importance to facts. One single tree can be many things.

Quad-Realism

LOGICAL Trees exist. Their existence is independent of ours and has no meaning beyond material reality.		
MIND 1 Trees have as much right to exist as we do. Trees deserve equal consideration.	**MIND 2** Trees can be above us or below us; they can be sacred and worthy of worship and protection or only have value in relation to how we choose to use them.	
A-LOGICAL **ANTHROPOMORPHIC** Trees can have deep and important meaning, but only as determined by one or the other of the moral minds through which we view them.		

The sun is necessary to our existence. How do we make sure it comes out and shines tomorrow? This is an important question. Is the sun a god or a ball of fire? Does its continued existence depend on our worshiping it? Do we need to be right with a god-creator of all things, lest he make the sun go dim? Will the sun shine regardless of our worshiping it? Answering these questions is important. Morally, we can answer them in any of these ways. Survival depends on applying the proper truth to our fact.

In modern times, we have figured out that the sun will shine reliably regardless of our disposition toward it. But this was not always known. And its shining was important. So, way back when people imagined they needed to pray to keep it blazing above us, it made sense to do just that. It also made sense to see as dangerous anyone who refused to pray. The sun existed, that was a fact; we depended upon it for survival; that was a fact too. We had to do whatever we could to be sure it continued to do what we needed it to do. The sun had a cultural meaning and it needed to be understood and addressed in a certain way; that was the truth. People who did not adhere to our truths might put the rest of us in danger.

FACTS AND TRUTHS: HOW DO THEY DIFFER?
The rational and a-rational

Truths are a-rational. Beauty is in the mind of the beholder, beauty is a truth, and beauty is a-rational. A human child can be beautiful to a human parent; but it is just dinner to the mosquito or the tiger.

Facts are different. Facts establish and affirm knowledge, which exists beyond us and which describes what happens outside of us, in the world of cause and effect. Facts are independently verifiable. Facts are rational. The happy parent and the hungry tiger physically observed the same things when they looked at the child, but they did not psychologically see the same truth. The tiger saw the baby as a dinner not unlike that of every other it has eaten; the parent sees an object of irreplaceable uniqueness and inestimable value. Truths conform to needs and delineate desires; facts conform to external reality outside of desire. The physical presence of the child was a fact to both tiger and parent. The subjective value of the baby differed. Internally the tiger valued the meal. Internally the parent valued the life. Both shared the same facts, but differed in their truths.

The following are not facts; all are truths held by someone. When there are no longer people who hold these views, they will no longer exist:

- *All men are created equal.*
- *Men are not equal - and to treat unequals equally is not justice.*
- *The only thing we have to fear is fear itself.*
- *Allah exists.*
- *A human is more intrinsically valuable than a flea.*
- *The Unites States of America exists.*

All are truths; none are facts. All can be felt, none objectively verified outside of humanity. All are dispositions; none are physical reality. A fact is any event before, outside of, or unaffected by our emotional dispositions. The sun exists; labeling it as good or bad, or calling it a god has no effect on it. The location, the area, the borders, boundary length, coastline, etc. of the land we refer to as "the United States of America" are all geographical facts about its territory. But as a socio-political entity, with its own history, culture, values, traditions, way of life, and beliefs, the United States of America exists only in truth. The terrorist does not hold the same truths about the United States of America as does the patriot – or the immigrant, or the visitor, or the foreigner on a student visa. And even among its own citizens, the meaning of what it is to be American varies widely.

A person was killed by another person; this is a fact. That the person deserved to die, or did not deserve to, are matters of internal moral judgment. The man is dead - that is a fact; that his killing was justified or was not justified is a truth.

If we conclude his killing was unjustified by either Moral Mind 1 or 2, we might react by demanding justice. Justice is giving something what it deserves, as understood by one of our two moral outlooks. Depending on which Moral Mind we are operating in, we see justice differently. Justice is shaping events appropriately in order to be seen as right by our Moral Mind 1 or 2.

Mind 1 Sympathetic horizontal equality	Mind 2 Ethical verticality
The culture that produced the killer must be considered.	The killer is responsible; the culture is also damaged by his act, and we must protect the culture as well as the individuals in it.
The victim has no more inherent value than the criminal.	The criminal proved by his act that he is of less value to the culture than his law-abiding victim.
The criminal still has value; an effort to correct and rehabilitate should be attempted.	The criminal needs to be punished, exiled or eliminated, not only to protect society from his further misdeeds, but as an example to other wrongdoers.

If a man openly and publically threatens us, we might get scared or we might get mad, but what can we do about it? That depends on our culture. Proper action is both a personal and a cultural thing.

In former Mind 2 times of vertical self-reliance, we had to defend ourselves. If we live in a Mind 1 leaning society – as much of America lives today – we live in a culture of wealthy social dependence on the group. If we feel threatened, we are no longer thought morally justified to act alone. We are encouraged to call the police. In a Mind 1 culture, the group handles the problem for us.

If we are part of a severe Mind 2 culture and our family is insulted, we may kill the aggressor on the spot, or challenge him to a duel. In a Mind 2 culture, what others think of us matters. Because it is a Mind 2 culture, we know that times are tough. In lean times, government is too small to handle every personal dispute. We are individually responsible for our own wellbeing. Both methods can be right. Calling in a social arbitrator can be right in a Mind 1 world; reacting with personal violence to an insult or a threat can be right in a Mind 2 period. We are successful because the morality that guides our actions can vary to meet our circumstances.

Verifying truths and facts

Our subjective and internal feelings are fundamentally different things from the *reality* of external sense experience. But feelings are real to us, just as real as the objects of our senses. To the individual, both are real at once. But with others, only external reality can be a shared experience. We never really know by immediate experience what other people are feeling, though we know what they are seeing or hearing. We are only clued in on their feelings by how they act.

Our internal reality of feelings may be similar to the internal feelings felt by others, but our feelings are immediately knowable only to us. External reality is knowable to everybody. Action becomes a relationship between both. Though the internal is a private world of subjective motivations and the external a public realm of cold and uncaring cause-and-effect facts, our flexible brains comprehend each of these as parallel and equally valid spheres of reality.

Consciousness is our name for the point where these two worlds meet; consciousness is the apprehension of internal desire meeting external physicality. Consciousness is where the subjective meets the objective. To us, our hunger is as much a reality as the empty plate staring us in the face. But the hunger is a truth known only to us; the empty plate is visible to all. Hunger is a truth; the empty plate is a fact.

Truths are subjectively verifiable; facts are objectively verifiable. The two processes are similar but not identical. Truths are not facts. Yet, at the level of consciousness they are treated similarly.

Truths come to us through introspection. They are our goals, beliefs, values and virtues verified differently from facts. Truths tell us what to make of facts. It is a truth that adults should protect children and shield others from harm. It is a truth that your puppy is cute and the neighbor's dog a menace. It is a truth that you should not rape, kill and steal. These are subjective human beliefs; they are not physical laws of the universe. They are not facts.

Truths are verified inwardly. Truths are shaped to conform to either our Mind 1 or Mind 2 morality. Our two moral methods construct them. This explains why truths often contradict each other. It is a truth that though *thou shalt not steal*, it can also be true that it can be right to steal when taking from those who have more and giving to others who may die from having so much less. We can have it both ways. *Thou shalt not steal* is a command from above, issued from a vertically higher authority, so we know it is a Mind 2 outlook. Taking from those who have too much to equalize and share with those who have too little is a Mind 1 sympathetic and equalizing outlook. Both points of view can be felt by us. We are vertical and horizontal creatures with a dual morality.

Mind 1 truth struggles to recognize and react to the injustice of the gap between richer and poorer – to see the herd in terms of haves and have-nots; justice in our Mind 1 comes through redressing these wrongs and reforming the wrongdoers. Mind 1 justice is recognizing that everyone has something to offer. Mind 2 truths keep us on guard against rule breakers, thwarters of custom, flouters of decorum, foreigners, outsiders and physical danger, Method 2 finds it true that some of us are better than others; through it we understand that there is justice in punishment and proper retaliation. Which variant of *truth* we feel, believe and adhere to is determined by the situation at hand. In easy times, we focus on Mind 1 sharing; in tougher times we lean toward Mind 2 prioritization of people and resources.

Outside our world of truths exists the world of facts. Reality to the conscious mind is the interplay between them. Any morally challenging situation – for example, what to do about crime – can be diagramed to show how the problem is addressed by the truth of each moral mind, and also looked at amorally or ultra-morally.

Criminality

LOGICAL
Behaviors are animalistic expressions with no moral components.

MIND 1
People are not good or bad; only their actions can be. Bad behavior needs to be rehabilitated and corrected.

MIND 2
People can be good or bad. We know which of these they are by how they act. Deviant behavior should be punished, the deviant removed from society if necessary.

A-LOGICAL ANTHROPOMORPHIC
Ultimate punishment or ultimate rehabilitation and forgiveness can be possible.

We label as facts the objects and actions outside ourselves and beyond our truths. Facts are verifiable by others. They are known by looking outward. When we look at things "factually" or "objectively," we are looking at them impersonally and would diagram this outlook near the top of our chart. When we look at things as truths, we see them from a psychological vantage diagrammed at the lower portion of our chart.

As an example, let us look at a case of simple assault. A guy I do not know approached me in an alley, demanded my wallet, and when I was slow in turning it over, he stabbed me. Our mind understands the interaction in a number of ways. It is a fact I was cut with a knife. It is a fact I reacted to it by calling for help. But it is only a truth, and not a fact, that it was done undeservedly, and by a villain. It is also a subjective truth that my wounds hurt. It is a moral position – a truth, and not a fact – that it was unjust. And it is a truth, not a fact, that I should either retaliate or turn the other cheek. The physical details are facts; the motivations, goals, and emotions behind them are truths. Morality is truth in action. *Living is the process of turning our truths into facts.*

SURVIVAL DEPENDS ON THE INTEGRATION OF TRUTHS AND FACTS
Subjective and objective relevance
Hume's/Schopenhauer's fact/value distinction

Armed with two ways of feeling truth - our Mind 1 and Mind 2 – we have two standards by which we can interpret right and wrong behavior; and as herding creatures, we can only survive with the assistance of others. Therefore, understanding and getting along with other people (agreeing with their truths) is vital. Second in importance to getting along with others in our group is the requirement to understand the world. We cannot survive if we cannot figure out the world beyond the herd (understanding facts). The world of animals and physical processes is vital to our survival also. We are humans, but we are humans who exist in a non-human world. Understanding both truths and facts is imperative.

Things have objective and subjective relevance. Mom exists as another being and she exists as our mother. What and who she is, is determined objectively and subjectively. She exists objectively as any other creature and subjectively in relation to us and our group. Our moms exist subjectively with a relative value unique to us personally or to humans generally. To the universe outside human morality, mom is just a particular jumble of atoms.

These two things – the world of humans and the world of everything else – are as distinct as two separate universes. The way in which we deal with one has no relation to how we must deal with the other. To deal successfully with humans, we must act rightly in the realm of truths. To succeed in the world outside humanity, we must ascertain facts. Facts exist outside the world of right and wrong. Truths and facts are two different things. Our survival depends on the proper integration of both.

The world beyond our human herd is not experienced as truth; it is a place completely dominated by fact. The sun does not react to our tears; the rain does not respond to our prayers; it could never be enough that we understood this external world only subjectively. To make the most sense of the non-human universe, we have had to develop some ability to understand it logically, that is, understand the world *outside* of our own subjective truths. We had to grasp that there is a world that exists without us, and that goes on existing regardless of what it means to us.

The great division of human understanding is not between our two subjective lines of truth; it is not in the ends sought in the subjective battles going on within us between our Mind 1 truths and our Mind 2 truths. The greatest challenge in human comprehension comes in trying to unite the subjective internal world of our feelings with the objective external world of physical reality. Survival depends on deciding in every moment how to act. If we are hungry and we come across a tiger eating a deer, what do we do?

Do we act right now as if what mattered most is our own human desire, or do we act right now as if our desires do not matter as much as the impossibility of getting that deer away from the tiger? Wanting the deer and actually getting it from the tiger are two different things.

Mastering the first, the world of the subjective, the world of human truths, is necessary for us to best deal with other people. But these human subjective values have no impact on the external non-human world. It has been by understanding and conquering the non-human world of the objective that we have been able to rule nature. Mastering the subjective world allows us to deal with humans; mastering the objective world allows us to deal with everything else. Without a viable plan to overcome the strength of the carnivore, we survive by accepting the "fact" that we will not be eating deer today. We have internalized this realization. This means we have accepted that this fact is also now a truth.

Suppressing truths to allow facts to reveal themselves

The mind allows us to ascertain fact, to understand reality outside of human need. We accomplish this by suppressing our urges to truth, by mitigating our impulse to apply human meanings to non-human things. The less strongly we feel our truths, the more clearly we see the facts. In order to understand the sun as a plasma of ions continually involved in nuclear fusion, we first had to grasp that it was not a god and not an object placed in the heavens to provide for man.

This way – *seeing the world as it is rather than how it relates to us* – opens up a new perspective on the universe. The spring rains come or do not come depending on factors completely outside humanity. Our rain dances have no real effect on them. The sun exists; it rises and it sets, not as part of an integrated whole that includes humans, and not as an object whose existence depends on us doing our part to keep it shining; the sun exists independently of humanity. In this separate and objective way to see things, the rain and sun are in no way reliant upon us. Both existed before man, will exist after man, and neither takes any account at all of man. Our religious sacrifices, our hunger, our thirst and our drowning matter not to them. Neither our love nor our hatred of them makes any difference at all. If the sun died out tomorrow, it would not, could not, care. Only *we* care about human things. Caring about anything is not an aspect of the rain or the sun.

Quad-Realism

LOGICAL The sun exists independently of us and its existence is not related or dependent on human action, need, or existence.	
MIND 1 **Horizontal Subjective** The sun is a coequal part of the shared universe alongside us that we both fit into.	**MIND 2** **Vertical Subjective** The sun is an object that fits in to the scheme of things above or below us. What it does for us or what we do for it matters.
A-LOGICAL/ANTHROPOMORPHIC The sun exists for human purposes; its existence has meaning only in how it relates to us.	

Using the four-sided pictograph above, we can show how someone is emotionally relating to an object. People who are relatively objective thinkers, that is, they prefer objective facts to subjective truths, show up near the top. If they lean objective but have conservative expectations of others, they would be marked at about the two o'clock position. If a person is a deeply subjective liberal who puts her ideals of right before arguments of feasibility, they might be at the eight o'clock position. A guru or monk looking inward and dismissing all the cares of the outside world might be at six o'clock on our diagram. In a large community, we are surrounded by all types of people. Each one of us can feel it correct to look at any situation from these different vantage points. Each of us can be objective and logical, sympathetic Mind 1, ethical Mind 2, or spiritual. Collectively, an assortment of people feeling things in all these possible ways makes up our human herds. Working together, we watch for danger and look for opportunities from every direction.

Figure 5-4

Medical people coined the term "neuroplasticity" to describe the pliability of the brain in allocating resources to deal with the challenges it faces. If one part of the brain is damaged, it might convert other undamaged portions to a new use. In a similar vein, we understand humanity as having a certain amount of psycho-plasticity. Like the hand, which evolved to be flexible and suited for many uses, our psyches have an enormous range of cooperative capability. Our personality and character develop not only in accordance with a genetic predisposition, but also in response to the challenges of the real world we move in. A person facing constant danger is likely to develop a psychological profile different from the person who lives constantly in the lap of luxury and safety.

We are internally motivated through two directions of truth in order to best protect and provide. We protect and provide by sometimes focusing on dangers and inequalities from within the group (Mind 1 truths) and other times by watching for trouble from outside it (Mind 2 truths). Most of us develop the habit of feeling consistently one way, either as a Mind 1 type or a Mind 2 type. By being a member of a herd, we are assured that there will always be those among us who look out in the other direction (moral individuality). But both these outlooks are human-focused and herd-directed; they have no bearing on any world beyond humanity. The Mississippi river does not care that your child is healthy or terminally ill.

We can never turn our truths completely off. After all, the reason we need to understand the outside world is to better acquire what the inside world (our subjective desires) demands of us. We need to retain the capacity to minimize the application of our subjective truths to better understand what we objectively observe. There is a greater world around us, apart from human desire. To satisfy our needs, we had to comprehend success as a relationship between subjective desire and objective (non-human) reality around us.

When our two internal moral task masters run up against the unbending laws of nature and the amorality of other creatures, survival often depends upon our moral compulsions yielding. When we cannot pray the mosquito away, we must kill it; when we cannot kill them all, we must protect our babies with mosquito netting. Our subjective desires must be able to bow to objective reality. When they do this, we survive.

Figure 5-5:

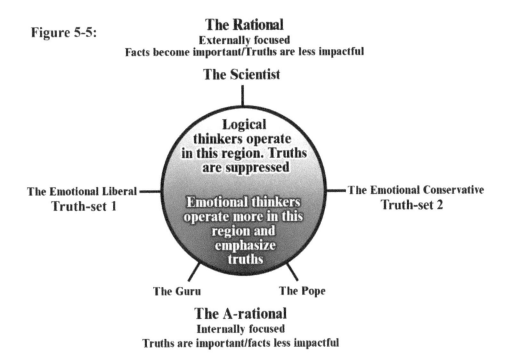

Life is the meeting of the internal and subjective with the external and objective

We are hungry. We may want to eat the buffalo, but we cannot until we figure out how to make and use the spear. The spear does not get made just because we wish it. The hardest part of making a spear is the initial conception of it. Until we could do that, nothing like it could ever be used. The spear can be invented only after we acquired the capacity to imagine a world where it might exist, along with a mastery of the physical environment that allows us to create it by combining sticks with sharpened stones. We pick up a stick and throw it at the animal; others pick up stones and hurl it at the beasts. Then, one day, someone attached the stone to the stick and changed the world.

We suppress desires in order to understand the world as it really is (or as we assume it to be) outside us. Those better able to do this we call the unemotional or logical type. These folks seem a bit more capable than others in grasping the events of the world physically and unsentimentally. When we suppress both our Mind 1 and Mind 2 urges to apply meanings to facts, we see things as we presume they really are. People vary in their ability to do this. Not everyone can suppress his or her own urges to morality in the same way.

Life is lived at the point where the internal and subjective meets the external and objective. The living are distinguished from the dead by their assignment of purpose and meaning to the physical reality around them. They have goals and assign values. The tiger gets hungry and looks around for a meal. The big cat must identify, run down and kill its dinner. The tiger takes no account of the hopes, dreams, and urges of the deer or the human it destroys and consumes. That the human or the deer is a mother or a leader in their own herd makes no difference to the tiger. The tiger, like the human and the deer, lives at the meeting point between its own subjective urges and objective reality. We have no moral value to tigers beyond being food.

Quad-realism: Two examples

With four ways to understand the world (quad-realism) – a logical and amoral outlook, a deep and completely moral and anthropomorphic outlook, and between these poles two moral patterns of human right and wrong (sympathetic and ethical) – understanding anything grows complicated.

For example, sex is a great source of pleasure, and the family it produces is a necessary component for the continuation of the group. Having sex, getting more sex, and controlling sex consume a great deal of personal and social energy. So what is the proper attitude toward having and watching other people have sex? Does sex have a moral component? The answer in our own mind becomes both Yes and No.

The quad-realism diagram below outlines the range of moral attitudes that we routinely adopt towards the practice, enjoyment and control of sex, and classifies them into strong and weak expressions of our dual moral outlook.

Quad-Realism
Sexuality/Pornography/Abstinence

LOGICAL
Truths are suppressed and no meaning beyond the physical is applied.

Sex is simply human reproductive animalistic behavior.

MIND 1 Horizontalism **The good of the individual comes before the good of the group.** Sex and even pornography are justified and accepted as simple personal pleasures. As long as no one is hurt, anything goes.	**MIND 2 Verticality** **Sex may be wrong and bad unless performed under the proper circumstances and for the right reasons.** The good of the group should be considered before the personal pleasures of the participants. Sexual control is paramount to ensure such a strong instinct is directed to accomplish proper ends.

A-LOGICAL
ANTHROPOMORPHIC
For the purpose of ultimate proper guidance, sex might be completely eliminated, promoted to excess, or ceremonially performed as is required.

Violence, like sex (and everything else), is looked at in two subjective ways (Mind 1 or Mind 2). Violence can be right or wrong, depending on which subjective viewpoint dominates us at the moment. These moral feelings can also be felt *strongly* and extremely, or *weakly* and mildly so that our feelings about them hardly matter at all. This gives us a four-way pattern by which we might look at war, violence, and militarism too.

Quad-Realism
Wars and personal violence

LOGICAL
Territoriality and protective aggression are common to many animals and are manifested in humans as wars or personal battles.

MIND 1
Wars and violence are always wrong. Everyone is a loser.

MIND 2
Violence is often needed to protect the group from dangers posed from without or miscreant behavior from within the herd. Killing can be justified.

A-LOGICAL/ANTHROPOMORPHIC
Ritualistic violence or its complete elimination can find their justification in the subjective needs of humanity. Ritualistic human sacrifice or the complete repudiation of harm, even to the smallest creature, can be justified in a purely internally facing viewpoint.

We can tone down (though never quite turn off) our moral minds and see these acts, and all others, from a logical vantage. In the illustrations above, we have created neat boxes into which we separate our capacity to understand the world into four patterns. The illustrations make them appear clear and distinct. But in reality our moral outlooks blend slowly one into the other. As a moral Mind 2 outlook weakens with safety and security, it passes over the top of our moral compass through an amoral period where neither moral mind holds sway, and then into a weak Mind 1 point of view. Passing from a Mind 2 point of view into a Mind 1 outlook requires we pass through a period, however brief, of psychological amoralism.

We possess the ability to jump back and forth and all around our moral compass. We can view, that is, "morally interpret," the same event in a number of moral ways, before we settle upon the proper or "best" way to feel about something. When we find ourselves in a position of abundance, with more food or more money than we need, we debate within our own mind about the "right" thing to do. Do we share it with others? Do we keep it all for ourselves? We know it can be "right" to do either. And often we choose to do a little of both.

The rationality of fact and the a-rationality of truth

We experience and evaluate life in four dimensions, three of them social and personal – god/country/family – and one of them scientific and logical. Our personal and public lives are lived in the light of internal truths, which, carried to extreme, we call "god," or "religion" or "ultimate right." Then again, our personal and public lives can be lived more in relation to the external world of non-human fact; we call this "the world of science, mathematics, and technology."

Taught the methods of family, we learn how to interact with people personally. We are taught our group's politics and we learn trades and social relations. We are taught our clan's religion and we are given an ultimate base for moral goals and traditions. We are taught the world beyond human desires; we are introduced to lions, volcanoes, and gravity – things that seem unresponsive to human need. As we move toward the top of our moral compass, we are responding in more logical and unemotional ways; toward the bottom, we are more emotional and a-rational.

Figure 5-6

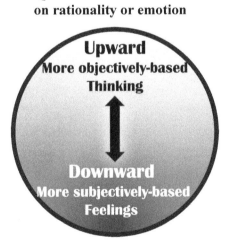

Questions decided based
on rationality or emotion

TURNING FACTS INTO TRUTHS AND TRUTHS INTO FACTS

We have already seen that truths assign meaning to facts. For example, if your neighbor calls you a jerk, his action can be viewed in three ways:

Figure 5-7

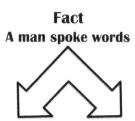

Fact
A man spoke words

Their Moral Meaning	**Their Moral Meaning**
Mind 1	**Mind 2**
His opinion means no more than mine or anyone else's. I should ignore him.	He openly insulted me. I attacked him in justified retaliation.

Objectively, words were spoken. But how do I interpret them emotionally? If I am in a Mind 1 frame of mind, I might interpret his utterance as just one opinion among many, which he is quite entitled to express, and pay it little heed – it's a free world! From a Mind 2 perspective, on the other hand, I might view it as a deliberate insult, an assault on my character, and feel called upon to react in some way. His behavior, I feel, is rude and uncivilized.

The same facts – the spoken words – can be interpreted in different ways to reveal different truths about the world. Is the world a place where everyone is equal and free to express whatever opinion they happen to possess? Or is it a world where verticality and social propriety demand courtesy and respect between neighbors?

Turning facts into truths assigns meaning to the world.

Since facts can mean multiple things to us, the way we react to them will be a function of their meaning to us. Facts, by themselves, don't move us to action. We must feel some way about the facts in order to feel motivated to act. I might react to being insulted by ignoring it, or I might strike out at my verbal assailant. Justice is doing what is right, but justice can be seen in different ways. If we are of a Mind 1 persuasion and we discover one man has punched another in retaliation over an insult, we might be appalled and demand justice – that is, we might demand the fighter be arrested and controlled. If we are of a Mind 2 persuasion, seeing a man react to an insult by ignoring it might indicate the insulted party was a coward or that any man who allows himself to be insulted probably deserves to be. Right, in Mind 2, might be to punch the insulter in the nose. A Mind 2 leaning judge looking at a case where the person who openly insulted someone was punched in the face might dismiss the case as an instance of understandable provocation that had been settled on the spot.

Both points of view can be right. But logic cannot be right. Logic is just logic. Logic is not justice. Logic favors no act over another. Logic is not right or wrong. A person looking upon the scene in a purely rational and logical outlook cannot judge which action was right or wrong, justified or not. In a strictly logical outlook, there is no moral pronouncement to be made.

How miscreants are dealt with are matters of moral, not logical, outlook. We may punish, kill and torture (Moral Mind 2) or we may parole, attempt to reform and try to rehabilitate (Moral Mind 1). The "whys" justifying our actions are subjective and a-rational and have only circumstantial association with facts. Moral outrages, doing a good deed, doing one's duty, or simply acting rightly, are all subjective moral concepts. Our physical efforts, our acts and our lives are reactions to these subjective conceptions. All voluntary actions are based on subjective emotions. All action is an attempt to turn our truths into facts. *Making our facts conform to our truths gives meaning to life.*

Turning our truths into facts assigns meaning to life.

To be human is to imagine our truths might somehow be *objectively* valid. This is the great illusion of life. Subjective reality assigns meaning to ostensibly objective and meaningless action. Without subjective motivation, there is no reason to prefer life to death, food to poison, eating a fish to eating a Finlander. Our moral codes of Mind 1 or Mind 2 can discern right from wrong, but as any act relates to objective reality, it cannot be right or wrong; it can only be a fact or a fiction.

It is not right or wrong that the sun rises in the east and not in the west. But it can be right or wrong, advantageous or disadvantageous to human beings if we fail to get up at sunrise and go to work. Facts and truths are two separate methods of understanding reality; looking outward for confirmation about what is "real" or looking inward for what is "valuable." The opposite of a fact is a fiction. When operating from our logical outlook, "truths" are seen as fictions too. The opposite of truths are lies in the bottom quadrant. And facts can be seen as lies if they contradict long held beliefs. For the ancient Roman, the "fact" that Zeus does not exist seems a "lie." For the Roman operating in a logical frame of mind, the existence of Zeus is a "fiction."

- The deliberate misrepresentation of a fact is a "fiction."
- The deliberate misrepresentation of a truth is a "lie."

Figure 5-8

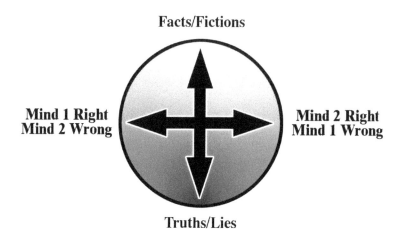

Executing or trying to rehabilitate murderers is never *factually* the right thing to do, and can only be *truthfully* the right thing to do as it coincides with our moral outlook. *"The right thing to do"* can never be a matter of fact; it must be a matter of truth. This is not easily understood.

Getting married or not getting married, or being homosexual or heterosexual are all truths that have relevance for the herd we are a part of. They have no objective significance in a physical world where it does not matter if we even exist or what we do. Actions have meaning to us, not to the world. Meaning is subjective. When we act, we are trying to influence the world to make it conform to our desires.

> *We add meaning to life when ...*
> *what we __feel__ is "truth" subjectively,*
> *we strive to __know__ as "fact" objectively.*

Turning our truths into facts is a liminal potentiality. A truth and a fact are forever insuperable things. But our mind deals with them in a parallel fashion and does so, so casually that distinguishing one from the other is not always easy — and not always productive either.

The country must be defended, the kids need to go to school, we need to put Christ back into Christmas, and a fat Santa has recently become a bad example for the kids. All are truths being put forward by somebody as candidates to be made into facts. We struggle to influence.

Culture, habit, politics, and religion are social configurations perpetually employed at convincing us that our truths could be, should be and must be made facts. Turning truths into facts is how we protect and provide for ourselves and the herd.

THE RELATIVE IMPORTANCE OF TRUTHS AND FACTS

Which is more important to us: truths or facts? The question answers itself. Importance is a concept of internal relevance. Importance is a concept certified only through truths. Truths must be more important than facts, because without truths, we are indifferent to facts. Outside human existence, the pine tree is no more important than the pebble, the chicken no more important than the child. But within human culture, one may be far more valuable and important than the other.

We love our own children more than we love other people's children. But can we ascertain if our children are *factually* most worth loving? Does this make sense?

If it can be demonstrated empirically that the neighbor's children are *in fact* better and more worthy than our own because they are smarter, kinder, have won beauty contests and spelling bees, do we conclude that *we should* love these other children more than our own? Of course not! The thought is absurd on its face. The phrase "worth loving" indicates we are operating in the world of the subjective. Worth is a condition of truth and not fact. In this sense, we recognize that we love children, or anything else, not because they are "worth" it, but because they fulfill some subjective purpose for us. We do not necessarily love those people who are objectively *worth* loving; we love those we are supposed to love We can factually determine better from worse when it comes to physical conditions, like the fastest runner. But we cannot determine better from worse in personal relationships, which are based on subjective relations of truth.

We can no more hinge our love for our children on their relative worth than we can determine our love of country or of our gods based on how they stack up to other nations and other people's deities. None are conditions of fact. Love is not a condition of fact.

Everyone assumes each parent loves his child most, and we would be suspicious if anyone suggested otherwise, or who asked us such foolish questions. Love is based on truths, not facts. We do not "objectively" decide who is worth loving; it seems to be "subjectively" decided for us.

That Neptune is almost three billion miles from the earth is as much a fact as that a grain of rice can be grown and used by people for food. That one of these facts is more vital to human existence and therefore "truthfully" more important to know is a subjective condition. Being wrong about the rice affects us more than being wrong about the planet.

Intention is a matter of truths. With no emotional value, no one deliberately misrepresents a fact. One can be mistaken, but one is only purposefully incorrect to promote or subvert a truth. Politicians may technically lie when they promise to cut federal spending or cure homelessness when they know neither will factually happen in their lifetime. But it is the truth of the statement we look for, not always the fact. Proper intent counts more than the likelihood of the result in a world dominated by truth.

All voters acknowledge and excuse his politicians' lapses in factuality as long as they are convinced their leaders are struggling to promote a shared truth. We trust that as long as the office holders are trying to guard the herd from dangers we believe are upon us, the details are dispensable. Liberal Democrats who watched their leader, Bill Clinton, team up with Republicans to pass legislation limiting the growth of the welfare state in 1994 felt betrayed. Yet most citizens supported his re-election in 1996. Why? His campaign promises still seemed more in step with their subjective truths than the words of his political opponent. What our politicians do is far less important to us than what they promise they are trying to do. Truths always matter more than facts, because facts only matter at all in relation to how they affect our truths.

A restaurateur advertises his spaghetti is the best ever cooked. Car insurance is peddled to us by an animated talking lizard suggesting it is the cheapest we will find. We look the other way at the absurdity and hyperbole when we understand that both are getting across a truth that the meal is good and the needed insurance is as cheap as possible. Truths identify our ends; facts are merely the means we use to achieve them. We tolerate factual inaccuracies and exaggerations as long as our truths are upheld.

When my daughter lies to me about a bad grade on her school report card, I get angry. But realizing that she hid the grade to both escape punishment and avoid disappointing me, I calm down. Her fear of punishment is sympathetically understandable; and her trying to remain good and capable in my eyes is ethically proper. I realize she wanted to do better and I trust she will try harder in the future. Should the day arrive when she no longer feels badly about a poor grade, and when she no longer cares what I think of her school performance, then I will really be angry. When that day arrives, I will realize that she no longer shares my truth, which is that it is vital she do well in school. Should that day arrive, I will wish to return to the days when she lied to protect herself and me, guarding our shared truth.

SHARED SELECTIVE ABSTRACTIONS: THE CASE OF "GRIZZLY MAN"

In 2005, a film documentary was made about a man named Timothy Treadwell, titled "Grizzly Man." It was a compellation of home movies made and narrated by a man who voluntarily went to live among bears in the wild. He set up his camera and filmed himself moving close to the beasts as they ate, fought, and otherwise meandered around. Treadwell, the Grizzly Man, gave them names, knew the male bears from the female, and believed the growling behemoths reciprocated his respect. He survived for a while. His camera was filming and recorded his screams as he, probably inevitably, was eaten alive.

Director and narrator Werner Herzog, commenting on the spectacle, marveled how Treadwell, the Grizzly Man, could have imagined that these wild bears recognized him and accepted him as a companion. Truth for Treadwell was apparently not truth for the bears. When one old bear became too retched or too ill to catch fish or gather food, Treadwell became the handiest item on the menu. As he died in agony just off screen, we are left to wonder if he imagined himself a fool, or felt betrayed by a pal.

To be a fool or to believe you were betrayed would require imagining that your initial truths were incorrect. This I doubt he could do. He probably just believed he strayed a bit too close. Up until the end, I think he felt his truths were right and unassailable. He probably believed he erred in fact by getting too near to a sick bear, but right up to the end it is likely he did not question his truths.

Should Treadwell, the Grizzly Man, have filmed the bears in such a way? What is right? Psychologists devised a phrase, "selective abstraction," to describe people who pick out events or things and give them undue weight and unjustified value. If this definition is correct, then all behavioral diversity can be understood as mere selective abstractions.

When I recognize that your personality and character differ from my own, it is just another way of saying we subjectively value things differently. We can ask ourselves, how much should we value something? Such things are at the root of understanding when we ask questions like, "Was Treadwell's life wasted?"

How can we answer that? Who is to be the judge? A Mind 1 leaning person might shrug it off, saying he died doing exactly what he wanted to do. A Mind 2 person might condemn it as a life wasted in pursuit of a personal extravagance that in no way contributed toward recognized social values.

We are trying to present a truth as if it could be a fact. How a life is valued and when it is right to be given up depend on subjective notions of truth and cannot be answered in terms of facts. The fundamental division of subjective morality into Mind

1 horizontalism and Mind 2 verticality can both justify and condemn the result. His life can be seen as both having been worth living and having been wasted. Right can also be wrong.

Was Timothy Treadwell's Choice of a Lifestyle Right?

LOGICAL

There is no inherently moral component to life or death. His actions prompted reactions. Neither his life nor his death matter in any absolute way. There is no such thing as a correct lifestyle.

MIND 1

His life is his own, and he should do with it as he pleases as long as he harms no one else. One choice is as good as another. His life and death had meaning to him and the others with whom he interacted. Each lifestyle is correct for the person who chooses it.

MIND 2

His life was wasted. It was neither lived nor lost for any other purpose than his self- indulgent pleasures. Customarily and traditionally, people do not go to live among bears. Nothing was gained by his death except to serve as an example of a bad way to live and a foolish way to die. His lifestyle was wrong.

A-LOGICAL/ANTHROPOMORPHIC

His life and his death had deep and important meaning, though it may be debated exactly what that meaning was.

RATIONALITY, A-RATIONALITY AND IRRATIONALITY

Behavior is a-rationality seeking to be made rationality

All human emotions, feelings, desires and motivations are, by their very nature, a-rational (or non-rational). That is, they are not within the domain of what can be understood by reason; they are not observable or measurable by others and are not understood in terms of logic or cause and effect. We cannot observe others feeling want, fear and need, or desiring love. These are internal, emotional and therefore a-rational intuitions, known immediately only to the individual. Others can never predict with complete accuracy when and how you feel these things. Loves, hates, and appetites emerge from your psyche irregularly. Our a-rational desires are not graded in the same way as facts.

"A-rational" does not mean the same thing as "irrational." It is a-rational to fear a bear, but it is not irrational. However, it is irrational to fear a common housefly. In everyday conversation, we often apply the words "rational" and "irrational" to emotions in order to distinguish between ones that appear to be reasonable responses to causes and effects in the real world and ones that seem to arise out of nowhere, with nothing in a situation to explain them. So we say that it is irrational to fear a housefly, because there is no fact about houseflies that indicates that they can hurt you; but it is rational to fear Grizzly bears, because you know for a fact that they are very large and strong and that, if threatened, will attack and kill you.

We often use the terms "logical" and "illogical" interchangeably with the words "rational" and "irrational." Logic is simply the rules and principles of valid reasoning, so if something is considered rational, it is also considered logical, and vice versa.

As we have noted, something is considered rational and logical only insofar as it can be related to factuality and cause and effect. Desires, wants, needs and truths are a-rational in that they do not reflect a matter of fact that can be objectively observed. However, we may call them "rational" or "logical" if we can reasonably assume that they arose from real-world facts that would normally elicit such a reaction, or "irrational" or "illogical" if we can find no grounds whatsoever for such an assumption.

But what about actions? On the one hand, an action is a fact, insofar as it is observable and verifiable by others. On the other hand, it embodies an intention or an "end" — a desire to fulfill a need — that is itself unobservable. We refer to the observable part of action as "behavior." Behavior is action stripped of all subjectivity — of all desires, motives and intentionality. It is the observable tip of the iceberg in the image below. But actions have both an objective and a subjective side. The subjective side is represented by the unobservable part of the iceberg that lies below the surface of the water. Human action is thus the meeting ground between our internal subjective desires and the cause-effect relationships of the external world, which constrain and direct our actions towards the attainment of our goals, allowing us to turn our truths into facts (observable behavior) and assign meaning (truth) to the facts we observe.

Figure 5-9

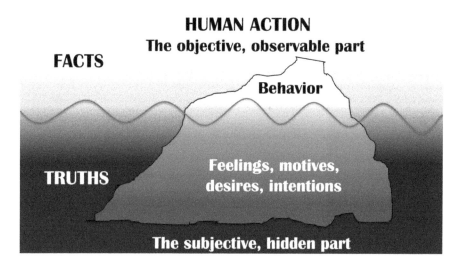

An action is presumed by others to be supportive of whatever end the actor is seeking. If everyone imagines that the action taken will likely lead to the end sought, it will be considered rational and logical. The actions of Timothy Treadwell – to live in close association with wild bears – would be considered irrational or illogical by most, as they would not be presumed to lead to a long, happy, and prosperous life, which we presume he was seeking.

It is a-rational to want to paint your bedroom blue rather than green, but it is not irrational. However, it is irrational to want it blue but to deliberately buy a can of green paint. It is illogical to act in a way where experience has shown that we will likely wind up with facts that do not satisfy our desires.

Rationality and logic are exercised when we attempt to satisfy our desires through action. The close interplay between our subjective truths and impulses along with the acts which emanate from them gives rise to the many words we use to describe the events; rational and irrational, reasonable and unreasonable, logical and illogical, emotional and unemotional.

Behavior gives form to feeling

Every conscious act, human or animal, is an expression of desire attempting to be sated, truth struggling to be made fact.

In common parlance, irrationality is a pejorative term. To say someone is irrational is an insult. It is to suggest they lack sound judgment. But to be human is to be a-rational, which is not the same. Living in any fashion is in some sense counter-factual. That is, we know something is alive when it acts in ways that indicate it is not inanimate and governed solely by physical laws. Concepts like "animal will" emerge in our philosophies.

Gravity brings us down onto the earth. When something appears to willfully stand up and oppose gravity, we confirm it is alive. To live is to prefer one thing to another. Logic and facts do not determine preferences. To prefer is to be, in a sense, acting counter-factually, that is, beyond mere cause and effect. Living things are less predictable because the motives that provoke their actions are inaccessible to the rest of us.

If I throw a ball at a window, and the window breaks, we can say that the physical act of throwing the ball with a certain force and from a certain distance *caused* the window to break. But what "caused" me to throw the ball at the window in the first place? Was I trying to get the attention of my girlfriend by lightly tapping the window of her bedroom, but miscalculated the force of my throw? Or was I exacting revenge on my neighbor for some previous injustice he did to me? This type of "cause" is not a *physical cause*; it is a *motive*. Rather than acting as a "force" that pushes us to a predetermined effect, a motive acts more like a magnet, pulling us in the direction of our preferences, which are subjective, variable and relatively unpredictable.

PROPER AND IMPROPER TRUTHS AND FACTS

Immorality occurs as a result of improper truths or sometimes as a result of proper truths but incorrect facts. Using either "bad truths" or "bad facts" can make us go wrong. For example, we may be properly motivated to feed our kids – this is a good and proper truth shared by the group. But when we do so by feeding them sand, we have misjudged the relationship between our truth and the fact about where such action would take us.

Improper truths

If our children are hungry and we have plenty of money to acquire copious amounts of food but neglect to do so, or if we feed our children sand – knowing it will do them harm – because we are pleased by their pain, then we are not caring rightly; we have "bad truths." Our facts are sound. We understand clearly that the sand will hurt them, but we desire they be hurt.

Neglecting our children and not feeling distressed by their hunger is improper a-rationality. We are not feeling the proper truth. Without proper truths, no action, logical or otherwise, can be moral. Morality, like criminality, lies in intent. We must attempt to act rightly as understood by Moral Mind 1 or Moral Mind 2. *Immorality occurs when we have improper truths motivating us.*

It should be noted, of course, that, since we are dually moral, we have two standards by which we distinguish proper from improper truths. Our Mind 1 and Mind 2 truths often contradict each other, so that what is a proper truth in Mind 2 might be considered an improper truth in Mind 1, and vice versa.

For example, parents who favor the Mind 1 approach feel that children should be allowed, indeed encouraged, to express their individuality and indulge in their own personal tastes and preferences. Hence, children get to eat what they like and when they like, and are not forced to eat what they dislike. Parents who favor a Mind 2 approach, by contrast, believe that their primary role is to pass on to their children the standards and traditions of the group, and this extends to eating habits and behavior around the table. Children are expected to eat when the meals are served, use good manners at the table, and finish everything on their plate, whether they like it or not. For a Mind 2 parent, allowing children to eat whatever and whenever they please is improper. It endangers their health, risks obesity, and fails to teach them the valuable lesson that sometimes we have to forego an immediate pleasure, or accept a bit of displeasure, for the sake of a more important goal. For the Mind 1 leaning parent, on the other hand, the Mind 2 rules and traditions surrounding the supper table are too rigid and out-of-date for today's contemporary life, and constant monitoring, supervising and controlling everything children eat constitute an improper and misplaced display of parental authority that fails to respect children's individuality. We are morally ambidextrous and adapt our approach to the demands of the situation; but, just as most of us are easily identifiable as left-handed or right-handed, so too are we identifiably as left-moralists or right-moralists.

Proper truths, incorrect facts

But what if we have proper truths but we get the facts wrong? Are our actions immoral in such situations? Here the issue gets murky. Is ignorance of the facts sufficient grounds for avoiding moral blame?

Suppose, for example, that a mother unknowingly gives her young child something to eat that he is allergic too. It is the first time she has ever fed him this food, and she is unaware (up to now) that he has an allergy to it. Indeed, it's a rare allergy and there would be no reason to be suspicious of it. Nevertheless, the child becomes very ill and dies. Mom had good truths but bad facts.

In such a tragic situation, it is unlikely that we would hold the mother morally responsible for her child's death. It would not be reasonable for us to expect her to know about her child's allergy, particularly since even the pediatrician didn't know about it. We would not deem that she had acted immorally.

Suppose, on the other hand, a mom feeds her infant coca cola instead of milk, because he seems to love it and drinks it up every time. She takes pleasure in feeding him what he likes, and thinks to herself, "What an extraordinary baby I have!" However, the child eventually suffers from severe malnutrition and dies.

In such a situation, we are much less likely to excuse the mother's ignorance. We would probably argue that, as a new parent, she had a duty to inform herself about how to care for an infant; there are free pre-natal classes everywhere, and there's no excuse in the 21st century for anyone to be that ignorant. So, although her heart was in the right place – she wanted to feed her child things he enjoyed – her head was not. But this time, we feel that it should have been; this time, we feel that she acted immorally.

So, in situations where we act on good truths but bad facts, our actions are sometimes deemed immoral, and at other times not.

From this we can conclude that:

- Immorality always and necessarily occurs when we attempt to satisfy culturally improper emotions, whether we do so successfully or not (bad truths; any facts).
- Immorality *may* occur (but not necessarily) when we try to satisfy proper emotions by ineffective means (good truths; bad facts).

In easy times, like those we live in, we are not too concerned with the truths held by others; we only pay attention to their facts. It does not matter that the neighbor hates the president, but if he acts on that hate by attempting to assassinate him, we put the neighbor in jail. In poorer times, or in socially disrupted and dangerous times, people often feel they cannot risk waiting around to see if an improper believer will become an improper actor. In hard times, what a person believes is as important as how they act. People have frequently been jailed, killed or re-educated so that others could be sure they held proper beliefs. Combating heresies through inquisitions or communist re-education camps are matters of replacing bad truths with good ones.

DIFFICULTIES DISTINGUISHING FACT FROM TRUTH
Knowledge vs. belief

It's not so much that he doesn't know,
it's that he knows so much that isn't so.

We acquire what knowledge we possess in two ways: through direct personal experience, physically or psychologically, or by having things told to us. Most of our social knowledge is gained through this second method.

We know something because someone said it was so. If a number of people, or just a single person in authority, tells us that George Washington existed, we believe them. We assume that the memories or stories coming from others can be trusted as if they had been facts experienced by us through our own senses. We believe we could have sensed what others relate had we been there ourselves. Our truths and facts conflate.

I have never been to Moscow, but I know it exists. My geography teacher said so. I don't know much about potassium, but a chemist told me that if I drop some in water, it will explode. I believe them. For herding creatures, the knowledge, conclusions and experiences of others can be passed on. Information stored in the minds of others in my group is available to me.

I have not actually seen Moscow, but I believe I could see it if I were in the right place. I have also been told by my teachers that Jesus rose from the dead. Others have taught me that Krishna is the eighth incarnation of the Lord Vishnu and is worthy of worship. At some future time, I am assured, I will be able to affirm these as facts as well. Is Krishna as much a fact as Moscow if I have personally never seen either?

We may presume Allah or Jesus exists as superhuman entities because someone told us so. If someone else didn't tell us, we wouldn't know it. Neither is experienced through direct evidence. If we do not come from cultures that pass on beliefs in them, we would not be aware of them. There are a billion people who *believe in* Krishna. But Krishna is not a fact.

We can find people who will not only claim to have experienced Moscow with the senses, but who can take us there with them. Most of what we know comes from the minds of others. But we relegate their stories into the realms of facts or beliefs, depending on how available the object is to our own senses.

Someone told us that the Grand Canyon exists. We *believe* him. The Grand Canyon is a belief in us until we factually witness it. But through the testimonials of others, we take it as a fact as if we had experienced it ourselves.

It is easier to believe in a Grand Canyon than a Grand Creator. The Grand Canyon exists as an external reality regardless of our need. The Grand Canyon does no special thing for or against humanity. The Grand Canyon requires no proof beyond the senses, and no subjective desire is satisfied in relation to it in our culture.

Creation stories may be invented involving the Grand Canyon. Some native tribe may have viewed it as a holy place. But once the last member of that tribe died, whatever gods occupied the great ravine perished with them. We assign purpose and value to people and things to satisfy our own group's subjective needs. For most Americans today, the Grand Canyon is not worshipped.

As we interact with people, we adopt their mannerisms and react to their fears. We are empathetic creatures. Others react to us too. We are born into a world where culture is introduced to us through individuals who put their own emphasis on things. Cultures change.

The interplay of truths and facts impacts every aspect of life. Discerning proper truths and struggling to make them facts goes on in trivial matters as well as in matters of great theological or philosophical importance. All deliberate actions are concerned with this interplay between truths and facts.

Figure 5-10

My daughter returned home from college and though she had not seen me in weeks, her first reaction to the sight of me was a combination of disappointment and disgust. She came over to me and told me that she had just spent the morning with a few friends discussing better and worse things. The group concluded that it was nearly an indisputable law of decent society that the better people made sure that their shoes matched their belts. Who could disagree?

Then she came home and took one look at her poor old dad and shook her head. Apparently, my shoes did not match my belt, and therefore I was among the miserable. I didn't argue. Her truth became my fact, as she brought me a matching belt to wear.

Memory

I put a dollar into my pocket and walk to the store. There I meet a friend who asks me how much money I have. I answer *truthfully*, "I have a dollar."

I reach into my pocket and, unbeknownst to me, discover that there is a hole in it and my dollar has fallen out. In fact, I have no money. So when I answered, "I have a dollar," I was telling the truth, verified by looking inward upon my own memory. But my truth was not a fact, as verified by looking outside myself and into my pocket.

I believed I had a dollar, but independent verification demonstrated that I did not. The truth did not match the facts. After that, I no longer claimed to have a dollar, so I altered my understanding of what was true to correspond with the facts.

Our truths are often "recollected facts" reached by looking inward. But our memories are often wrong, inexact and emotionally distorted. Police investigations frequently reveal that eyewitnesses routinely misremember facts - the details of events they recently witnessed with their own eyes.

The truths we were told in youth were presented to us as facts. Family history proudly informed us that grandpa died a hero in the big war. That is what everybody always told us. Then one year, grandpa's sole surviving sister pulls us aside and tells us that her brother really avoided the draft by running away and that he later died while robbing a liquor store. She still weeps remembering her older brother. She loved him regardless of what he did. She accepted him for himself.

Grandpa's sister looks at him in Mind 1; the rest of the family squirms at this. What good does that (more factual) memory do for the rest of us? The rest of the family imagined they were doing the grandchildren a favor by distorting truth away from fact. By depicting grandpa as the man they wished he had been, instead of as the man he really was, they reshape and improve the memory of him and turn it into the better example. It is no disgrace to die in a war (at least in Mind 2). It is disgraceful being shot robbing a liquor store. For his sister operating in Mind 1, her brother's disgrace is not a factor. She does not reflect on her brother's life in terms of what his memory does for others. She recalled him personally.

Being shot by the enemy brings glory; glory and disgrace are Mind 2 moral concepts. Glory and disgrace are truths that relate to our vertical position in the herd (higher or lower). The family was not so much interested in the *facts* of grandpa's death as the *truths* that might be made of it. More than this, valuing the past in any way is a Mind 2 priority. Whenever we look to the past for examples, we tend to give the nod to our Mind 2 outlook. An outsider can be recalled as bad, but a family member should be remembered as good and decent.

A father talking to his child might exaggerate the obstacles he had to overcome when he went to school. The effort to recall the past and look for meaning in it is a Mind 2 avocation. In Mind 2, sacrificing yourself for the superior object is virtuous. Dad tells his child he had to walk five miles to school and do two hours of homework each night. He misrepresents the facts to better support the invaluable truth he attempts to portray – that going to school is worth sacrificing personal pleasure.

Truths pose as facts with meaning

My wife is beautiful and my kids are smart, but my daughter-in-law is an idiot and a loudmouth. Are these truths or facts? Truths are things that I feel certain about; facts are verifiable and confirmed through others. Truths are what I *feel*; facts are things we all can *know*. Truths might become facts through action.

When anticipating the actions of others, we try to ascertain what their truths or beliefs are. We want to understand what is in their minds so that we can better predict what they will try to make a fact. If I know another man is a diehard democrat, I might anticipate our conversation turning to politics. I can predict his effort will be to persuade me to support the candidates he favors. He will warn me that my life will be made measurably worse unless I vote as he does. He tells me that future facts will conform to his unpleasant truths unless we act to prevent it. In this case, we have the truths presented to us first, with warnings that facts will follow that I will not like.

Sometimes it is the other way round. We have to try to figure out what the truths are behind the facts. When we discover that our sister Mary is divorcing her husband and has moved in with his best friend, she mixes truths and facts in just the right proportions to support and justify her actions:

> *I left my husband because he always ignored me, and I think he had a porn addiction because he was always on the computer. I was so disgusted with him.*

That she and everyone in the family knew for years that her husband was not particularly attentive and did not hide the fact that he watched pornography are beside the point. That neither she nor anyone else seemed overly disgusted with him in the past is also beside the point. She wanted to justify her act of hurting him and flaunting a social custom by suggesting he deserved to be hurt and that she was in extenuating circumstances.

Once her husband's pal began showing her some attention, the habits of Mary's husband probably did become intolerable to her. We try to tolerate what we cannot change. When we can change something, our mind informs us through feelings that we no longer should put up with it. When Mary had a better option, her emotions shifted to encourage her to change her situation. She felt in new ways, which encouraged her to act in new ways. Once there was somewhere better to go, her mind emotionally moved her to go there.

Was Mary lying? Would Mary have left her husband if his friend had never found her attractive? What are the truths behind these facts? How can we know? Mary said she could no longer tolerate her husband's inattention and his pornography. This had not been her truth for years, but it became her truth when circumstances changed. She supported her new truth with the fact that she left him to join another. Her old truth had been made fact before; her new truth was reflected in the different fact everyone saw now.

That she left him was certainly a fact. That it was only based on his cool demeanor and his interest in watching naked women is the truth that is debatable. After she left her husband for his friend, we have to wonder if she would have found another excuse to leave him, if the pornography watching had not been so readily available. Her family debates it behind her back.

My wife is beautiful and my kids are smart. I bring up these truths to others often, and no one contradicts me. So I take their silence for agreement and presume my subjective truth has been verified as objective fact. Others have seen what I do and have judged it in the same way. My daughter-in-law is a loudmouth; anyone who knows her will tell you so. Therefore, it is more than a belief; it is a fact.

Aristotle points out that human action is not like mathematics; we cannot precisely predict what others might do. The past is not always prologue. With two moral minds, we always have the option of concluding two ways to see right, or two ways to find wrongs; at least two courses of action can be known to us, either of which can be seen as right or wrong at the very same time.

Eating garlic prevents heart attacks; Jesus is God and will be returning soon; mankind is causing the atmosphere to heat up to dangerous levels; my wife loves me; children should be seen and not heard; and buying a home is a good investment. Each of these propositions is a truth and there are people everywhere trying to convince others that they are also facts.

On the other hand, there are people around who will say Jesus is not God, mankind is not responsible for the heating of the atmosphere, and the presumptions about family life are questionable. They challenge these things as "truths," and do not concede them to be "facts."

The parade of truths dressed up as facts

We are internally motivated in many ways: to appear desirable, to eat, to sleep and to protect ourselves. Opportunities are forever popping up to satisfy these ends. They present themselves as facts to pin against these truths. The latest mineral supplement is peddled as an anti-aging miracle; the restaurant around the corner promises us the best food we have eaten in years; if we stop worrying, we will sleep better; and by watching television commercials of growling men breaking down the doors of defenseless women and children, we are persuaded to buy home security systems. A selected series of facts are presented to us as offering the means by which we might satisfy the truths we seek. We want to be healthy, eat the best foods and protect our families. Advertisers tell us these truths can be turned into facts by purchasing their products. Politicians, scientists and priests reassure us with similar arguments, all promising to help us make our dreams come true, turn our desires into reality and transform our truths into facts. Doing so defines progress in life.

Culturally agreed-upon truths serve as facts

It is important to me that your truths match mine; otherwise I think there is something wrong with you. I presume you love your kids most. This is a truth that conforms to my own: that I love my kids most. If you act as if this is a truth of yours, I understand your motivations and can explain your actions. I can get along with you. If you suddenly act like one of my kids is more valuable to you than your own children, I grow suspicious. Something about you isn't right.

If you love your kids most and I love mine most, we share a truth, though we differ in facts. The fact that our loves are directed differently is understood as natural and proper. Our facts did not have to be identical as long as our truths agree.

In truth, we both agree we should attend the baseball game dressed comfortably. But if I go to the game in shorts and a tee shirt, and you go there in a suit and tie, I will laugh, thinking one of us must be joking. If I am not joking and you say you are not joking, I will probably think you are a bit weird. If you go to the game naked, I will be more than uncomfortable with you. I may have to call somebody and actually intercede and act against you. We cannot get along if your truths deviate too much from my own. I ascertain which truths you believe by your actions. Your actions reveal your truths. How you act is who you are.

The fact that you understood comfort to include nudity told me that our truths did not agree after all. "Put something on for Pete's sake!" If you do not voluntarily conform, it is right that you be made to. The group may have failed to properly mold your truths, but we can certainly force you to conform to the facts we prefer to experience.

Facts tell us what is; truths tells us what ought to be. Facts describe the world around us; truths tell us how much we care about it. Facts tell us what happened; truth instructs us on what we want to happen. The two are easy to distinguish conversationally, but in practice it is almost unavoidable that we get our own actions, our own "truths-becoming-facts," intermixed with each other. Facts and truths become jumbled and almost hopelessly intertwined when explaining human action.

Science and religion

"Do you believe in science or religion?" I have been asked this question before. The first reaction is to dismiss the question as misstated. Science is not a belief system. The scientific method allows for experimentation and independent verification of fact. Through science, we achieve knowledge, not belief. Facts exist whether we believe in them or not. Belief systems, on the other hand, disappear as soon as the last believer dies. I have stated the argument this way many times. But after reflecting, I don't think it is quite that simple.

Belief is subjective; facts are objective. I can believe both Moscow and Atlantis exist. But only Moscow is considered a factual entity. The existence of Moscow can be independently proven. I can take a plane there.

I can say, "I love my child." And I can demonstrate that love through my support, teaching and nurturing. When we look at a mother nursing her baby, she is in the act of loving it. Her love is made a fact through action. But love is a subjective feeling too. A wet-nurse who holds no love for the baby can be hired to feed the baby as well. Is love not a fact? In this way, we often treat our truths as "personal facts" only confirmable through ourselves.

Subjective reality exists for the subject. It is as real for him or her as if it were objective and physical. It is simply a reality that cannot be shared through the five senses. Subjective reality is shared by creating an empathetic response in others, which lets them understand what our emotional position is. When a mother claims to love her child, we take it as a fact without need of demonstration. If we see a woman day after day caring for her child, we know through her actions that she loves it. How we act is who we are.

Subjective feeling motivates us to moral or immoral actions, that is, to actions that conform or do not conform to the subjective truths of those around us. We are sensitive to emotional imprinting in youth. We learn who our family is, which society we belong to, and how to seek and find absolute right. These four spheres of social existence - family, country, religion and technology - are presented to us pre-memory. As a member of a herding species we are receptive to learning them, bind to them, love them and believe in them without need of factual argument. After we are taught, we cleave to the facts that seem to support what we already believe. We don't need it demonstrated to us that our family, our country and our religion are worth loving and protecting. We use the same terms to describe fidelity to these social concepts. We say we are *loyal* to our god/country/family; we *protect* them; we *have faith in* them; we *stand behind* them. Our feelings toward others are subjective and not always apparent to others, but they are known to *us*.

The feelings of loving my family or my country or my gods and hating my enemies, or even sentimentally remembering an old hound dog I had as a kid, are feelings as apparent to me as the images before my eyes. Objective knowledge is verifiable by others. Subjective knowledge is only immediately known to us. But from the point of view of the individual, both are valid.

I know I love my child and I know I am composing this book. At the level of the individual subject, truth and fact become one. For a person sitting beside me, the writing of this book is a fact. They have to confess that their position on my love for my child is only a belief. One they can confirm; the other they suppose.

Atoms exist, the center of the earth is molten metal, and Jesus raised the dead. Are these beliefs, or have we seen them for ourselves and so can confirm them as facts? Most of science, technology and history come to us as beliefs. Someone tells us, and we believe him. Robert E. Lee was defeated at Gettysburg and the angel Gabriel was sent by Allah to visit Mohamed in a cave. Are these truths or facts?

Historians and scientists assure us that they deal in verifiable accounts, physical evidence and logical deduction. Outside these methods lies mere belief, not knowledge – truths, not facts. We can all agree on this in theory, but in practice all take the form of beliefs. I believe the scientist who assures me atoms can be shown to exist. I believe the historian who assures me there is verifiable physical evidence for the battle of Gettysburg. I believe the preacher when he repeats the harrowing tales of Moses, through accounts recorded in his holy book from eyewitness testimonial. From my point of view, it is faith in the authority that decides the issue. It is not in any way dependent on my personal ability to discern facts from truths, subjective beliefs from objective knowledge. I will not independently verify any of it.

Aristotle tells us that the Pythagoreans taught that the comets were like the planets, only appearing at great intervals of time.[2] We do not call it knowledge, since they did not support their claim in any demonstrable way. We call the Pythagorean's good guess a "correct belief." Their view on comets was a truth; it was not a fact. At least, it was not yet a fact.

Do we believe in science or religion? How we answer this question reveals not just what we happen to feel or personally think; it informs others which authorities we follow. As a herding creature, we do well by following the best examples. In easy times, we can each do well believing the world is 4.5 billion years old as the astrophysicists tell us, and we do alright believing it is only 6000 years old as Clement of Alexandria and other religious figures suggested. We do okay if we sign on to the Darwinist idea that species evolved, and we suffer no ill effects if we want to say we were all blinked into existence by the miracle of spontaneous creation. For most of us, both are beliefs.

For cultures where science has been promoted, technological progress has been remarkable. For those who stuck closer to a subjective and religious version of the universe, little has changed in 4000 years. Truth needs to be suppressed to reveal facts. Obviously the culture developing in an atmosphere where moral truth is subdued comes to differ markedly from truth-based cultures. When facts are freed from the anchor of truth, what can be done with them can change rapidly. One scientist can think differently and challenge the notion of other scientists. For the scientist and historian, the evidence that counts most are the details that exist outside of any of them personally.

Each of us has the capacity to lean more heavily on beliefs than on facts. The factors that push a culture to produce people more of one persuasion than another has more to do with how often they are forced to deal with others who believe differently from them. Fact-based cultures are usually production, trade, traveling and reading cultures – all those things that undermine parochialism and serve to get people in the habit of putting their own comfortable belief systems in abeyance and allow for fact and experience to dominate their outlook more than past practice, customs and belief systems. We all want to believe, but more and more, and whether we like it or not, facts seem to get in the way.

SHARED CULTURE
The harmony of everyone's truths and facts

Culture is a particular relationship between a group of people to their facts and truths. Being raised in a particular culture is to be taught what to make of the things we will invariably see, hear, taste, smell and touch. These things we call facts. We are given explanations for these external facts and told what to make of them. What we make of our facts we call our truths.

We are told how to address the internal urges we will invariably feel. We are taught to direct our urges to eat toward the proper foods prepared in the safest and best ways as worked out by others in our clan long ago. We are told what to drink, when and where to reproduce, and how to associate. These are the truths of our culture. Truths inform us of the proper manipulation and use of facts.

We look outside ourselves for facts and inside ourselves for truths. A shared culture is the harmony of everyone's truths. We share a culture when we all believe we should eat three meals a day and breakfast should include eggs, fruit or cereal. A shared culture means we agree on the facts too. When we look into the sky we see stars, burning giants of hydrogen gas; we don't see gods or angels traveling round attached to heavenly orbs as other cultures observed. Definitions are the bridge between truths and facts. We believe that what our neighbor sees is what we see, and what he smells is what we smell; but the value or purpose of the things we both see and smell tells us if we share the same culture or if we have differences. We not only strive to factually experience the same things, but to interpret those experiences in the same way. We want to see the same things and feel about them in the same ways. We seek social harmony.

If I am a relatively conservative person living in a run-of-the-mill middle class neighborhood, I can be expected to look, act and dress in a certain way. If a family of nudists moves in next door to me, I will be discombobulated. We both see the same things – clothing or skin – but we react to them in different ways. We share the facts, but our truths do not match. How I will interpret those facts differs from my new neighbor. He feels he is doing right and I feel he is doing wrong. Our facts match but our truths do not. We have social disharmony.

Culture addresses each of our subjective desires and matches them with objective methods that assist in their attainment. If we need food, our culture teaches us what we can eat, when we should eat it, and even how to eat in the proper way. Born Taiwanese, we might learn to prepare rooster testicles; if from the southern United States, we could enjoy pigs' intestines; and if we are from South Korea, we can buy cans of caterpillars to munch on. In Mexico, it is rice and beans, and in New York, it is pizza and deli sandwiches. What is the best thing to eat becomes more a matter of culture than science.

How we should satisfy hunger is addressed in both Mind 1 and Mind 2 ways. We learn what to yearn for and what to detest. In Asia, chocolate-covered bugs are available; in most of America, they are detested – but not always. Just as with everything else, we look to satisfy hunger by seeing right in two ways. Insects are not a part of traditional American fare, and so they are suspect. But eating a bug might be a fad, done on a dare, or resorted to in times of starvation. In Mind 2 traditionalism, where what was done in the past is valued most, bugs are not eaten. In Mind 1, right is a thing determined in the present moment, and though eating a bug might not be the right thing to do traditionally, it might be right in the now.

How we act is who we are. We are known by what we do. We are taught the proper way to satisfy the desire for warmth and modesty with pants, hoop skirts, kimonos or fig leaves, depending on which group we belong to. When we do what others are doing, we do right. We mimic those around us or those above us. Our logical capacity is not involved in the process of setting goals or establishing values. Logical mind only takes over when the moral direction – Mind 1 or Mind 2 – has already been set. Logic guides us as we interact with the non-human world. Should we eat a bug? If we subjectively decide the answer is yes – that is, if the idea of eating a bug appeals to us; if we feel that we can eat whatever pleases us (Mind 1) –

then our logical mind will guide us to acquiring and eating it. If we have subjectively decided no – if the idea of eating a bug revolts us and we feel we should eat as we have been taught (Mind 2) – then our logical mind will help us steer around it. Logical mind guides our actions, brings in information to be evaluated, but it never sets our goals.

LOGICAL
The eating or not eating of an insect has no moral component. The external physical or social need faced by the animal may make eating insects the logical thing to do.

MIND 1
Maybe: What is happening right now determines what is right. Impressing others or answering the needs of the moment is what matters.

MIND 2
No: It has not been condoned by past practice; revulsion for them has been established. It would be a low and disgusting thing to do. Better people in better situations to not eat insects. What is right in this matter has been decided before; our duty now is to recognize and respect that.

A-LOGICAL/ANTHROPOMORPHIC
We look within ourselves for the answer.

We need social belonging. The culture we are born into teaches us how to behave toward the others of our group and what help or criticism we can expect from them. We are taught group dress, group language and group songs; we praise the group's cultural leaders, fear the group's enemies, and worship the group's deities. All social needs are addressed satisfactorily by showing us how to fit in as we pass from our mothers' wombs and into the greater herd. We are taught our place relative to the major social constructs of moral mind – religion, tribe, family, and the external physical world – as a relationship between our own subjective "proper" truths and the objective facts.

The circumstantial nature of truth

Are stealing and destroying the property of other people bad? It depends.

If we desire to kill a rival, burn down a city or steal a vehicle, these deeds may be possible, and even moral. Stealing cars and killing people is deemed immoral at home and in times of peace. However, in war, and against another herd, or in self-defense, such actions are cheered. Facts are facts; truths are circumstantial. We are expected to hold the same truths as our neighbors and leaders. When our group goes to war, the individual is expected to support it; when married, we are expected to support our spouse. For a group to remain congenial, their truths must be shared and coincide. We must do what is expected of us.

If I had been an American sent to war against the Nazis in the 1940s, and I wanted to kill Nazi soldiers on sight, I would share a truth with most of my fellow infantrymen. My truth would be good and right. However, if I also wanted to kill German women and children on sight because they might be Nazis also, many would think I was going too far. My fellow soldiers would not have shared this truth and would have tried to dissuade me. If I had been seen by them, putting my beliefs into action, turning my truths into facts, and killing the German kids and their mothers, many would have tried to stop me.

Finding happiness for a herding species depends on learning to mimic the desires felt by others, and to internally generate our own proper, matching, desires – that is, to feel truths within us in similar ways as others in our group do (in either moral outlook). Correct a-rationality, our herd's version of proper moral outlook and customs, is required. To be considered "morally sound," we must seem to feel it "right" and "correct" that needs be satisfied in ways similar to those that are acceptable to others of our group. Concerning clothing, right is dressing in ways similar to others in our group. With religion, Christians eat pork and beef, Muslims do not eat pork, and Hindus do not eat beef. We are not born feeling any of these as "right" and "proper," but we are born receptive to being taught to feel properly. We are born equipped to learn how put those feelings into action – that is, to "think properly" – and we are born to carry out what we have been taught – that is, to "act properly." Feeling proper truths means feeling how others expect us to feel, to feel as they do. When we reflect and plan our actions based on proper truths, we call it "thinking rightly." By *feeling rightly*, which leads to *thinking rightly*, others can rely on us to *act rightly* - that is, to behave properly and predictably in shared social situations, to behave in a morally acceptable way.

To get along well with others in our herd, our desires need to be similar to theirs, and how to satisfy those desires needs to be in line with how they satisfy theirs. The group needs to be able to anticipate our actions relative to others. If the group approves of satisfying sexual urges only through marriage, then prostitution and extra-marital sex will get you a mean look or worse. We turned our shared truths into acceptable and unacceptable facts.

Culture teaches us what right is. A Catholic raised in 1966 knew it was wrong to eat meat on Fridays. This was true for him. And by not eating meat on Fridays, the Catholic acted upon his truth and turned it into a fact. A Hindu holy man finds truth in the belief that it is wrong to eat beef on any day. An American born at any time in the past 40 years has been taught that it is bad to give alcohol to children. The specifics of our truths are malleable things.

Recognizing the value of doing what others do, and doing these things ourselves, are the starting point of tradition and culture. The details of culture are less important than the fact that we share them. That Roman women tended to wear yellow on their wedding day and English women preferred white since Queen Victoria chose it more than a century ago are incidental details. That women tried to learn and attempted to follow what others did in similar circumstances is the important and vital point. We do what others do to demonstrate we are steadfast, dependable and good.

How tolerant of differences can we be?

The easier the times, the more likely we are to shift to a Mind 1 position and tolerate changes in traditions. In easy times, good Roman girls didn't have to wear yellow on their wedding day; and in easier times, American girls do not need to wear white at their wedding to still be considered "good." In harsher times, flaunting traditions makes one morally suspect. In easy times, daring and risking often bring positive attention and acclaim. To stand out from the crowd can be a good thing. In the 1950s, almost every American bride walked down to the isle to the sound of Mendelssohn's Wedding March. By the end of the century, the brides were entering to the tune of whatever popular and current song they favored at the time. And for some, the selection of the wedding song became a closely guarded secret not revealed to their friends until the ceremony.

MIND 1	MIND 2
Custom can be changed to suit my whim.	My whim must be changed to suit custom.

An American born 20 years ago knows aborting babies can be right, decided by the mother as she perceives her circumstances. An American born a hundred years ago knew aborting a baby was never socially right, regardless of the circumstances. If she resorted to it, it was likely when facing a desperate or life-threatening situation. An American aborting a fetus one hundred years ago required that she reject her culture's view of right and wrong. Any women having an abortion then probably experienced feelings of guilt, shame, and remorse. They are the biological/psychological by-products of a herding creature thwarting its herd's expectations.

Customs change. What is not changeable is that there will be customs and examples to follow, and that we will feel morally compelled to follow them. What are unchangeable are the moral templates of Mind 1 and Mind 2, which frame our desires and channel our actions towards their satisfaction. Within these general guidelines, the details of truths vary with circumstance.

- The goal of philosophy as it pertains to (subjective) feeling is to become properly a-rational – to feel the right truths.
- The goal of philosophy as it pertains to (objective) action is to become properly rational – to behave in the right ways – to create the proper facts.

The ultimate goal of all philosophy, then, is to meld proper a-rationality with proper rationality – to feel what is right, and do it. The common term for this is "wisdom." And since we assume that we will act in accordance with our own feelings and desires, the best way to ensure proper actions is to ensure the right truths. If people believe rightly, they will act rightly.

Influencing and being influenced

As herding creatures, we learn to have our needs met by copying the actions of those around us and following the examples of our leaders. We do as others do -- and others do as we do. Early in life I discovered I had an interest in the writings of historians and philosophers. Why I cannot say; no other family member had the affliction. I have collected many written works considered by some as the greatest writings of all times, the greatest thoughts of man stored outside the human brain in written form for others to savor at their leisure. Some have called all this book writing and such "extelligence."

To pursue an interest, we must first imagine it has value. Shortly after my marriage, I recognized that my wife had never read, nor shown any interest in, books such as these. Her reading focused on modern magazines, childcare, health, and novels. Certainly hers is the more common and typical reading fare of the citizenry. But is it the best?

Feeling smug, a bit superior, and justifiably self-righteous, I asked my wife, "How long would you have to be alive before you'd get around to reading the books recognized by one and all as the greatest writings in human history?"

She responded without a blink, "Longer than one human lifetime."

In other, less sarcastic words, she had not read them, felt perfectly fine about not reading them, had no desire to read them, anticipated no intention of ever reading them, and could not be made to feel guilty about it. She suggested she might read the *Koran* or Copernicus on the same day I read her stack of ladies' magazines piled in our bathroom. Between now and then, she was headed out to the movies with her sister to view some love story and I was welcome to join them or I could stay at home with my friends, Plutarch and Plato, and we would see who ended up having a better time.

I stayed at home. She does as well in this society ignoring Plato as I do taking no notice of her magazines. Such is the advantage of a herding animal in easy times. It is not merely that we can be ignorant of some things without suffering for it; *it is that we must be, and are probably better off for being so.* In order to dedicate our brainpower to our own specialty, we are compelled to discount what we can rely on others to master. Because my wife can rely on me to bring to her attention whatever the philosophers might have to teach us, and because I can have at my disposal – through her - the wisdom contained in this month's stack of magazines, we both benefit by having diverse interests.

We enjoy the luxury of plentiful times. We can be different. Individuality can make itself known. But we are still herding creatures. Sometimes it is best to do what others are doing around us and in this way demonstrate we know better from worse, right from wrong. Even in these easy times, it is occasionally necessary to subjugate our personalities for what others view as proper character. There are only 24 hours in a day. If we both read and did the same things, our children would have had a more narrow range of interests to learn from. Doing different things, and trading, has made us intellectually wealthier as a group.

My son tells a funny story of wooing a local beauty when he was in high school. She was very religious. What does this mean? Largely, it means truths prevail and elbow out facts in her psyche. Using our familiar moral diagram, being strongly religious means she feels at the lower end of our moral compass. Her truths are strong; for her, facts were of less importance.

She attended a Pentecostal Holiness church. The customs of her faith put great store in speaking in tongues. In an attempt to win her affections, my son accompanied her to a church service. He later told me:

> It was a Pentecostal church and we sat near the front. Before long and to my surprise, people started speaking in tongues. I had never seen such a thing. The preacher moved first up one row then down the next, pointing to each congregation member in turn. As his finger fell upon one of them, they would begin blathering incoherently. He

> came to the row in front of me and went along person-by-person. Each dutifully spoke in some strange tongue. Then he got to my row, and he moved along until he got to my girl sitting next to me. I was taken aback when, to my surprise, she began babbling in tongues too. Then he pointed to me.

His obvious social dilemma had me on the edge of my seat. I asked him, "What did you do when he pointed to you?" He responded matter-of-factly, "I spoke in tongues of course. What else could I do?"

We want to move up in the eyes of those around us. What else could he do? He was no rabble-rouser. He was not there for a theological dispute. He just wanted to get the girl. So he did what he thought was best. This was right. In the moment, cooperating with a would-be girlfriend's truth made more sense that conflicting with her about facts.

Was his conforming to expectations an aspect of his personality or of his character? If he did it to advance his own goals and ideals, we can say it was a matter of personality. If he conformed to the practice as a matter of respect to the institutions or people he was trying to impress with his presence, we might say his performance was a display of character. In Mind 1, we call the totality of a person's habits and disposition his personality; and in Mind 1 we are equal. In Mind 1, a person's personality is his or her own business and one is as good as the next. In Mind 2, we gauge the totality of a person's outlook in relation to how he or she conforms to what is expected and call it "character." A person can be of good character or bad.

Vicarious prestige

We excel in almost nothing, and we concede superiority to others in just about everything. Yet we have an inner desire to be recognized for our own achievements, to be acknowledged in some way as superior. We do this by patting ourselves on the back for picking the winning side. I am smart because I follow smart people. I am more right than you if my candidate attains office in the upcoming election and the person you supported loses. I am a winner if my team wins the Super Bowl.

Bragging about the accomplishments of my ancestors, my countrymen or my heroes, I somehow imagine I share in their reflected glory. I do not have to write the plays of Shakespeare; I can gain by claiming I read and enjoy them. If you follow my lead, I count you not just as a fellow admirer of Shakespeare, but an admirer of me. Imitation is the sincerest form of flattery. When you do as I do, I gain. You confirm I was right.

By pumping up the reputation of the authors of my books to my wife, I was indirectly pumping up myself. By suggesting these were superior works, I was hinting that anyone who reads superior things must, *ipso facto*, be superior in some way. And my wife, not looking to gain points with anyone who would find the reading of Aristotle as meritorious, saw no advantage to it.

The vast portion of our emotional life centers on gaining vicarious satisfaction from the accomplishments of others. We cleave to a political party and feel good when they win elections and bad if they do not. We look upon the history of our nation with pride, as if, by being fellow Americans, we are somehow partially responsible for Edison's invention of the phonograph or man landing on the moon. We share the limelight because we are of the herd that did these things.

In their personal lives, parents revel in the accomplishments of their children. As each child learns to cross the street or hold a job, the parents feel pride as if they themselves had accomplished something new. I play for you the music I enjoy, hoping that you will enjoy it too, not simply for your pleasure, but to achieve a temporary superiority by gaining status as the person who brought it to your attention. Others doing as we do is important social feedback for a herd member, confirming position, acceptance, and status. Most conversations find us propagandists for our own preferences in movies, restaurants, political candidates, family, and hobbies. When our group is pushed up, we are raised. When my truths are turned into facts for others, I gain.

Moral agency

The role of culture in shaping our moral inclinations cannot be denied. To admit this, however, does not entail subscribing to some form of cultural determinism. For one thing, in most cultures, even the most rigid ones, you can always find some individuals who adopt values that deviate from the group's norms. We only have to look at some of the great social and political leaders throughout history who have challenged the authority of the existing social structure – Jesus, Martin Luther King, Lenin, etc. - to recognize this. But even ordinary individuals can occasionally be non-conformist with respect to one or more of the accepted truths of their group. How can this be explained?

We are all born with a natural capacity to learn how to feel, think and act properly, and this natural capacity is dual in nature: we can feel things properly in either a Mind 1 or a Mind 2 way. That is, we can feel that we must share and are inherently equal and equally able to judge right from wrong, or we can feel that some people and ideals are superior to others, particularly those from our group's past. But this capacity is not preset in any particular direction (Mind 1 or Mind 2). Like the capacity to acquire language, it must be triggered by exposure to the values ("the language") of the culture in which an individual is raised. So it is quite likely that a person will acquire the values (the truths) of her own culture first. If she grows up and continues to live in a very closed, uniform and authoritarian society, with little or no exposure to external influences, it is likely that her truths will remain unchanged. But even then, she will, at the very least, have two Minds, two ways of feeling, because, she will have experienced both family morality at home and social morality outside the home, so a certain degree of flexibility is already built-in. So even in a very controlled and vertical Mind 2 culture, you will find some individuals who do not conform, but this can be explained, because everyone has been exposed to two ways of feeling and acting right from the start. Individuals who live in a more open and culturally diverse society – such as a democracy – are likely to be even more flexible in their moral outlook, just like the polyglot whose linguistic competence has become more flexible as a result of his exposure to different languages.

With two ways of judging right and wrong, it is easy to see how we often view things in different ways. The mind is not one, but apparently many competing and cooperating sub-minds making their needs known to us internally. We satisfy as many of them as we can, acting under the guidance of some combination of our temporal outlooks. This allows us to conceive that at times one type of feeling/thinking occurs and at other times we feel/think in a wholly different way. Or maybe we can do both at the same time. Sometimes we have two explanations for the same thing, and both can seem right. I re-emphasize this concept as the single most important proposition put forward in this book:

> *I can feel that two opposing and even contradictory things are both right. Both can be right and both can be wrong at the same time, depending on the attitude of mind dominating consciousness at the moment.*

We go back and forth within ourselves, in our own hearts, trying to figure it out. And no matter which path we take, the other tugs at us and suggests we may have made the wrong decision. We call it guilt. *Guilt is one of our moral minds crying out that the other should not have won the argument.* This is the foundation of moral agency.

ARISTOTLE AND CLASSICAL MORALITY
Aristotle (c. 384-322 BC)

Aristotle studied medicine, rhetoric, mathematics, poetry, law, and, we can presume, everything that was considered worth knowing. His pupils included political leaders and the future king, Alexander the Great. The schoolbooks he used were the constitutions of the assorted Greek city-states, the poems of poets like Homer, and the natural world.

In his book called *Rhetoric*,[3] Aristotle instructs us on the *three ways* we must appeal to the minds of others whenever we wish to sway them. Influencing others was a threefold process. In his book, he uses the example of how a lawyer might try to convince a jury on the validity of an argument. To be most convincing, he tells us, our arguments must appeal to the three aspects of our mind, which he called "Pathos," "Ethos" and "Logos."

Aristotle does not put forth these three outlooks as fundamental biological aspects of moral mind in the same way I have done here. He never tries to explain why these three methods exist and why they should work. He just tells us that they do. What he notices is that we are persuaded in a combination of three ways. He puts forth these ideas in the setting of a speaker trying to convince an audience of the guilt or innocence of his client.

He tells us that there are three aspects we need to satisfy to completely convince other people. The first is by the social standing, character, or authority of the people giving testimony for or against the accused; the second comes with our natural sympathy with the situation or with the victim/accused person; and finally we are moved by the cold hard facts of the evidence.

Aristotle's three aspects of thought addressed by the good lawyer

LOGOS
We examine the bare facts outside either moral component.

PATHOS
We judge actions as good or bad in relation to their impact on individuals - either the accused or the victims. What would we do in the same circumstances?

ETHOS
We judge actions as good or bad in relation to how they conform to standards set by the group and outside of current human whim. What actions the accused should have taken to have been in accord with customary morality

Aristotle doesn't say why we are persuaded in these ways; we just are. Our attitude of moral judgment is not restricted to cases of law, but informs us of right in every instance. When anyone tells us anything, we use *Ethos* or our ethics to first judge the credibility of the witnesses. Are they honest and likely to know what they are talking about? Are they superior experts or are they just gossips? We then use our *Pathos* or our sympathy to determine how we might relate. What would we do in a similar situation? And we use our intellect (*Logos*/logic) to interpret the meaning and significance of any facts as they are told to us.

Aristotle points out that we intuitively trust and believe those we deem good more readily than those we deem evil. If the prosecution presents the accuser as a decent person and diligent follower of custom who has achieved a high social status, and if the accused is shown to be of bad repute, we judge readily that the accuser is telling the truth and the defendant lying. Our Ethical aspect of mind favors accepted actions and condemns practices not allowed by our group. We see this at work every day when somebody is arrested.

The mind naturally leans toward the side of law and authority. To be accused is to be presumed guilty. We have a criminal justice system that is supposed to count us as innocent until proven guilty, but there is a natural bias in most of us to stand on the side of established authority. Whenever someone is arrested, it is the custom of many law-enforcement agencies to release the most unflattering pictures possible of the accused. A slovenly dressed and slouching person in handcuffs standing next to a well-put-together officer in uniform already begins to sell the case to us.

We also have the ability to empathize with the hurt or the downtrodden. Lawyers for the defense try to present their client in the most sympathetic light possible. The prosecutor tries to detail the suffering of the victims, hoping to elicit enmity for the accused; the defense suggests to us that if we were in the position of the accused, we might do as he or she did. Each struggles for our sympathy or for our social indignity. They state the facts, and then try to apply the appropriate moral outlook to them. Presented with the factual evidence, the details of the act itself lie outside of feeling and beyond excuses. Facts are facts.

We see today what Aristotle saw then. His ideas fit in easily with the method we have presented here. His *Pathos* we call Mind 1 or Sympathetic Mind; Aristotle's *Ethos* we have called Mind 2 or Ethical Mind; and his *Logos* we refer to as Logical (morality suppressed, outward looking) Mind.

In all situations, we apply the same old familiar methods to set our course of right action. From job seekers to the boy trying to impress the girl, each ascertains advantage through the mastery of these outlooks. We sell ourselves to bosses and mates sympathetically, that is, on the merit of our being interesting and fun people, but also ethically, in terms of being trustworthy and honest. Combine these with the facts that we are smart and accomplished too and we become irresistible. We sell ourselves to others based on the ideals we intuitively understand as important – sympathetically/ethically/logically.

Office seekers win our loyalty in the same way. They assure us that they are kind dog owners, generous givers to charity who are regular folks like us. They add to this an appeal to our virtues by touting their regular church attendance and their college degrees; and finally, they convince us logically by telling us they have mastered the current threats and have the remedy for all our present woes. The politician is emotionally exuberant about solving our problems. And since they are good people, worthy of our trust, and know the facts, we support them. What was apparent to the Greek sage two millennia ago remains true in every generation since.

> We believe good men more fully and more readily than others; this is true generally whatever the question is, where exact certainty is impossible and opinions are divided...Secondly, persuasion may come through the hearers, when the speech stirs their emotions...Thirdly, persuasion is effected through the speech itself when we have proved a truth...
> -Aristotle[4]

THE SYMPATHETIC, ETHICAL, LOGICAL, AND ROMANTIC
Different strokes for different folks

Most of us can be categorized as habitually leaning toward one or the other of our broad patterns of truth. We are known to be either Sympathetic people (Method 1) or Ethical types (Method 2). Either we look to the emotions of others personally when determining what is right for them, or we think it best to adhere to rules or laws for indications of what is right. We are judged as being the liberal or conservative type.

Those who are liberal and Sympathetic are more likely to be ever vigilant against the hoarding of wealth, unbalanced distribution of goods, and to see right as no one being left behind. They are on guard against dangers and wrongs emanating from within the group. For those in this mode of truth, equality matters most – majorities should rule, equality should reign, and no one should be seen as inherently better than anyone else.

<u>Mind 1 truths</u>

- Let he who hath no sin cast the first stone.
- With malice toward none, with charity for all.
- Free men, wherever they may live, are citizens of the world.

- We hold these truths to be self-evident, that all men are created equal.
- Forgiveness doesn't change the past, but it enlarges the future.
- The danger comes from the rich getting richer while the poor get poorer.

The Sympathetic type emphasizes that we are one like another, that a weakness exhibited by a neighbor today may be exhibited by us tomorrow. Those among us whose psyches lean to Mind 1 assume the strong may be oppressing the weak, the rich are depriving the poor, and that what the neighbor is doing personally is nobody's business as long as no one is hurt. The predominant social outlook is: *The greatest dangers now are likely to come from imbalances inside our group.*

If conservative and Ethical, we are more likely to be vigilant for threats from outside the group. The Ethical type looks at the group's rules before the individual's feelings. Ethical people remain on alert for dangers emanating from outside the herd and see real danger in transgressing cultural customs and breaking the law. The good of the many outweighs the good of the few or the one. Moral absolutes in the form of right and wrong are the arguments that appeal to those of us in this type. Right is understood as better people doing better things. The worst types of people are known because they do the worst things. People and things are categorized. A vertical classification of superiors and inferiors pervades morality.

Mind 2 truths

- Honor thy mother and thy father.
- Everyone must stand when the national anthem is played.
- All cars must drive on the left side of the road.
- My country, may she always be right; but my country, right or wrong.
- Those who fail to learn from the past are destined to repeat it.
- You break it, you pay for it.
- Don't trust people greatly different from us.

Ethical arguments are the types of conversations that hold sway almost always with vertically oriented (Mind 2) people. Ethically leaning folks are comfortable knowing there are rules of conduct and codes of behavior that need to be upheld. The law is the law, we should learn from the past, self-control is a virtue, and it is never right to do wrong. Some folks are better than others. The foreigner needs to be watched. Our traditions and past practices are best. Life is tough; it's tougher if you're stupid. The predominant social outlook is: *The greatest dangers now are likely to come from outside the group.*

The third common division of type, the Logical (suppression of both Mind 1 and Mind 2 urges) corresponds to our objective outlook. But it is a mistake to think this type of feeler is distinct from a Mind 1 or Mind 2 person. Logical people favor arguments and a logical outlook that is unemotional; they appeal to naked rationality, to cause and effect. Logical types are most easily swayed by emotionally indifferent arguments and facts. The Logical is not a different type of mind, but mind when both moral components are toned down:

Facts

-   His fingerprints were found on the murder weapon.
-   He confessed when brought in for questioning.
-   I think, therefore I am.
-   The sun rises in the east.
-   Assembly-line specialization has increased production.
-   Hydrogen and oxygen can combine to produce water.
-   Two + two = four.

For the Logical, the most important things are the facts, as stark and unfeeling as they may be. The Logical Mind looks first to these considerations; the rest of us may lean to other minds first, but we all have the capacity to recognize logical considerations. We are all Logical, Ethical, and Sympathetic. Conclusion: *The extreme Logical types do not see the world in terms of dangers. It matters not if anyone lives or dies.*

Facts are given precedent when both our moral outlooks are suppressed. We look to what happened, not why things happened or how we should feel about them.

What Aristotle ignored we account for here: the moral absolutist, the religious, and the spiritual. People at the opposite moral extreme from the Logical look at events in light of their own "pure truth." Here, facts are irrelevant and maybe even illusory. All that matters is absolute faith in proper belief:

Ultimate Truths

-   Ultimate right exists and can be known.
-   There is an absolutely correct way to justify acts and purpose.
-   Ultimate good and ultimate evil are real.
-   Truths are presented as facts to others. For example:
    -   Jesus Christ is the Son of God.
    -   The world and everything in it was created by God in six days.
    -   After death, our souls are reincarnated in a different physical body.
    -   Muhammad is the Messenger of God.
    -   There are extraterrestrial entities operating unidentified flying objects that have visited Earth in the past and continue to do so today.

The Religious or Romantic outlook is not in itself another form of moral mind; it is simply our dual outlook giving internal feelings extreme priority over any mitigation by external facts. It gives absolute precedence to feelings over physical experience; it puts truths before facts. It does not matter if a religious outlook makes no physical or historical sense; what matters are the truths behind it. Conclusion: *Danger comes from a faith in facts and a loyalty to the outside world; real understanding comes from the truths discovered or revealed within us.*

Whenever we face a challenge, we run our options over each of these alternatives to determine a best course of action. Usually we try to satisfy the needs of all outlooks. For example, when determining what type of education is best for our children, we want something that will satisfy each aspect of mind.

Quad-Realism:
What type of education is best?

LOGICAL Training to accomplish whatever production is demanded.	

MIND 1	**MIND 2**
One that allows children to fit in and feel good about their place in the group. Self-esteem is vital. Everyone has equal value.	One that makes these students better than their competitors and teaches them to outperform others and lead a superior life.

A-LOGICALAL ANTHROPOMORPHIC
Religious education that recognizes that there is ultimate right and ultimate good and we should feel compelled to seek it and follow it.

Pure emotional subjectivity, free from facts, at the opposite end of logical thought, is an important aspect of psyche we will discuss later. To illustrate our current point in another way, we return to the diagram we have used earlier. The diagrams above and below are two different ways to visualize the same thing:

Figure 5-11

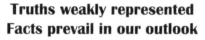

Truths weakly represented
Facts prevail in our outlook

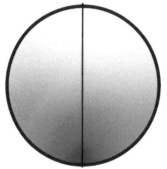

Mind 1 Truth Set
Trying to be made fact
- Aristotle's Pathos
- I Ching Yin
- Liberal
- Horizontal/Equal

Mind 2 Truth Set
Trying to be made fact
- Aristotle's Ethos
- I Ching Yang
- Conservative
- Vertical/Superior-Inferior

Facts weakly represented
Truths dominate our outlook

The Ethical type is sometimes conflated with the Logical
"Conservatives do not care about the little-guy"

The Ethical feeler is sometimes conflated with the Logical and unemotional outlook, since both appear to disregard sympathetic emotions and hold righteousness as a standard that exists outside of the condition of any one individual. When the Sympathetic Mind feels it is never right that someone should have to die, both the Ethical and the Logical outlook seem to object. The Ethical Mind believes there are social goods worth dying for, and a Logical outlook simply accepts mortality as a fact of existence. But from the point of view of the Sympathetic Mind, the Ethical and the Logical both seem cold and uncaring. For the Sympathetic Feeler, everyone is worthy of concern. From an ethical standpoint, this isn't always so. And logically, human life is of no special or particular concern at all.

When we control and conceal emotions, as we do in Mind 2, it makes it easy to confuse us with someone who lacks them. In an ethical state of mind, we may tolerate the execution of a guilty person as an unhappy necessity. But in a purely logical outlook, we do not merely tolerate it; we are indifferent to it.

Seneca was the most famous of the ancient Stoics. The stoics were great promoters of self-control and so are easily identified as holders of a Mind 2 truth set. Two thousand years later, we still refer to people who act unemotionally as "Stoics." Seneca also jumbles the two concepts of Ethical Mind and Logical Outlook when he praises lofty fearlessness (Ethical Mind) and lack of desire (Logical Mind) as the key to happiness. Here he is, circa 65 AD, expressing, not logic, but a pure Mind 2 emotionalism:

> For what prevents us from saying that the happy life is to have a mind that is free, lofty, fearless and steadfast – a mind that is placed beyond the reach of fear, beyond the reach of desire, that counts virtue the only good, baseness the only evil...[5]

The desire to be beyond desire is itself just another desire. Seneca mistakes the proper control of desires with the elimination of them. He promotes the holding of his set of truths as best. The desires that have their roots in Mind 1, like pleasure and emotional expression, he rejects as base and indulgent. The "emotions" he promotes – virtues, dedication to duty, and emotional control – he regards as not emotions at all, but some higher calling.

The modern Jewish or Muslim person in America is prohibited from eating pork. Those among them dominated by an Ethical Outlook say that you simply don't do it, and they condemn other Jews or Muslims when it is discovered they have done it. The Ethical types do not wish to be asses about it, but right is right. For the Sympathetic among them, the pork chop looks so good and people get hungry; and besides, who among us hasn't bent rules on occasion? To each his own. The Muslims or Jews who lean towards a Logical Outlook fill their bellies with the best food available, dismissing the dietary restrictions as so much superstitious tomfoolery. For the ultra-religious and orthodox, not even the pain of death could get them to eat what is prohibited.

The Ethical may be looked upon as Mind 2 leadership by authority corresponding to the baboon style of association. Vertically, the Ethical big cheese is at the top, lieutenants are underneath, and women and children occupy the center to be protected. The best sacrifice for the group. We are one for all.

Sympathetic Mind 1 authority corresponds to a sardine style of socializing. We empathize with the neighbor, follow the crowd, majorities rule, and what the group demands (not what the superior or the leader commands) defines proper social action. There is no sardine leader that stands out as always in charge. Leadership is rotated and we are all for one.

The Logical understands the world as free as possible of any subjectivity. It takes no account of a person's place or position, or even of majorities, and tries to find right governance in principles outside of human moral considerations. And for the religious, it is only human understanding of human impact on the world that matters. A herd of dinosaurs polluting a small pond and making it unusable to most forms of life is natural; a group of humans doing the same thing is condemned as immoral. To the religious, spiritual, or truth-oriented, what humans do is almost all that matters.

THE ARTS AND SCIENCES:
TRUTHS AND FACTS

We have developed words that reflect which types of thinking we are applying to an event. Depending on the language we use, we are letting it be known which mind is being brought to bear on a subject.

Language is a mental struggle to put our psychological concepts into the heads of others. Dealing with multiple moral minds, we develop different words to express which of our mental outlooks we are bringing to bear on a subject. When investigating the broad outline of human experience, we divide our outlook into the objective or the subjective, the logical or the emotional, the rational or the a-rational, the externally based or the internally based.

Words explain not only what we are seeing but in which mind we are viewing things. Take art, for example. Why is there art and how is it that some people seem more artistic than others? In Plato's dialogue, *Phaedrus*,[6] and in *The Republic*,[7] the philosopher suggests that artistic people are just born of God; there is no explanation of how they came to be that way; they just are. Plato was a subjective feeler and he explained things in the subjective manner of inner truths. Plato also loved logic and mathematics. Plato's philosophy is the great struggle of trying to synthesize truth with fact.

We have no better explanation for why some are artists and others are not. But we live in a technologically based, logically oriented society. We use updated terminology to answer the question and we now say that genetic variation causes some to be endowed with greater artistic abilities than others.

When looking outside ourselves for facts, we use terms referring to fact-based activities like those at the top of the diagram above. If we are using the inward-facing mind, we use terms signifying truths like those at the bottom of the diagram. We understand that knowledge is like belief, but not exactly the same. We can experience the conflict between our minds telling us one thing and our hearts another; we can label someone as a thinker more than a feeler, or vice versa.

Our language has evolved to reflect which moral mind we are operating in. Sometimes we use terms that are similar in their denotation – that is, in their literal meaning – but not identical in their connotations – that is, in their social overtones, cultural implications and emotional meanings. The differences in the respective connotations of certain terms often correspond to the differences between our two moral minds. The terms "pleasure" and "happiness" are an example of this, where "pleasure" connotes the satisfaction of one's immediate desires (Mind 1) and "happiness" the long-term satisfaction with a life well lived (Mind 2). "Personality" and "character" are another example, where "personality" connotes a collection of morally neutral psychological traits and "character" connotes the collection of morally significant virtues and vices that define a person's moral worth.

Figure 5-12

Rational/Externally Verified
Fact Driven:
• The Sciences • Associations • Thinking
• Knowledge • Understanding • Behaviour
• Homo Sapiens

A-rational/Internally Verified
Truth Driven:
• The Arts • Loves/Likes • Feeling
• Belief • Faith • Virtues & Values • People

The impact of dual morality on language use is explored in greater detail in Chapter 25, Extrapolation 16 ("Worship Words and the Profane").

THE GOOD

In philosophy, concepts like goodness pop up again and again. So we ask: What is good or what is right? And how do we know it?

In 50 B.C., Caesar conquered the Gallic tribes and the Romans believed it to be good. The Gauls undoubtedly had a different opinion. Joan of Arc was a divinely inspired prophetess to some, but when her English captors burned her at the stake, they felt they were doing right. Alexander of Macedon destroyed the Persian Empire and the Western world believed the feat was more than good; it was great.

Destruction carried out in the name of goodness is common. When something is of such obvious advantage to us, the bad is overshadowed by the good we gain. And the deed usually considered evil is relabeled "good." Historians often suggest that the monumental nature of a task somehow justifies its temporary or circumstantially terrible consequences. We find such leaders described with phrases like, "He was too great to be good."

The most famous investigation of the good is found in Plato's *Republic*. There he suggests that the ability to recognize something as "good" is the most important and vital power we possess. The capacity to ascertain what is good and being able to distinguish it from what is not good allows us to successfully navigate the world. In the quote below, Socrates tells us that the recognition of the good confirms the value of both "facts" and "truths" and is therefore superior to both:

> Now that which imparts truth to the known and the power
> of knowing to the knower is what I would have you term
> the idea of the good, and this you will deem to be the cause
> of science, and of truth in so far as the latter becomes the
> subject of knowledge; beautiful too, as are both truth and
> knowledge, you will be right in esteeming this other nature
> as more beautiful than either; and … science and truth may
> be deemed to be like the good, but not the good; the good
> has a place of honor yet higher.[8]

G. E. Moore, in his book *Principia Ethica*, published in 1903, also confers a special and exalted place for our idea of good when he writes, "… how good is to be defined is the most fundamental question in all Ethics."[9]

Moore holds that our capacity to label, feel, identify, or connote something as "good" is fundamentally ineffable, non-definable, and non-natural. That is, the "good" cannot be confirmed by looking to the external and physical world; it is confirmed within us. For Moore, whatever "good" is, it lies outside of science or logic, and is embedded in the realm of truth.

Figure 5-13

Amoral Intuition
"Mathematics"
The intuitive system that describes cause and effect

Moral Intuition
"Goodness" and "Greatness"
The intuitive labels of rectitude

The words "good" and "right" – along with their opposites, "bad" and "wrong" – have a number of connotations. They can indicate "correctness" (or incorrectness) with respect to matters of fact, as when a teacher tells a student that his answer on the science quiz is "right" or that his spelling of a particular word is "wrong." And they can also indicate propriety (or impropriety) in moral action, as when we say, "Sally was only trying to 'do good' when she gave the baby all that candy," or "Cheating on an exam is 'bad'." Applying words like "good" and "right" to both matters of fact and matters of belief exacerbates our tendency to conflate truths and facts.

Distinguishing facts from truths has been the subject of this chapter. At the uppermost logical extreme, we suppress moral emotions and examine our world with an amoral intuition that deciphers causality. This form of intuition systematizes our understanding of cause and effect. We call this intuitive ability "mathematics." Here goodness has no place. The formula 2 + 2 = 4 is neither good nor bad, it simply "is." At the other extreme we have our truths. Human goodness is found there.

Truth ultimately passes into mysticism, into a sort of transcendental reality where ultimate goodness becomes greatness. At the ultimate extreme of fact we discover mathematics. At the ultimate extreme of truth we find God.

The philosopher Frederick Copleston tells us, "… the problem of God" is *the* metaphysical problem…"[10] But that problem will not be examined here in this chapter. Before we can get to our gods, we must further examine ourselves.

CONCLUSION

   The preceding chapters presented the broad outline of the philosophy of dual morality. The following chapters focus on specific aspects of our social behavior. The next four chapters are devoted to the four great spheres of our social order and human endeavor that emerge from our biological morality - country, family, religion, and technology. Each is a permutation and objectification of social urges. Every institution, no matter how large or complex, has its beginnings in the quad-realism of the human psyche.

   Following these four chapters come a series of short chapters extrapolating ever more narrowing particulars.

Notes

   1. G. K. *Chesterton, Orthodoxy* (Nashville, TN: Sam Torode Book Arts, 2009; originally published 1908) 27.

   2. Aristotle, *Meteorology*, trans. E. W. Webster, in *The Great Books of the Western World* (UK: Encyclopedia Britannica, 1952, 1990), 8: 449.

   3. Aristotle, *Rhetoric*, trans. W. R. Roberts, in *The Great Books of the Western World* (UK: Encyclopedia Britannica, 1952, 1990), 9.

   4. Ibid., 9: 595.

   5. Seneca, On The Happy Life, in *Seneca's Moral Essays*, trans J. Basore (Cambridge: Harvard University Press, 1935), 2: 109.

   6. Plato, *Phaedrus*, trans. Benjamin Jowett, in *The Great Books of the Western World* (UK: Encyclopedia Britannica), 7.

   7. Plato, *The Republic*, trans. Benjamin Jowett, in *The Great Books of the Western World* (UK: Encyclopedia Britannica), 7.

   8. Ibid., 7: 386.

   9. G. E. Moore, *Principia Ethica* [Online] (1903, cited 19 December 2016); available from <http://fair-use.org/g-e-moore/principia-ethica/chapter-i>.

10.   Frederick Copleston, *Logical Positivism and Existentialism*, in *A History of Philosophy* (London: Bloomsbury, 2015), 11: 227.

SECTION II
The Derivations

OVERVIEW OF CHAPTERS 6-9

The unabridged version of *Our Human Herds* contains 23 additional chapters detailing how dual morality has shaped everything from political institutions to science, religion, psychology, history, philosophy, education, art and every other human endeavor. These are divided into two sections: The Derivations and The Extrapolations.

This section presents a brief overview of Section II, The Derivations, which explores the four major social realms of family, country, religion and technology, and the institutions that emerge within them to support our moral urges.

CHAPTER 9
Jobs/Commercial Life
Logical, rational Amorality
Science/Technology/Nature

CHAPTER 6	**CHAPTER 7**
Personal Life	**Public Persona**
Private Morality	**Public Morality**

CHAPTER 8
Spiritual Life
Ultimate Morality

CHAPTER 6
Family

This chapter explains how the morality that developed to guide the family life of mother and children has overflowed into our social life, and how social morality, once best suited for relationships between adult males outside the home who were charged with protecting territories and competing with each other, is brought into the home.

Some of the topics discussed include the biological differences between males and females; the evolution of gender roles; marriage; monogamy; homosexuality; virginity; sex and violence; prostitution; feminism; and romance. Each of these topics is presented in its historical context, illustrating how our attitudes towards them have evolved and vacillated between our two ways of viewing "right" and "wrong."

CLASSICAL MORALITY

INSIDE – with the adult female The moral pattern that developed to protect individuals	OUTSIDE - among the adult males The moral pattern that developed to protect the group
Share and care for every member.	Some deserve more than others.
Every voice counts; listen to the needs and desires of the little ones as well as the big ones.	Some are better than others. The direction of these leaders should be given more weight than others.
Everyone must survive.	Some must be sent to die or left behind if they are too weak to keep up.
To get the closest attention, be smallest, weakest, and cry loudest.	To command attention, be biggest, strongest, fastest, and stoically impervious.
Those who act wrong are corrected so that they will act right the next time. Deviants are re-taught and rehabilitated.	Those who act wrong or who are incompetent are ridiculed or punished; corrected lightly with laughter or rebuked harshly with punishment.

MIND 1 AND MIND 2 FAMILY MORALITY

MIND 1	MIND 2
The family is organized horizontally, with all members equally deserving. Parents are more like caregivers than authority figures	The family is organized hierarchically, with Dad at the top, then Mom, and finally children, with males before females.
There are very few rules (except those regarding non-violence), and the few that exist are usually "negotiated."	There are rules of conduct and a regimen – e.g. bedtime, homework, household chores – that kids are expected to follow and obey.
Children's individual preferences are taken into consideration when planning family meals or activities.	Children are expected to conform to the family's traditional preferences regarding food and social activities.
Not much discipline is expected; everyone is "rewarded" equally, independent of "merit"; corporal punishment is not acceptable.	Discipline is enforced; good behavior is rewarded and bad behavior punished; corporal punishment is acceptable.
Children should be allowed to be children and not be weighed down prematurely by responsibilities. Adults seek to find their "inner child."	Childhood is a preparation for adulthood, a time for children to learn about and adopt the standards of the group.
Parents "respect" their children as individuals with their unique personalities, tastes and preferences.	Children look up to and respect their parents as "models" to imitate.
Children should express themselves.	"Children should be seen, not heard."
Failures at school damage a child's self-esteem. "Making an effort" and "doing your best" is what counts.	A "fail" at school is unacceptable and must be corrected through extra remedial homework.
Parents usually side with the child if he/she has been reprimanded or disciplined at school.	Parents generally side with the teacher or principal if the child is disciplined at school.
Guests to be welcomed are treated like family, with everyone feeling relaxed and open. Language and dress are informal.	Guests should be honored, given the better place at the table. We should be on our best behavior and show due respect in language and dress.

MIND 1	MIND 2
Who cares what the neighbors think? Reputation is not important.	Being recognized by our neighbors for reliably living up to social standards – i.e. having a good reputation – is important.

INDIFFERENCE, TOLERANCE, INTOLERANCE

Both individuals and entire cultures can be plotted along the moral compass in terms of their relative indifference, tolerance, or intolerance towards opposing moral outlooks.

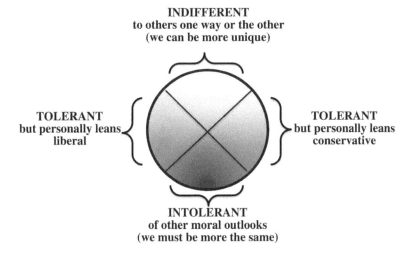

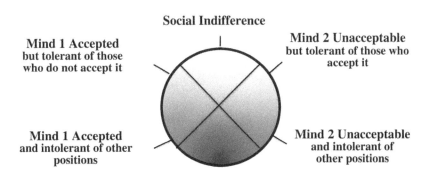

Quad-Realism
Attitudes to Sex

LOGICAL
Sex is merely an amoral biological activity. Sex work is just a technical specialty like any other with no moral component.

MIND 1	MIND 2
Sex is enjoyed as a simple pleasure. Taken to excess, the groupie or the promiscuous male or female is a hedonist.	Lack of sexual control or non-standard sexual practices condemns one (male or female) as a whore or gigolo.

SPIRITUAL
Sex can take on ritualistic significance: Tantric sex practices, the Roman Vestal Virgins, the Virgin Mary.

Love is our strongest social emotion. It is the glue that binds us together and links us to our purpose. It can be felt and expressed within a range of moral intensity.

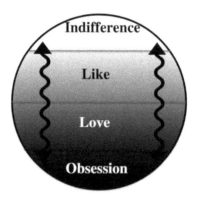

Mind 1 culture has its biological roots in ancient female-to-child patterns of behavior. Examples involve caring and support at the level of the individual, such as nursing, care giving, social work, and motherhood. It emphasizes the equal importance of each of us.

Mind 2 culture has its biological roots in ancient male-to-male patterns of behavior. Examples are the military, male prisons, organized crime, motorcycle gangs and everywhere males dominate. Mind 2-guided groups are hierarchal and ritualistic, with some members being more important than others.

Social systems that include concepts of class, caste, and rank inform us that a Mind 2 moral structure is dominant. The origin of the expressions, "classy" or "having class" comes from the notion that better people (higher in social standing) act in certain identifiable ways.

Males tend to write history and recall the doings of other men. Most of history simply ignored the goings-on among the women, and so because they are seldom mentioned, we mistakenly imagine they were less significant.

The social milieu of yesterday has often been described as "a man's world." If wealth and safety continue to increase as a result of democratization and commercial expansion, it is likely that the social environment of tomorrow will be described as "a woman' world."

Prolonged security and plenty brought about by wealth has allowed the Mind 1 family morality to be loosed in the streets. In a Mind 1 leaning culture, every voice deserves respect and everyone's drawing deserves a place on the collective refrigerator.

Our culture is described as weak, sensual, vulgar, codling, dumbed-down and profane. Much of this is factual and we argue whether it is also true.

Conservatism is not so much what was done 200 years ago, but what we imagine was done a generation or two ago.

CHAPTER 7
Country

In this chapter, we examine how our social morality, developed in adult male-to-male relationships with its emphasis on territoriality and social hierarchy, influences everything from politics to corporate structures and prison gangs.

We address the question, *What is good government?* Is the best government a government by the people? Or maybe the best government is leadership by the best person? The chapter explores a variety of topics within their historical context – the limits of government; liberalism vs. conservatism; individualism vs. authoritarianism; provision vs. protection; dictatorship vs. democracy; the impact of production and trade; libertarianism; civil rights; private property; progressivism; and so on – and shows how these have been differentially addressed by each of our moral minds.

LEADERSHIP

MIND 1	MIND 2
Leadership is horizontal. Everyone has an equal voice. The leader stands shoulder to shoulder and is one of us.	Leadership is top-down vertical. Some voices are more valuable than others. The leader sits atop a ladder of increasing superiority.
The leader is a sympathetic friend who will make sure everyone has enough.	The leader is a tough decision maker who will cull the weak when necessary.
Ask what your country can do for you.	Ask what you can do for your country.

The Democratic Period

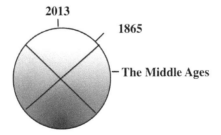

Democracy is the outcome of government's inability to control the growing wealth, as well as its production and distribution, from a single point.

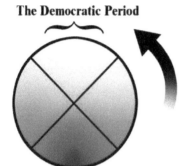
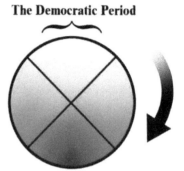

Democracy is the face of a commercial society; dictatorship the pinnacle of a non-commercial one.

In Mind 1, inequality is a never-ending problem, which leads us into a world where social imbalances must be perpetually addressed. ... Judged through our Mind 2, inequalities are not dangerous; in fact they are distinguishing.

Government can no more make unequals equal today than it could make kings divine in former times. But we seek to turn these truths into facts nonetheless.

Democracy does not create equality; equality creates democracy.

Political discourse is the effort to convince others that the things we fear are the things most worth fearing.

Regardless of the situation, the group benefits if some of us operate in one mind while others see danger in a different way. Always having both types about is like having sentries keeping watch in all directions.

Figure 5-4:

The Mind 1 socializing efforts going on all around us now inexorably run into the same necessarily authoritarian challenge. The effort to redistribute wealth presupposes the central authority is morally obligated to control and commandeer as much of anybody's wealth as it sees fit. And the authority that commandeers the wealth is not a god but real live human beings endowed with all our frailties and an overabundance of power. All social authority is theoretically surrendered to "the community," but in practice this must eventually turn out to be wielded by a small cadre of leaders, themselves directed by the strongest personality. In Mind 1, horizontal intentions lead unavoidably to vertical results. Mind 1 morality passes the culture back to Mind 2.

In the democracies, this drama, the moral back-and-forth between the Mind 1 all-for-one collectivists and the Mind 2 one-for-all rugged individualists, repeats itself in every election. Democracy is fundamentally a mid-point of government representing a culture caught around the northern point of our moral compass, wavering between Mind 1 and Mind 2. With ever increasing prosperity, Mind 1 is coming to dominate us culturally, but Mind 2 is far from eradicated. Nor can it ever be. We are creatures of a dual morality.

The battle between conservatives and liberals goes on in a fury. Mind 2 sloganeering emotionalism warns us of the dangers of big government collectivism, that is, the danger of listening to our Mind 1. From the other side, we hear cries against falling victim to a rich man's cold and uncaring rugged individualism. Political campaigns are defined by emotionally pubescent slogans like, "The rich get richer while the poor get poorer"; or glaringly self-serving bribes like, "Vote yourself a farm," used by Abraham Lincoln; or Ralph Nader's slogan in the 2000 election, "Government of, by, and for the people … not the moneyed interests."

Real politics, really lived, is a perpetual battle between our dual moral outlooks.

CHAPTER 8
Religion

This chapter examines the social institutions that emerge as our moral urges are taken to extremes and we are pressed to believe in, seek out, find and inplement "ultimate right." This sometimes leads us to do what others view as "ultimate wrong." When we seek to do wrong, we kill in ones and twos. When seeking to do right, we kill in the thousands and even millions.

The chapter provides examples of dual morality in some of the major religions, and explores such topics as faith and science; cults; alternative conceptions of prayer, miracles, sin, divine punishment, and heaven; arguments for the existence of God; literal vs. metaphorical interpretations of scriptures; and Eastern religions.

The Peace and Love Commune   **The Quasi-Nationalist Militia**
(Branch Davidians)   **(The Ku Klux Klan)**

In this chapter, we explore why most moral codes focus upon the great trifecta of moral action — the control of sex, the limitation of violence, and the proper distribution of resources.

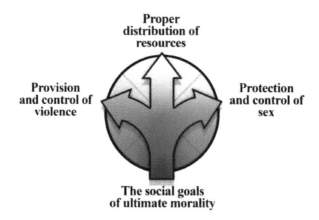

MIND 1	MIND 2
The tenets of all major religions hold truth. All religious practices are valuable.	Our religion is more truthful and our religious practices are better than others.
The practices and ceremonies of my religion can change and be updated to suit what is needed now.	The traditional practices and ceremonies of my religion need to be passed on and carried forward by the current generation
The good of the present matters most.	Supreme good and the good of past and future matter most.
Everyone has an equal chance at being saved, eliminated, or rewarded.	Better people will attain rewards; the worst will be punished or at least unrewarded.
Love thy neighbor as thyself.	If you lay down with dogs, you get up with fleas.
We are all equal before God.	Priests, rabbis, teachers, a religious hierarchy distinct from laymen, are right. Better people are loved most and will be closest to ultimate good.
Religion serves us.	We serve religion.

Understanding quad-realism, it becomes clear why the ascetic impulse manifests itself in similar ways across all cultures and religions.

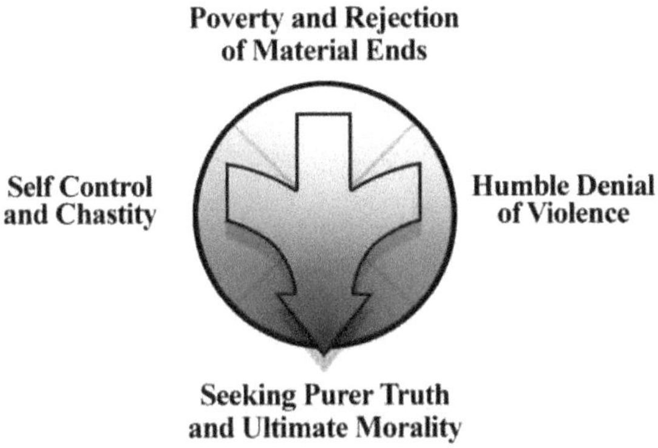

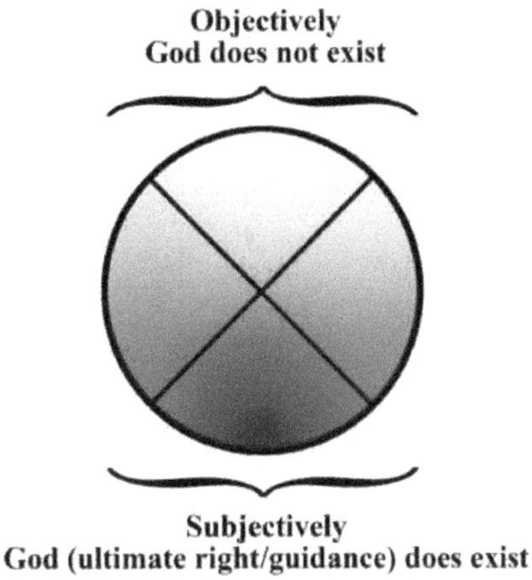

Morality doesn't get us into heaven; morality keeps life on earth from becoming hell.

Religion does not create morality; morality creates religion.

We are not born with religion; we are all born potentially religious.

Religion is the search for absolute truth, just as science is the search for absolute fact. Life is lived somewhere between these extremes.

It is a mistake to believe that religion exists because its adherents are not trained in science. It is an error to imagine that atheists make their claims based on a stubborn obstructionist attitude to the revealed word.

Claiming to be a believer or an atheist does not make us unequivocally one or the other. We are all atheists; we are all believers.

CHAPTER 9
Science and Technology

This chapter examines human action when moral impulses are suppressed and when we view the world in a materialistic and "top-of-the-compass" fashion. This comes about as a result of increased production and trade, which has an equalizing effect on the population as more and more people interact with each other for mutual gain – the butcher provides meat to the baker, who provides bread to the tailor, who provides clothes to the teacher, and so on. Economic expansion thus creates an atmosphere of equality. After a critical point, the older hierarchical system of dictators or kings is replaced (usually with violence) by a leadership structure that reflects the production-based and equal social structure of the society beneath it.

Under these "democratic" circumstances, we come to understand the world in terms of cause and effect and define what it means to improve our lives in terms of how much we increase our material goods. We have passed out of the condition where the world was viewed in terms of right and wrong and where the better life was understood as the life lived in conformity with the "moral good." It is thus in democratic circumstances that science and technology grow and flourish.

The debate at the top of the compass is therefore an economic debate, not a moral debate (since our moral impulses are suppressed). It is primarily a debate about how resources are to be handled. In early democratic times, despite equal representation at the political level, a Mind 2 social outlook still prevails, where merit (the best deserve more than the worst), private property and limited government prevail. As production continues to expand and everything gets easier for everyone, a more Mind 1 social attitude takes over, where sharing our wealth and taking care of the weakest and poorest become our priorities.

Democratic societies waver back and forth between these two outlooks. The Mind 2 "survival-of-the-fittest" policies are called "capitalist" by the Mind 1 folk who disapprove of them, while the Mind 1 "share-the-wealth" policies are called "socialist" by the Mind 2 folk who don't like them. The political arena is occupied by leaders who argue over policies that seem too socialistic to some or too capitalistic to others. This back and forth occurs at the top of the compass, as we are driven by *a-moral* economics making us all richer and more independent.

Democratic Times

Socialism   Capitalism

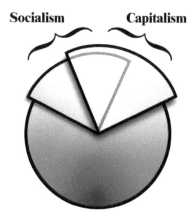

Whereas the building blocks of religion are subjective truths, the building blocks of science are objective facts. However, human action is driven by human motivation, which is based on subjective desires. Consequently, we are never satisfied to simply "know the facts," but are always driven to apply our scientific knowledge and our technological expertise to advance subjective human aims; technologies are the means we create to manipulate external reality for our benefit. And since our aims are divided along dually moral lines, and felt either strongly or weakly, the uses to which we put our scientific and technological advances can also be viewed quad-realistically.

The chapter explores some examples of quad-realism in the domains of science, technology and the world of work – management theory; scientific theories and their interpretations; economic and political theory – and concludes with a discussion of commercialism and the "valuing" of material possessions, whereby a fundamentally *amoral* pursuit can be viewed as "immoral" when it becomes an end-in-itself.

The philosopher and economist, Adam Smith, defended capitalism on the grounds that material prosperity was the key factor in civilizing man, and that it was by increasing material abundance that we promote moral advancement.

However, In spite of the fact that fantastic levels of manufacture and assembly have allowed Mind 1 goals of provision and Mind 2 aims at protection to be attained more completely than ever before, moralists of both persuasions find capitalism's material and amoral outlook suspect.

Quad-Realism
The Morality of a Free Market Economy

SCIENTIFIC **Adam Smith** A free market economic system is good because unrestrained production and trade improve the material prosperity of a society.	
MIND 1 A free market economy becomes immoral when it increases the inequalities among citizens and downplays the need for sharing and generosity.	**MIND 2** A free market economy becomes immoral when it replaces the worthier goals and values of sacrifice, honor and nobility with the pursuit of wealth.
RELIGIOUS It is better to give than to receive. A free market economic system is immoral because it promotes the pursuit of self-interest over and above morality and the desire to be good.	

Should the day arrive when we are visited by aliens from another planet, it is likely they will not share our morality. They may have five different sexes, and may have no trouble eating their own children. They may be as different from us morally as our imagination can devise, but they will be like us in their science. Science will tell us what they are. Our morality will tell us who they are, and why they are here – and if they are friend or foe. We need the one to help us with the other.

SECTION III
The Extrapolations

OVERVIEW OF CHAPTERS 10-28

Any area of life or human activity – from art to politics, from education to history, from logic and wisdom to good and evil – can be shown to exhibit a pattern of dual morality, which can be felt at different levels of moral intensity and represented quad-realistically in terms of its Logical, Mind 1, Mind 2 or Spiritual expression.

CHAPTER 10
Art and Creativity

This chapter explores a wide variety of forms of artistic creation, ranging from the purely aesthetic fine arts (art for art's sake), to the vast array of industrial arts (art for utility), along with the whole range of decorative arts that fall somewhere in-between. Different approaches to the role and function of art are explored – art as entertainment; art as personal expression; art as the repository and transmission of culture; art as an expression of group identity; art as a commodity; art as leisure; art as ornamentation; art as a civilizing force.

ARTISTIC QUAD-REALISM

Applied/industrial/medical arts
Creativity focuses on physical responses

Door bells, crutches, skyscrapers, toilets, rockets, pencils, penicillin, computers

MIND 1 Art
The physical art supports
Mind 1 emotional reactions

Video games, rock-and-roll, baseballs, whoopee cushions, Barbie dolls, movies

MIND 2 Art
The physical art supports
Mind 2 emotional reactions

Placemats with the pictures of all the presidents, the flag, the national anthem, the maple leaf emblem

Fine Arts and Literary Arts
Creativity focuses on emotional responses

Rembrandt painting, Gregorian chant, ballet, poetry, the rosary

Art is human psychology in physical form

LOGICAL - Utility

MIND 1 – Personal/Aesthetic

MIND 2 – High Position

SPIRITUAL
The imagined thrown of God

Mind 1	Mind 2
The artist is the judge of his creation, of what is right and what is best.	The group or the public who view the art can judge what is best and right. The more educated they are in these matters, the better their judgment.
Art is individual expression, done for the satisfaction of the artist. If others can appreciate it, all the better, but this is not a necessity.	Art is recognizable by others. The best art is that which creates constructive emotional responses in the observer.

Mind 1	Mind 2
The artist should strive to please himself, or promote Mind 1 values such as peace, sharing, and inclusion.	The artist should strive to please others, particularly those above him, or to celebrate Mind 2 values, such as duty, honor, service to one's country or God.
Eclectic art, modern art, cubism, impressionism etc., express "truth" and "beauty" as the artist knows them to be.	Classical art expresses "truth" and "beauty" by conforming to objective, pre-established standards known to all.
The standards of classical art are too rigid and confining to allow the creative spirit to flourish by exploring and experimenting with new forms of artistic expression.	Modern art is hedonistic, self-serving and objectively meaningless. It hardly qualifies as "art" at all. If I come across a pile of junk somebody somewhere has declared to be "art," am I obligated to see it as such?
We should not regulate the fine arts because what the artist produces is personal and not the concern of the public. One person's art is as good as another's, and no one other than the artist can really stand in judgment of his work.	We should regulate the fine arts to prevent them from becoming too obscene, disrespectful of traditions, and unpatriotic. The artist, as the judge of his own works, tends to moral excess.
There cannot be art critics because art is in the mind of its creator. What is wonderful to some might be abhorrent to others. A child's drawing may be more beautiful to him than a Vermeer. The beauty is there for him, even if it does not exist for anyone else.	Art can be judged. There are more educated people who know better things and higher standards. Superior art and inferior art can be judged objectively. A child's finger painting is not as good as a Vermeer, even if the child, and his parents, prefer it.

CHAPTER 11
Pleasure and Happiness

Pleasure and happiness are internal reward systems that focus on present satisfaction (pleasure) and/or the long-term completion of moral aims (happiness). In a Mind 1 environment, the pursuit of pleasure and material wellbeing is considered a legitimate goal, while in times of trouble and danger (Mind 2), pleasures are few and people are encouraged to pursue the long-term goal of happiness.

MIND 1 Have fun in the present	MIND 2 Honor the Past
Christmas means Santa Clause will visit us.	Christmas means it is the birthday of Jesus.
Fourth of July celebrations mean barbecues and fireworks.	Fourth of July celebrations recall the sacrifices of the revolutionaries.
Memorial Day weekend means a visit to the beach.	Memorial Day recalls the sacrifices of past warriors.
Thanksgiving is all about football and Black Friday shopping.	Thanksgiving is about giving thanks for the fortunate events of life.
Wedding anniversaries are about celebrating "us" with parties and current celebrations.	Wedding anniversaries reaffirm our dedication to our loved one and our commitment to uphold this mutually beneficial social arrangement.
All pleasures are equally good. It is a matter of personal tastes and preferences.	Pleasures can be ranked as "superior" and "inferior." The intellectual pleasures are superior to the sensual pleasures.
Pleasures are distributed according to need, not on the basis of hard work or achievements.	Pleasures, when they are acceptable, are given as reward for hard work, effort and superior achievements.
Happiness is achieved when we are all safe, equally cared and provided for, and respected.	Happiness is achieved when we succeed in achieving the traditional aims and ends of an accomplished member of society.

CHAPTER 12
Aristocracy

Here we examine the leadership that evolves in prolonged times of want, or in times of extended threat, when not everyone can have enough and many routinely do not survive. Under these conditions, some form of *aristocracy* emerges. It may be in the form of a military leader supported by a close group of subordinates, a central party figure, or a long-established family. But one way or another, social structures and cultural leadership become a vertical arrangement of most to least important people. The group is governed by the few, usually with some head figure emerging at the top. Such social arrangements also develop in areas where all wealth comes from one easily controlled resource (such as oil).

No one cares that the poor of today live better than the rich of yesterday. But many care deeply that the poor of today live worse than the rich here and now.

Forced wealth redistribution does not ensure equality so much as it guarantees a universal subservience to the redistributive authority.

The concept and justifications for charitable giving differ between our two moral outlooks:

MIND 1 COMPASSION: THE PLIGHT OF THE POOR SPURS GENEROSITY. We give because the poor need it. The richer give to the poorer because in no way do the poor deserve to be in a lesser condition than the rich. We give to family as parenthood obligates us to do for our smallest and weakest members. We give to more equally distribute the advantages of living in our society. Generosity benefits the people in a lesser condition. The rich miser who does not give lacks compassion.

MIND 2 NOBLESSE OBLIGE: THE NOBILITY OF THE RICH SPURS GENEROSITY. We give because generosity is an aspect of superior character. The poverty or weakness of others in no way obligates anyone to give to them or support them. Generosity confirms the recognition of some as deserving of being in a superior position. The rich miser who does not give lacks noble character.

CHAPTER 13
Democracy

Democratic culture is safe culture. It emerges in periods of widespread production and trade, and withers in times of ongoing war and danger, which destroy production and limit trade.

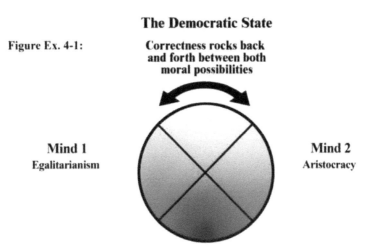

The Democratic State

Figure Ex. 4-1:

Correctness rocks back and forth between both moral possibilities

Mind 1
Egalitarianism

Mind 2
Aristocracy

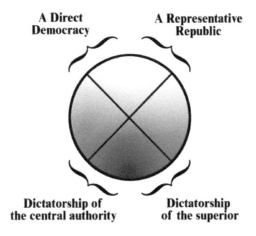

Figure Ex. 4-3:

A Direct Democracy

A Representative Republic

Dictatorship of the central authority

Dictatorship of the superior

In a democracy, when the carpenter goes to a restaurant for lunch, the waitress becomes his temporary servant. The next day, when the carpenter shows up at the waitress's home to install her cabinets, she becomes his master.

Democracy is dispersed social authority sometimes seen as a never-ending parade of protests.

In times of increasing poverty, women retreat back into their home, not because they feel like returning to more private lives, but because it is from there they can do the most good for their families.

CHAPTER 14
War

This chapter addresses war with a focus on the struggle to change the form of government itself, from either the aristocratic to the democratic pattern or vice versa. These fundamental forms of governments change in response to new social conditions and personal arrangements of the society beneath the level of government. When the people change from aristocrats and paupers to co-equal traders and producers, the leadership above them must change to benefit society the most. A variety of historical examples – Ancient Rome, Ancient Greece, the Glorious Revolution, the Russian Revolution, the American Revolution – are analyzed from a dual moral perspective, and the changes that motivate the turning of one form of government to another are elucidated as well.

Acceptable range of political viewpoints in 1860/1960

The right wingers like Jefferson Davis accepted democracy, the franchise for adult white males, and social participation short of voting for females, but accepted the historic need for slavery, with no social mixing between the races.

For the left wingers like Abraham Lincoln, black emancipation and the end of slavery was called for, but a general social mixing of the races with interracial marriage was still not acceptable even to most of them.

By 1960, the range had moved leftward. The 1960s' right winger believed in voting for all, but with limited social mixing of races, while the left winger encouraged social racial mixing.

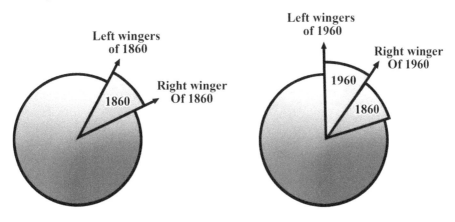

CHAPTER 15
Logic & Wisdom

We use logic and reason to determine the best means of achieving our emotional ends. But logic and reason do not tell us what ends to choose. Our instincts and impulses, which are necessarily filtered through our Mind 1 or Mind 2 outlooks, determine our ends.

The process of turning our truths into facts is twofold: first we look inward to discover the ends we seek, and then we look outward to find the means of satisfying them. Seeking the proper subjective ends is a matter of morality, and employing the efficient external means is a matter of logic. When we do both, we are wise.

Having two moral codes means we have the capacity to seek two different goals in every social situation, and hence two different means of achieving that goal. In a dually moralistic world, what is logical to some can be illogical to others when their actions are linked to dissimilar ends. When we see right in two ways, justice can be more than one thing. *Justice can even be injustice – logic can seem like illogic, and reason can be unreasonable*

Scenario 1: I am in charge of organizing a children's footrace

	Logic and Reason in the Service of Mind 1 Ends	Logic and Reason in the Service of Mind 2 Ends
End	I feel it is most important for all children to have fun and feel positively about themselves.	I feel it is important for children to have an opportunity to improve their skills through competition and to witness the rewards of superior performance.
Means	At the end of the race, we will give every child who participated in the race a trophy with the words, "You're a winner" inscribed on it. (Every participant is a winner.)	At the end of the race, we will give a trophy to the child who crossed the finish line first, with the words, "You're the winner" inscribed on it. (The participant whose performance was superior is the winner.)

WISDOM = MORALITY (proper ends) + LOGIC (effective means)

Wisdom
Using efficient facts to promote proper truths

Our wisdom is divided. We disagree about where we should be heading and what pitfalls we should be avoiding.

Today, Mind 1 personal values have replaced Mind 2 traditional virtues as moral standards, because plenty has replaced want. When was the last time you called anybody virtuous?

Mind 1 Focus	Mind 2 Focus
What the group can do for the individual	What the individual can do for the group
Improve the lives of individuals (end) by improving society (means)	Sustain and improve society (end) by improving the individuals within it (means)
Society and its "moral character"	The individual and his moral character
The Just Society – one that enshrines the *core values* of life, equality, peace, prosperity, fairness, but allows for variation in *personal values*	*The Virtuous Individual* – one that embodies the *moral virtues* of honesty, dignity, prudence, temperance, fortitude, courage
Doing good (actions) – the good citizen	*Being* good (character) – the virtuous person

CHAPTER 16
Education

This chapter addresses the questions, "What should we know and why should we know it?" and identifies the four quad-realistic approaches that have been used to answer them.

LOGICAL

Education is primarily job training. To be educated is to understand the physical laws of the universe and to have the skills and know-how to apply them to accomplish practical tasks.

Whatever you learn, it should help you to be productive.

MIND 1

To be educated is to have the skills and knowledge necessary to pursue one's personal and career goals, which may differ from one individual to the next. All pursuits are equally worthy. Differences among people are accepted, equality is promoted, and instances of bigotry, unfairness and oppression are detected and decried.

Whatever you choose to learn, it should satisfy your personal needs and increase your pleasures.

MIND 2

To be educated is to know the things superior people know and to display the habits of the better people, as defined by the culture. The better-educated act in exemplary ways, can identify improper behaviors in others, and are presumed to be the leaders in their fields and in life.

Education helps you to improve your social status and material conditions and leads to long-term happiness.

A-LOGICAL/ANTHROPOMORPHIC

To be educated is to know the ultimate truths. Proper belief is more vital than the knowledge of the physical world.

Whatever you learn, it should promote ultimate right and eternal truths.

This chapter explores such themes as the role of the textbook; the difference between education and training; universal education and the role of public schooling; affirmative action in education; and different educational models that are distinguished by how they define the ultimate goal of education.

Democracy is not a product of education (or sloganeering); it is the aftereffect of commercialization.

As culture moves into democratic eras, education takes on a commercial aspect – we believe we are educated if we are trained to make money. In prior, more horizontally structured times, formal education was a luxury of the leisure class. Education was a quality that distinguished the better from the worse. The modern curriculum of courses has its origins here. But in today's more democratic and egalitarian times, we often wonder why we are still subjected to learning such things as advanced mathematics, history, or philosophy, and we find students asking their teachers, "How will knowing this help me get to a job?"

In order to "get everybody educated," we needed to provide an education "everybody can get" – often shallow, undemanding, and superficial.

Educational paradigms

Specialists in curriculum have identified three educational paradigms, based on how each defines the goals of education. The cultural transmission paradigm, which has been the dominant paradigm throughout history, corresponds to the Mind 2 view of education as the passing on of the culture's traditions and values. As culture moved into democratic eras, near the top of the compass, preparation for the workplace became incorporated into the goals of the curriculum; hence, the transaction paradigm, which focused on skill and competency development, began to replace transmission. As we move further along into a Mind 1 culture, education takes on a "transformative" role, where the goal becomes change – either personal change (humanistic education), with its focus on the intellectual, physical and emotional development of the child as a unique person with his own individual identity, needs and preferences; or social change (critical pedagogy), with its concern to ensure equality for minority or marginalized groups.

The critical pedagogy strand in education is an outgrowth of postmodernism's rejection of Enlightenment principles, in particular, its confidence in reason and science. That confidence had been undermined by the rise of skepticism, nihilism, and romanticism during the Counter-Enlightenment, and replaced by an emphasis on feelings over knowledge and truths over facts. Spurred by concerns for equality, college campuses began to assign less importance to the Western canon of great works representing the "dominant" culture, and more importance to unknown or minor works representing minority or oppressed groups. In social studies programs, students are urged to challenge the status quo by exposing power relationships and patterns of inequality in society.

Critical pedagogy is thus a reflection of Mind 1 morality pushed further down the left-hand side of the compass towards the extreme. Parallel extremism on the Mind 2 side can be found in educational programs that reinforce religious or quasi-religious adherence to beliefs over facts (e.g. creationism) or strong ethnic or nationalistic commitments. While the former aims for absolute equality, the latter aims for absolute hierarchical ranking.

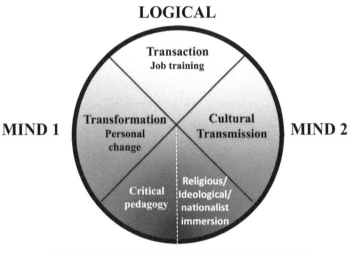

For more than a century, Mind 2 leaning educators have called for the need to return education to its roots in the great Western canon, with Mind 1 educators downplaying, to a greater or lesser extent, the significance of these works and advocating instead for greater variety and personal relevance in the content of the curriculum.

Mind 1 Education	Mind 2 Education
All books and authors are equally valuable and worthy of being taught. What one person appreciates may hold little interest to someone else. There is no objective hierarchy of value that can be applied to cultural products.	Some areas of knowledge are fundamentally superior to others. The *Great Books* of the Western canon represent the highest achievements in the philosophical, literary, and intellectual development of our culture and probably the world.

Mind 1 Education	Mind 2 Education
What is needed in the present determines what is best to learn now – whether it is job skills or the pursuit of a personal hobby or interest.	What was elevated and found valuable in times past is what needs to be passed on today.
Students are exposed to art and literature that is relevant to their personal lives and present interests, which may include works by obscure and relatively insignificant authors from their own or other cultures.	Students are taught the great works of classical learning in order for them to be recognized as "superior" people, elevated above the common masses.
Evaluation focuses on promoting learners' self-esteem. Students are not compared with each other in terms of superior/inferior. All learners are rewarded equally for "effort," or simply for participation.	Evaluation focuses on merit: The student who performs best is rewarded; those who perform poorly are scolded.
As education takes on a deeper Mind 1 aspect, Mind 2 aims and goals for education begin to look more like "social propaganda" than knowledge.	As education takes on a deeper Mind 2 aspect, Mind 1 aims and goals for education begin to look more like "social propaganda" than knowledge.
At the extreme Mind 1 position, the curriculum exposes students to the works of minority groups, which record their history and experience of oppression by dominant groups. With respect to the great works of Western civilization, students are expected to analyze them critically, with a view to detecting and exposing examples of racism, misogyny or homophobia. Collective identity (race, gender, sexual orientation) replaces individual identity.	At the extreme Mind 2 position, a strong sense of national or religious identity is enforced by demanding strict obedience to authority and a sense of duty untainted by any trace of self-interest or personal fulfillment. Students may be separated from their families/communities (e.g. boarding school) to avoid "contamination" from external sources. Collective identity (national, religious) replaces individual identity.

CHAPTER 17
The Rise of Libertarian Amoralism

This chapter explores the libertarian outlook characteristic of a top-of-the-compass position, where both our moral impulses are suppressed. Libertarianism is facilitated when a culture moves from times of hardship to times of plenty and people enjoy the kind of independence that comes with wealth. The chapter addresses questions such as, "What is freedom?"; "How are freedom and liberty differentiated?"; "How do we know if we are free?"; "Can some people in a culture be freer than others?"; and "What can free people do that unfree people cannot do?"

Wealth is the creation of material freedom.

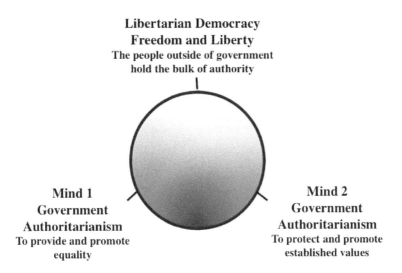

Mind 1- personal and family mind	Mind 2- public and social mind
Freedom is having a wide range of choices available and the ability/money to make them.	*Liberty* Is being unconstrained by leadership in the choices we are allowed to make.

Mind 1- personal and family mind	Mind 2- public and social mind
Freedom is threatened when choices are limited or when I lack the financial/social power to make them.	*Liberty* is threatened when I cannot influence leadership or when other groups impose their leadership's will and authority upon us.
Liberties can be sacrificed to improve lives – one should not be at liberty to discriminate based on race. This restricts freedom.	Lives can be sacrificed to preserve liberty. We can expect citizens to die to preserve our particular form of government, and though conscription temporarily limits one's freedom, it is done in the name of securing our liberties.
Liberty is trimmed to meet goals for personal freedom and equality.	Some freedoms need to be limited to preserve social liberty.
The wealth and status of individuals should be limited by government to promote personal equality.	Government power should be limited in order to promote and encourage unique accomplishment.
Profit is made out of the pockets of others. The businessman needs to "give back" some of his gains to others in the community.	Profit is the wealth created when both parties benefit from efficient productive transactions. The business owner's superior rewards are earned, just as they are earned by employees. The business owner is doing more for others than his peers have done and has already "given" to his community when he provides his product or service and employs its people.
The amount of charity should be determined by the needs of the recipient.	The amount of charity should be determined by the generosity and sense of the giver.
Natural resources are a shared collective inheritance. We should be forced by the wisdom of "group understanding" to save resources or to preserve nature itself.	There are no collective resources. We should be able to use resources or not use them as we determine, since we individually (not collectively) own them.

Beginning in the Middle Ages, the concept of a better life changed from being a better person "morally" to being better off "materially."

In a free market, where anyone can make or not make any choice, *choice itself* becomes the primary component of morality.

Should I be free to live my life as I choose? What if it means I end up with children I cannot care for, addicted to cocaine, illiterate, and living a hand-to-mouth existence one step outside the gutter? If the sum of my free choices places me in the life I just described, are my fellow herd members obligated (because they can afford it) to support my children, rid me of my addictions, and feed me?

When conceiving the world and existence from near the top of the moral compass, we view it physically and its meanings mechanically. From this vantage, we understand things deterministically, in terms of facts and cause and effect.

When apprehending existence from a place nearer the bottom of the compass, we perceive motives and actions as just springing forth from within, often seemingly uncaused, and in terms of truths. It is from this dichotomy in our own dually moral cognition that the battle between determinism and free will comes about in our own minds.

Determinism

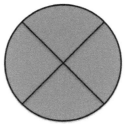

Free Will

CHAPTER 18
Politicians and Philosophers

This chapter examines philosophical and political orientations of notables from the past and how they fit in with our dual moralistic outlook. We examine the positions of philosophers, religious founders, psychologists, journalists, and economists – who attempt to explain not only how society works, but why it works as it does – and demonstrate that human psychology, given its dual moral makeup, lends itself to being described in predictable patterns.

The positions of philosophers can be plotted:

Fig Ex 9-1   **Fact-based and Material**

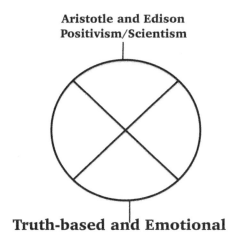

**Aristotle and Edison
Positivism/Scientism**

Truth-based and Emotional

**Plato and Lord Byron
Anti-Positivism/Anti-Scientism**

Philosophers, striving for wisdom, suggest we should act in certain ways in order to live the best lives. Our natural philosophers, the scientists and applied scientists like Francis Winslow Taylor and Stephen Hawking, tell us that it is through understanding the physical world that we can best understand ourselves and our place in it. Leftists like Noam Chomsky and John Rawls hold a different position from rightists like Confucius and Henry Mencken over the most satisfactory ideas of freedom, justice and social cooperation. And all of these see the world differently from spiritually oriented people like Kahlil Gibran and Gautama Buddha.

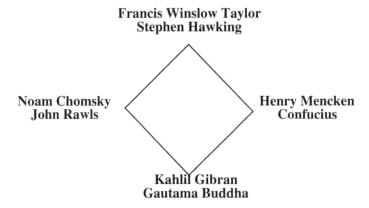

Positions on the moral compass are relative to each other. Furthermore, if we zoom in on one of the quadrants, we can see how the same pattern repeats itself, and if we continue to zoom in on increasingly smaller groups, the pattern repeats itself indefinitely. Below, we zoom in on the spiritual quadrant, and then even further on liberal spirituality.

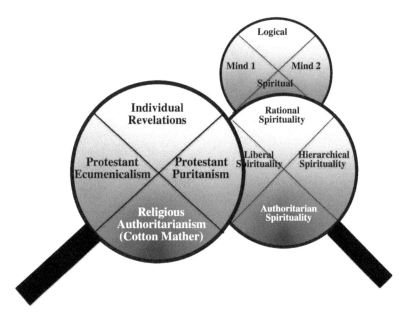

Similarly, although all economists are in the top quadrant of our moral compass, they can still be distinguished, relative to each other, as either more logical (or more liberal, or more conservative, or more subjective) than the others.

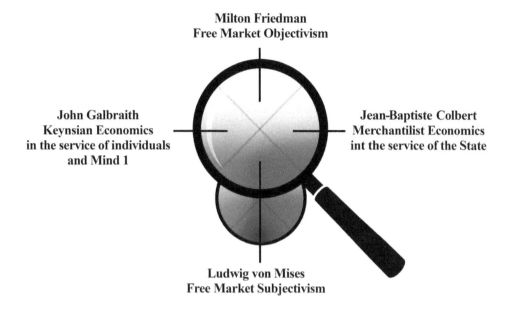

Over-production and wealth generation in modern Western democracies distort the normal distribution of moral concern and social authority.

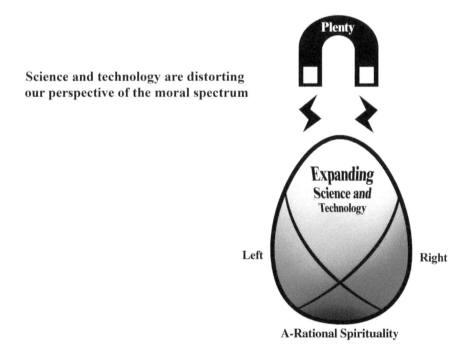

Political ideologies can also be represented quad-realistically. If we believe our truths are best realized by individuals acting on their own or in small groups, we lean toward the top of the compass. We move toward the bottom of the compass as individual freedom wanes and authoritarian collectivism is imposed, either to ensure equality among all groups (e.g. communism) or to preserve the hierarchical relations between groups (e.g. fascism).

As fewer and fewer factories, employing ever-smaller numbers of workers, produce everything everyone needs, wealth distribution, not wealth creation, becomes the dominant activity of leaders.

CHAPTER 19
Rehabilitation and Punishment

Law establishes codes of conduct outlining what individuals can expect from each other or what the group expects of its individual members. Fines, reimbursements, tortures, and imprisonments are used to achieve these expectations and are massaged to conform to our moral outlook.

Quad-Realism

LOGICAL
Rules concerning physical construction, transportation, and material organization. A procedural wrong more than a "moral wrong" (e.g. traffic laws, industrial regulations, physical laws of nature)

MIND 1
Civil law between individuals dealing with the private affairs of the community where the concept of "moral wrong" is in play.

MIND 2
Criminal or public law where behavior is construed to be detrimental to the society or to the state where "moral wrong" is employed.

A-LOGICAL
Religious laws often enforced by religious police (e.g. the Mutaween in Saudi Arabia today; the Inquisition of the 12th century Catholic Church in Europe.)

Our approach to miscreant behavior varies according to our moral outlook. From a Mind 1 vantage, correction takes the form of rehabilitation and reform, and its goal is to protect both the offending individual and the offended. From a Mind 2 point of view, the object deserving of concern is not the wrongdoer, and often not even the victim, but the protection of the "family" or the "society" or its beliefs and customs. Misbehavior deserves punishment.

Mind 1	Mind 2
Addiction is a disease.	Addiction is a personal failing.
Consumers need protection.	Let the buyer beware.
People cannot be judged as good or bad; only behaviors can be so judged.	How you act is who you are. Good people do good things and bad people do bad things.
Reforming behavior needs to be our aim, and the ultimate punishment can never be death, as it completely destroys the end that we seek: the correction and wellbeing of our individuals. When all individuals are acting correctly, society is well ordered.	Punishment, sacrifice, and the infliction of pain are the proper responses of the group when addressing misbehavior. Individuals need to recognize that the good of society is what matters most. They can and may be sacrificed unto death.

Political leaders compete to convince us to fear most what they promise to cure best.

CHAPTER 20
Good and Evil

It is easier to sloganeer for good and against evil than to define precisely what either is. This chapter explores how we view good and evil from two standards and therefore how something can be both right and wrong at the same time.

The Four Faces of Evil

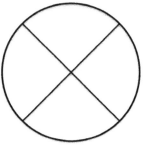

Evil or "wrong" as incorrect; inefficient production; physical or mathematical error

Evil as excess violence or subjugation to others

Evil as inordinate concern for self-preservation or self-satisfaction at the expense of the group or superiors

Evil as disloyalty to ultimate ideals

MIND 1 – Values	MIND 2 – Virtues
She is a person who did a bad thing.	She is a bad person.

Morality begins with feeling correctly under the circumstances. Having no emotions when some are called for identifies us as unbalanced.

Mind 1 Lack of proper empathy	Mind 2 Lack of proper respect for law & society
The psychopath	The sociopath

Philosophical Orientations to Good and Evil: Mill and Kant

Mind 1: MILL	Mind 2: KANT
Actions are good or bad as a function of their consequences.	Actions are good or bad as a function of whether or not they conform to the moral law.
The same action can be right or wrong, depending on its consequences.	An action is absolutely right or wrong, no matter what the consequences.
"Good" actions are those that promote the greatest happiness and the avoidance of pain for all concerned.	"Good" actions are those that conform to duty, whether or not they result in happiness or pain.
We cannot determine the moral quality of an action without considering its circumstances and effects.	The moral quality of an action is independent of its circumstances and effects.
There are always exceptions to general moral precepts.	The moral law is universal and admits of no exceptions.

Shame and guilt are two emotions that together guide us to proper moral action. … While shame is a reaction to social condemnation, guilt is a reaction to self-condemnation. Shame is the product of the moral judgments of others; guilt is the product of our "internal" moral judge.

Guilt is one of our moral minds crying out that the other should not have won the argument.

The conflict between good and evil is usually a debate between good and good.

CHAPTER 21

Suicide, Murder and Abortion

Suicide

Mind 1 Personal Morality	Mind 2 Public Morality
Suicide is tolerated. Your life is your own to dispose of as you wish. There is no obligation to the group before yourself.	Suicide for personal reasons is cowardice. It is frowned upon except to protect honor. Your life belongs to the group first and to yourself second.

Murder

One person's "murder" is another person's "justifiable homicide."

Mind 1	Mind 2
Private quarrels of a serious nature involve the group; they should be solved by the group. Private feuds can never involve violence.	Private quarrels do not involve the group and can be settled, even unto death, by the parties themselves.
Dueling is murder and should be prohibited.	Dueling (if recognized by tradition) is the honorable settling of a private disagreement and should be allowed.

Abortion

Mind 1	Mind 2
The deliberate killing of another human being is inherently wrong. It is the "individual's right" to dispose of her own life as she chooses, but not the life of another.	The deliberate killing of another human is circumstantially wrong as the group and tradition have determined. It is the "group's right" to retain or dispose of the lives of its members as is best for all.

	Mind 1	**Mind 2**
Pro-abortion	The fetus is not a human being; it is a part of the mother's body. Abortion is not murder.	Whether or not the fetus is a human being, abortion can be outlawed, permitted, or even mandated by the state if it serves the group's needs.
	The decision to abort or not is the mother's (pro-choice).	If abortion has been part of the culture's traditional practices, the decision can be left in the hands of the private individual.
Anti-abortion	The fetus is a human being from the moment of conception.	If abortion is banned by long-existing practice, religion or a significant part of the culture's tradition, then abortion will be viewed as wrong.
	The state is obligated to protect the inherent rights of the unborn child (pro-life).	Those who perform abortions and women who receive them have placed themselves above and outside the laws and traditions of their group.

A person dies, that is a fact. But what is the truth behind it? Was the death a murder? Was the thing being killed a person? These are matters of truth. At the extremes of our moral capacity, we are forced to accept that "logically" such questions have no real answers. Then again, we can also believe "emotionally" that these questions can be answered absolutely.

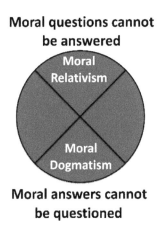

Moral questions cannot be answered

Moral answers cannot be questioned

CHAPTER 22
History

This chapter addresses the question: What should we remember and why should we remember it?

Quad-Realism
Historical "facts" are recalled to reinforce our present "truths"

LOGICAL MIND
History as a record of our technological and scientific achievements
(Maps; chronological records of births, deaths, dates of events, etc.; tools and technology; scientific facts and theories: archeological discoveries)

MIND 1	MIND 2
History as a record of Mind 1 struggles for peace and equality	History as a record of Mind 2 traditions and achievements
(Christian George; St. Francis of Assisi; Thomas Moore; Pullman; Jim Jones)	(Wars and military victories; famous leaders and noblemen; aristocracies and lines of succession; stories of bravery and courage)

SPIRITUAL MIND
History as a record of the words and teachings of our gods and prophets
- The Bible (Christianity)
- The Quran (Islam)
- The Torah and the Talmud (Judaism)
- The Tripitaka (Buddhism)

History is interesting because it focuses on the spectacular – current celebrity is interesting because it focuses on the salacious.

Knowing *what* happened is *history*; knowing *how* things happen is *science*; and knowing *why* things happen is *philosophy*. Understanding these things, we grasp that all wisdom begins with history.

CHAPTER 23
The better People

Colloquially, we still speak of people acting better or worse, or behaving with class or in a low-class manner, but it is no longer acceptable to imagine oneself as inherently superior to others. How to be "high class" is not taught in schools and no one is criticized for behaving like persons of the "lower orders." You may behave better in some specific technical circumstance, like playing basketball or reading, but you are not intrinsically a better human being.

Should we strive to be equal or struggle to be better?

Two hundred and fifty years ago, we all understood that there were better and worse types of humans, and there were culturally established ways to distinguish one from the other. ... Today, rules of etiquette are almost unheard of – as they are unnecessary. We all do as we please.

We can feel it correct that the best culture is horizontal, and we can, on the other hand, feel that it should be competitive, distinguishing, and vertical. Everyone's voice matters and maybe some voices matter more than others. We want to give everyone a participation trophy, while retaining in our hearts the hope of being proclaimed the only "winner." We can and do have it both ways.

Mind 1 Equality	Mind 2 Better and Worse
Participation trophies	Trophies to distinguish top performers

CHAPTER 24
The Problem of Competent Authority

For the herd member, *what* is right usually comes down to deciding *who* is right. This chapter addresses the questions, who do I listen to, who do I believe and who do I follow? Ascertaining competent authority is the great problem facing humanity.

By the time we leave home, we have learned almost everything we need to know to be a fully functioning member of our society. Mom has taught us how to dress, speak, and eat in ways acceptable to the group we are joining, and dad taught us how to drive, mow the lawn, and accept the harsh reality that if we want to eat, we need to work. After leaving home, we are expected to make many choices and it becomes easy to imagine ourselves as independent thinkers. This is largely illusory.

QUAD-REALISM
COMPETENT AUTHORITY

LOGICAL/OBJECTIVE

Competent authority lies in the scientists, technologists and professional experts who use the scientific method to uncover objectively verifiable facts.

MIND 1

Everyone is his/her own authority. Competent authority is equally distributed throughout the members of the group represented by the majority, or the crowd, and is transferred to the leader, who has been chosen to represent their interests.

MIND 2

Competent authority resides in the leader, who is the representation and guardian of the superior values, traditions and customs of the group.

SPIRITUAL/SUBJECTIVE

The ultimate authority is the word of God, passed down to us as divine revelation through the holy scriptures and words of the prophets and gurus.

The average man-in-the-street is allowed to select the president of the United States, but he is certainly not qualified (and not allowed) to have a say in who should be the manager of a department store.

Doing right is the same as doing good.

Advertisers and politicians are smart enough to appeal to both our moral outlooks. They recognize that we will be swayed by both superiors and majorities. "Not only is our brand of toothpaste enjoyed by all, but four out of five dentists also recommend it!"

We believe Moscow exists, not because we have ever been there, but because some competent authority above us, or some majority around us, believes it.

We are not experts and we need guidance in almost everything. We are as gullible as hope and as frightened as fear. Fear is our most reliable motivator.

Good parenting involves proper instruction over what to worry about.

The wise men of both East and West agree that moderation is best in all things. To worry wisely means to worry enough but not too much. We select our leaders, our "proper authorities," not only as our problem solvers, but also as our proxy worriers.

CHAPTER 25
Worship Words and the Profane

In this chapter, we explore how the twofold nature of our moral attitudes, felt at various levels of intensity, are reflected in our choice of words and in how we use language to express our moral meanings. A variety of topics are addressed, such as how the moral meanings of words change over time; the differences between the terms "liberty" and "freedom" or the terms "liberated woman" and "feminist"; the moral messages underlying buzzwords such as "diversity"; profanity and offensive language; and political correctness.

Communication Breakdown

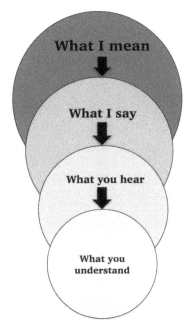

We use language to express meanings, and meanings are verified by comparing truths with facts. When we use language for informative purposes, we convey facts about the world that are easier to verify than subjective truth-based feelings. If I say, "This is an oak tree," my intention is to inform, and my meaning is verified externally and physically. But if I say to a friend, "I love oak trees," I am using language for expressive purposes. I am not conveying information about oak trees so much as information about my own subjective feelings towards them.

Quad-Realism: Worship words

LOGICAL
The advantageous is substituted for the moral:
- *Gain; Profit; Facts*

MIND 1	MIND 2
Words that support Mind 1 aims:	Words that support Mind 2 aims:
- *Empowerment; Unity; Fairness*	- *Decency; Distinction; Gallantry*

A-LOGICAL AND ANTHROPOMORPHIC
- *God; Belief; Truth*

Quad-Realism: The profane

LOGICAL
The disadvantageous is substituted for the immoral:
- *Loss; Error; Mistake*

MIND 1	MIND 2
Profanity creates social inequalities:	Profanity expresses the traditionally unacceptable:
- *Fat; Faggot; Nigger*	- *Fuck; Shit; Wimp*

A-LOGICAL AND ANTHROPOMORPHIC
- *Blasphemy; Impiety; Heresy*

Moral meanings

MIND 1	MIND 2
Before the Common Era / The Common Era BCE/CE	Before Christ / Anno Domini BC/AD
Fetus	Unborn baby
Sex trade worker	Prostitute/whore
Flag waiver	Patriot
Inuit	Eskimo
Sexually active	Promiscuous

MIND 1	MIND 2
The homeless	Bums
Gender reassignment	Sex change operation
Letter carrier	Mailman
Sexually dysfunctional	Perverted
Undocumented immigrants	Illegal aliens
Intellectual disability	Mental retardation
Challenged	Handicapped
Happy Holidays!	Merry Christmas!

Political Correctness and Identity Politics

The term, "political correctness" is of recent origin, but the basic concept of social acceptability is as old as socialization itself. Today, in our Mind 1 times, it refers to the use of language that reflects a Mind 1 preoccupation with equality, particularly for designated minority groups.

Banned Terms and Approved Alternatives	
Less correct	**More correct**
Best man for the job	Best person for the job
Waitress	Server
Fireman	Firefighter
Forefathers	Ancestors
Housewife	Consumer
Christian name	Forename
Homosexual	Same sex
Sportsmanship	Fairness
He/She	Zie

Political correctness is an aspect of identity politics, whereby individuals are categorized according to their membership in one or several groups. In Mind 1 times such as ours, these groups are defined by race, gender, ethnicity or sexual orientation; but a similar move occurs in Mind 2 when individuals are classified according to their religious or national affiliations. In both cases, the prevailing emphasis is on the group (collectivism) over the individual (individualism).

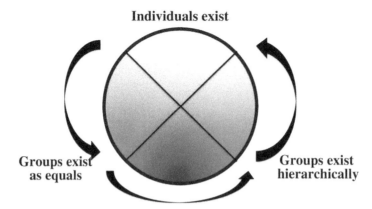

The liberated woman differs from the feminist in that the former sees herself as an individual who may choose to be a housewife or a CEO, a prostitute or a nun, according to her individual preferences, whereas the latter defines herself in terms of her shared identity with the "group" of other females, which is pitted against the group of males in an "Us vs. Them" confrontation.

In the top quadrant of the moral compass, you are not defined by what group you belong to, but by who you are individually. Your group affiliation is less important than your personal actions and abilities. As we move down the moral compass, we begin to be seen in terms of which group we belong to. On the right, our group affiliation serves to identify us as better or worse than others; on the left, it serves to ensure one group is *not* treated any better or any worse than any other group.

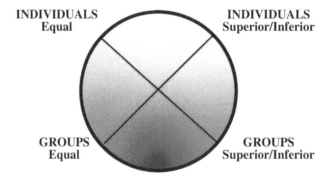

Critical pedagogy (Chapter 16), political correctness and identity politics are all outgrowths of postmodernism. We can plot the intellectual development of postmodernism along our familiar moral compass, labeling the mindset that dominated the Middle Ages as "pre-modern," the frame of mind prevalent during the Enlightenment as "modern," and recent Western thought as "postmodern."

While modernism replaced the supernatural, faith-based and collectivist orientation of the pre-modern period with a naturalist, scientific and individualist orientation, postmodernism represents a rejection of reason and science and a return to subjectivism and collectivism, where feelings triumph over knowledge and truths triumph over facts.

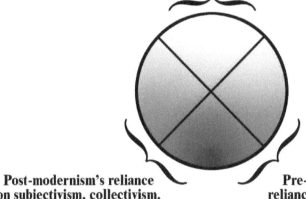

Modernism's reliance on individualism, perception, and reason

Post-modernism's reliance on subjectivism, collectivism, and egalitarianism

Pre-modernism's reliance on mysticism, faith, and custom

CHAPTER 26
Constitutions

Constitutions and other similar social contracts are put together by groups to codify and preserve their newly recognized or recently expanded rights, relationships and privileges. This chapter reviews and compares founding documents from different historical eras and for different countries, such as the British Magna Carta of 1215, the 1791 French Declaration of the Rights of Man, the Soviet Constitution of 1936, the 21st century Iraqi Constitution, the Canadian Constitution, and of course the 1787 Constitution of the United States.

What would the American Constitution look like if it had been written in our time instead of 250 years ago in Mind 2 times? We can figure it out. By understanding how the material circumstances of 1789 (the factor used to ascertain our condition of fear or want) created the society that wrote the constitution that was "right" for those times, we can grasp how the improvement of those material circumstances has altered our moral outlook now. Improved material circumstances puts pressure on us to "re-interpret" the old constitution to make it "right" for our times.

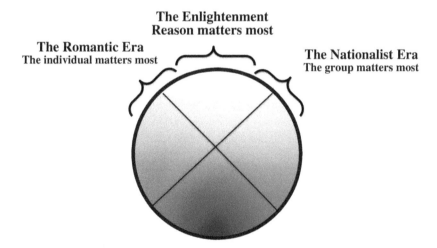

The American revolutionaries, who were seen as liberals relative to the prevailing culture, wanted to reduce the size of the state and move the culture counterclockwise, towards the top of the compass where reason prevailed. As wealth increased, political theorists strove to continue the move leftward, and to transform government into an aid to the people. Thus the prevailing vision of our

"Romantic period" began to replace the vision of the "Enlightenment." The prevailing effort now is to move society and its government past the 12 o'clock position and leftward toward a deeper Mind 1 moral understanding.

It is easier to ignore or "reinterpret" constitutions than to amend them.

Liberty and freedoms are not something listed; they are something lived.

Political campaign promises mean less to the day-to-day lives of everyday people than what is on sale this week.

<u>Concerning the Iraqi constitution Americans helped create</u>: America's founding document is a Mind 2 conservative-leaning libertarian constitution. It takes as axiomatic and self-evident that limiting government is synonymous with promoting liberty and freedom. The American revolutionaries struggled to throw off, and keep off, the yoke of an all-powerful central planner. The presumption that the state might make decisions for everybody to benefit everybody was the very thing the early Americans fought to destroy. Not so today's (Mind 1 leaning) Anglo-Iraqi equivalent.

The *thou-shalt-nots* found in America's Bill of Rights are replaced in the Iraqi manifestation by innumerable *thou shalts*. Iraq's Constitution is page after page of *government will do this, government shall do that*, and *government must do anything and everything that we now call good*. Where once limiting government was what promoted freedom, we now feel freedom is promoted by enhancing the powers of a *properly motivated and well-intentioned* state.

CHAPTER 27
What Should I Do and How Should I Live?

Each of us operates every day from many points around the moral compass. We switch our perspective as the situation demands and our temperament allows. The compass is a conceptual model, not a precise measuring tool. But by understanding that it represents who we are and the many ways in which we can "feel," it can help us to answer the question, *"How should I live?"* Right and wrong become debatable things.

The focal point of social leadership is what we call government. When times are harsh, it becomes concentrated in the hands of the few, or in the hands of the one.

Harsh Dictatorial Times

In easier democratic times, numerous influential groups command a voice in how the herd is managed. Government becomes a committee.

Easy Democratic Times

Affections
We use facts to determine who we like
and emotional attachments to determine who we love

THE GOOD LIFE: *The meaning of life is found in turning our truths into facts as we satisfy the demands of each quadrant of our dual morality. We are happy when we do well materially, when we are satisfied spiritually, when our family life is successful, and when we are respected by others and enjoy a healthy social life.*

Our job

Our family   **Our social standing –
friends & acquaintances**

Our religion

Attacks on the moneychangers, on usury, or on "capitalism" in one form or another will never go away. They are really the attacks on materialism and inequality and the means by which the former leads to the latter. They originate from within the self-righteous as an error of our character, how we mistakenly promote the means (money) at the expense of the end (humanity).

CHAPTER 28
Afterthoughts

This final chapter has been reserved for the most speculative ideas, the "leftovers," set aside until the end, and proposed as avenues of future reflection and exploration.

Several thought experiments are proposed, in which readers are asked to consider alternative viewpoints on a variety of topics, such as the notion of progress; the Bering Sea migration; slavery; the meaning of civilization; when our country was greatest; species equality; car control; the existence of the soul; and the allocation of tax dollars.

Morality evolved as a flexible tool to guide our actions in the present. It did not evolve to help us speculate on changing the past. Nevertheless, such hypothetical moral dilemmas as are proposed here through "thought experiments" help us to better understand the limits of human moral sentiment.

Thought Experiment #3: Booker T. Washington wondered – and suggested – that though African slavery was an inexcusable evil, one upside was that it was the only way impoverished sub-Saharan Africans could have found their way to the New World, and to its booming future prosperity. Currently, millions of white Americans as well as millions of African Americans exist here in the United States who would not be here, who would not be rich and free, were it not for slavery.

And so we ask: If we could press a magic button that would wipe out all African slavery from the American past, but by doing so we would eliminate virtually every African American from the Western Hemisphere – all the African Americans living here today would be instantly transported to one or another sub-Saharan African country – would this be a moral good? Would you press that button and eliminate African slavery from America's history, knowing this would be the unavoidable result?

And would such an outcome be favored more by black humanitarians or white racists?

The chapter uses dual morality as a lens to peer into the future. Assuming society continues to shift in a leftward direction as we become ever richer and ever safer, a number of cultural changes can be anticipated. For example, religions may continue to meld cross-denominationally; the world may move to a universal worldwide government; the traditional family may disappear; education will continue to transform to mere training and certification; the military court system as a separate legal path may be reigned in and even eliminated; and social androgenization will likely increase, as males and females strive to dress and look alike.

By helping us figure out yesterday and anticipate tomorrow, dual morality lays out a roadmap that details how we likely "felt" under past circumstances and why we are likely to "feel" certain ways under future conditions. Inevitably, nature and nurture combine with material want or prolonged plenty to guide our moral outlook. We can continue to enjoy material prosperity, providing we do not let our propensity for extreme behavior take hold and stifle widespread production and distribution.

We call the most intense expression of meaning "love." *In the final analysis, the meaning of life comes down to "who did we love and who loved us."* Our lives and our loves can be dedicated to God, to Country, or to Family, and through these social constructs we find our purpose. Having the capacity to travel all these avenues of desire and satisfaction, human history suggests that the fullest and most complete existence would be to include a place in our lives for each of these loves, in balance.

Get the "Big Book"

*Pursue the full meaning and application of the Theory of Dual Morality by reading the complete, unabridged version of *Our Human Herds*.

*More than 1100 pages of insight and reflection showing how, through the lens of dual morality, we can gain a clearer and more comprehensive understanding of all aspects of human life and our relationship to the world. Explore topics as wide and varied as:

- The biological basis for government and the creation of democracies (Chapter 13)

- A comprehensive philosophy of education, explaining why the various forms, meanings, aims and methods of education develop as they do (Chapter 16)

- The role of art in the transmission and preservation of culture and the expression of personal identity (Chapter 10)

- A complete philosophy of history (Chapter 22)

- A philosophy of religion, where Eastern and Western religious development are shown to be philosophically compatible (Chapter 8)

Now available as a hardcover, softcover, or Ebook at Amazon.com
and other online book retailers

CPSIA information can be obtained
at www.ICGtesting.com
Printed in the USA
BVHW020331070619
550315BV00002B/3/P